TEACHING: WHY NOT TRY PSYCHOLOGY?

John A. Glover
Royce R. Ronning
Robert W. Filbeck

University of Nebraska
Lincoln, Nebraska

KENDALL/HUNT PUBLISHING COMPANY

2460 Kerper Boulevard,
Dubuque, Iowa 52001

B   401772   01

PREFACE

This book presents a brief introductory treatment of educational psychology applied to teaching for students who have not had considerable exposure to psychological training. It is designed to make a learning oriented educational psychology experience pertinent to the classroom teacher.

Our book is not a traditional text nor is it a workbook. It falls between these two categories. This book was designed to model for you the techniques we describe in the following pages. We have emphasized the practical and the application orientation of educational psychology but not, we feel, at the expense of appropriate theoretical foundations.

We would like to acknowledge the assistance of Roger Bruning and Ken Orton who helped us bring the content and style of this book to its present form through a series of very fruitful discussions. Our hope is that our commitment to the value of educational psychology for teachers is reflected in this book.

John A. Glover
Royce R. Ronning
Robert W. Filbeck

CONTENTS

Chapter 1
INTRODUCTION

This text has been designed and written for the specific needs of undergraduate students enrolled in an educational psychology course. The material in this text is partly theoretical but primarily applied. It is a book designed to make your transition from student to teacher easier by moving you from knowledge acquisition to knowledge application. This book is designed as a supplement to your other readings in an educational psychology course and, while we feel it can stand alone, it is best used in conjunction with other course activities.

ORGANIZATION

There are several important features in this text that you should be familiar with in order to gain maximum benefit from reading it. Each of the following nine chapters is preceded by a list of behavioral objectives you are to meet by reading the text material. It is a good idea to frequently refer to the objectives as you read through chapters so that you can satisfy yourself with respect to how well your studying helps you meet the objectives. You will soon see that a properly written behavioral objective includes the behavior of the student after the objective has been met, the criteria for accepting the student's performance as satisfactory and the conditions under which the assessment of mastery is to take place. The behaviors you are to perform will be self-evident as you look over the objectives (e.g., write, list, construct, etc.) but the criteria and conditions shall only be addressed in a general way. We cannot be with you in person as you study this text, so we are suggesting that you set your own conditions for assessing your learning. You may check yourself out in any way that you see fit. The criterion you should set for determining whether or not your behavior is satisfactory should be your estimation that you are within 90 percent agreement with our responses.

In addition to the objectives at the beginning of each chapter, you will find exercises in many of the chapters or at the back of the book in a section entitled "exercises." You should very carefully attend to the exercises. You will see that those exercises appearing at the back of the book are printed on perforated pages that may be torn out and turned in to your instructor.

The materials you are to respond to for assessing your mastery of the objectives are contained in the "Summative Evaluation" section at the back of the book. These evaluation activities are also printed on perforated pages so that they may be removed from the book and given to your instructor. You should complete these as you complete each chapter. Your responses will be written directly on the pages and your instructor may decide to examine them or not as she/he sees fit.

Our answers to the summative evaluation questions are contained in the text itself. You should compare your responses to ours to determine if you agree with us at a 90 percent level of agreement. This estimation must be your own. If you do not meet the objectives at a satisfactory level, we suggest several alternative readings at the end of each evaluation section. These books are common and may be found in any university or college library and at most municipal libraries.

ORIENTATION

There were five people involved to some degree in the preparation of this book. All are educational psychologists with a particular bent for the "human learning" aspect of our field. You will find, we think, that we have placed great emphasis on the observable as opposed to the internal components of human life. We are, we suppose, pragmatic empiricists with an applicational rather than a theoretical orientation. Of prime importance to us is your ability to apply the text material in your own teaching situations. We believe that you will find us to be "subjective behaviorists." We emphasize the observable but we do not deny the inner and find that internal processes, thinking, problem solving, memory and so forth are necessary for us to understand behavior. We are not attempting to sell you our philosophy (after all, there are differences among those of us who conceived of and then wrote this book) as the only correct one. Obviously, excellent teachers adhere to all kinds of educational philosophies. Rather, our philosophy is evident as you examine our material and we present it as one good approach, certainly not the only approach.

AN OUTLINE

Chapter two, "Writing Instructional Objectives," is prepared to provide you with a series of readings and exercises that will allow you to be able to construct and use instructional objectives. Why instructional objectives are necessary, what instructional objectives are, how to write instructional objectives and kinds of instructional objectives are the topics in the first part of this chapter. The last portion of the chapter describes how we may devise learning activities for students to meet our objectives and how we may assess the learning of students via pre, formative and summative tests.

Chapter three, "Task Analysis," is written in order to develop your ability to perform task analyses and to use the results of such analyses in your teaching. Task analyses are performed for cognitive, psychomotor and affective learning tasks and the resulting hierarchy of "prerequisites" are then demonstrated to be the starting point for determining children's entry levels with respect to the task you plan to teach. Developing a pretest from your task analysis and using the results of this pretest to rewrite your instructional objectives are also discussed.

Chapter four, "Problem Solving and Cognition," discusses concept learning, principle learning, rule learning, problem solving and memory. Examples are provided for the analysis of tasks within each of these categories as are methods of teaching for objectives in each category. Many useful hints for the teacher involved in day to day instruction are described in this chapter.

Chapter five, "Individualized Instruction," describes the process of individualizing instruction and presents the Diagnostic-Prescriptive Teaching model. We describe how to organize the classroom for individualized instruction, how to manage learning materials, how to initiate the program and how to have students meet their roles in this form of instruction. Specifically, performing diagnoses, making prescriptions, supervising student activities, tutoring, and evaluating student learning are described with special emphasis given unique problems in individualized instruction.

Chapter six, "Operant Theory," outlines one of the major theories of human behavior. This chapter is devoted primarily to the identification and definition of factors that influence human behavior. Starting from the simple premise that "behavior is controlled by the consequences of behavior," the theory and its classroom applications are organized in a step by step approach. This is the most theoretically-oriented chapter in the text.

Chapter seven, "Behavior Analysis and Classroom Management," is built directly on the theory and terminology you learn in chapter six. The process of behavior analysis is described and several methods of gathering behavioral data are presented. A series of behavior management techniques are described with guidelines for their use including behavioral contracts, proclamations and several approaches for individual students.

Chapter eight, "Assessment," is a partly technical, partly application-oriented chapter that discusses the traditional concepts of assessment. Specific topics include reliability, validity, standardized and teacher constructed assessment devices and brief summaries of frequently overlooked sources of assessment. Particular attention is given to how a teacher may assess the learning of his/her students in a real life setting.

Chapter nine, "Mainstreaming," is a brief summary of the new laws in mainstreaming. The laws are described and the impact of the laws on the classroom teacher are stressed. The processes of screening, referral and placement are emphasized and the teacher's roles in these processes are clearly described.

The last chapter is a culmination of the material in this book written to help you apply the principles of educational psychology in day to day teaching. This chapter is designed as a model for your use of this book as a source in your teaching.

This book is designed for your use. The perforated pages, work space and so on are included because we expect you to "use up" this book. We are convinced that as you finish this text and begin your teaching that you will have developed some worthwhile skills as a result of your educational psychology experience.

Chapter 2

WRITING INSTRUCTIONAL OBJECTIVES

Any student-instructor relationship must be governed by goals on the part of the instructor and the student. The questions of what is to be taught and what is to be learned are the first questions we must answer prior to attempting instruction of any sort. In this chapter you will read about instructional objectives, long and short term, how and why they are used, how you may go about preparing them for your students in a way that will most likely ensure your success and how learning activities and evaluation of student learning should follow directly from well-written objectives. Your objectives in reading this chapter are:

1. Write a sentence telling what instructional objectives are.
2. List the three components of a behavioral objective.
3. Give five possible differences between long-term and short-term (behavioral) objectives.
4. Write a sentence telling what learning is.
5. Write a sentence describing the accessibility of learning to an observer.
6. List three uses of behavioral objectives.
7. Write one behavioral objective, containing the three necessary components of behavioral objectives for (a) concept learning, (b) skill learning, and (c) value learning.
8. List the five guidelines for learning activities.
9. Describe the learning activities you would use (including the five guidelines for learning activities) for the three objectives you listed for objective seven above.
10. List the three forms of evaluation of learning.
11. Describe the three forms of evaluation you would use for each of the three behavioral objectives-learning activities you have developed for objectives seven and nine above.
12. You will be able to identify correctly written behavioral objectives and identify missing or incorrect components of incorrectly written objectives.

The conditions under which the mastery of these objectives will be assessed are those you set for yourself as you respond to the exercises at the end of this chapter. Criteria for acceptance of your performance shall be errorless responding to the exercises at the end of this chapter. The criteria are more specifically detailed throughout the chapter.

LEARNING AND INSTRUCTIONAL OBJECTIVES

Prior to a discussion of instructional objectives we must review a few basic concepts taken from the broad field of educational psychology. Teachers are about the business of teaching students. Another way to say this is that teachers are involved in helping students learn. Teaching, your future profession, amounts to all the activities you engage in that somehow cause learning to occur in students. Learning, on the other hand, is some sort of process that means different things to different people. We can talk about accumulating knowledge, gaining insights, developing skills, changing attitudes and many other things that would fit into the broadest interpretation of learning. What exactly is learning? A common definition for learning is *a relatively permanent change in a person's behavior as a result of some sort of experiential factor.* In other words, we would say that if learning has occurred in an organism, then the observable behavior of that organism must be changed in a way that is relatively permanent.

Think about learning for a moment. Specifically, think about people you have "watched" learn something. Perhaps it was a roommate who suddenly stumbled across a method to solve his/her mathematics problems or perhaps it was a small child that was able to "figure out" how to open a box. What happened? What did you see? No matter how many examples you consider did you ever see anything other than the results of learning? Here is one of the most crucial points we can make about the whole business of learning and teaching. Learning itself *cannot* be observed. We can only look at the results of learning, a change in behavior, and infer from this observation that learning has occurred.

The process of learning is inaccessible to us. We can watch what a person does prior to learning something, we can watch them during the time that learning occurs and we can watch them after learning. All we can ever see is that person's behavior. We do not have the ability to "look into" a person's head to see what happens during learning. We can say what learning is, a change in behavior, but we cannot say how it happens. All the research in learning is based on this one inescapable fact, whatever happens in learning is not observable, but rather the result of learning.

An example should serve to clarify this problem. Suppose we watch (observe) a student who has no knowledge of medieval Russian read a short book about life in Russia during this time. Prior to reading the book we determined that he had no knowledge of medieval Russia by giving him a 25 question multiple choice test taken from the short book he is to read. He missed all the questions. We sit and watch him open the book and turn the pages as he reads through the essay. His eyes move from side to side and up and down and perhaps we see an occasional movement of the lips. He moves around in his seat and scratches once in a while. Finally, after an hour or so he finishes the book. Did learning occur? Well, from what we have seen we have no reason to decide one way or the other. If learning did occur, how much was learned and what was learned? Again, from what we have seen we have no way of making any kind of judgment. We have been watching a process, reading, which most of us associate with learning. In fact most of us would probably argue that reading is a good way to learn things. On the basis of our observations, though, we have no reason to believe that learning, or for that matter reading, has occurred. How can we find out if learning occurred, what was learned and how much was learned? Let's go back to our definition of learning. Learning is a relatively permanent change in a person's (organism's) behavior as a result of some sort of experience. Has something happened that meets this definition?

The only way that we can find out whether or not learning has occurred, whether or not our definition has been met, is to find out if our example's behavior has changed as a result of his experience with the book. As we look back at him he is sitting in the same position he sat in at the beginning of the book experience and doesn't seem to be behaving differently. We could just continue to observe him for the next several hours, days or weeks to see if we can pick up a behavior change that we could attribute to the book experience but we are impatient so we will take a more direct approach. Let us readminister the 25 question multiple choice test on which he missed all the items prior to the book experience. He takes pencil in hand and zips right through the test. We immediately score it and find out that he has chosen the correct alternative for each of the questions. Has learning, a relatively permanent change in behavior occurred? Yes. His behavior, choosing alternatives on a multiple choice test, has changed for a reasonable length of time. We could not see learning occur. We didn't really even know whether he was reading or not (he could have been faking it), but we have seen a change in behavior as the result of an experience with a book and from this we *infer* that learning has occurred.

How much learning has occurred and what, specifically, was learned? These questions can only be partially answered by what we have done. All we can say is that he could recognize 25 bits of knowledge taken from the book. For all we have observed this may be all that he has learned or he may have learned far more. Our inferences about how much and what is learned must be based on what and how many behaviors we observe to have changed. We could, we suppose, continue the testing process for an indefinite period of time until we were satisfied with our answers. Our student subject, however, is in a hurry to get to his next class and so we let him go.

7

One more example should allow us to close off this discussion. Picture, if you will, a small child just tall enough to stand on her tip-toes and touch the outer edge of a stove's "eye" in our kitchen. For the sake of this example we'll assume that she has always lived and visited other homes wherein the tops of stoves were out of reach. We are saying that she has never had any experience with the tops of stoves before. Let's assume that we have just finished heating a pot of coffee and that the top of our stove is very hot. While we are turned around, thinking that she cannot reach the top of the stove, we see out of the corner of our eyes that the little girl reaches up and touches the hot part of the stove. Immediately she retracts her hand and starts crying in pain and fear. We drop whatever we are doing and treat her very slight but painful burn. Has any learning occurred? Has the little girl learned that the top of stoves causes pain? How can we find out if learning has occurred?

Again, we have not seen anything that would indicate to us that any kind of learning has occurred. All we saw was a little girl that wailed very loudly as a result of a painful encounter with the stove. We can only infer that learning has occurred if we can note a relatively permanent change in her behavior. How can we do this? We could watch her to see if she repeats her exploratory behavior in the immediate future and if she does not, we would have a pretty good reason to believe that some learning had occurred. If, however, we were impatient, we might place her favorite toy on top of the stove (now cool) and see if she will reach for it. If she refuses and motions for us to get it, we could infer that she has learned that the top of the stove is not a good place for her to touch. Obviously, this is, at best, a very imprecise measure. If we were to ask what and how much, exactly, was learned, we would have to pass because our simple assessment would only allow us to infer that some learning occurred, nothing more. (Please note: While we felt that this was a reasonably good example of a learning situation, we certainly would never do such a thing on purpose.)

Our examples should have made the point that learning, whatever situation it results from, is an internal process of some sort that is not open to observation. All we can do is look at the results of learning, a relatively permanent change in behavior, and infer that learning has occurred from this evidence. Okay. What has all this stuff about the inference of learning from changes of behavior got to do with instructional objectives? All instructional objectives must be tailored to meet the problems inherent in the assessment of learning. Since we can only infer learning from observed changes in behavior, our instructional objectives must say what kind of changes in behavior we are looking for. Any other kinds of statements are likely to be misleading.

THE USE OF INSTRUCTIONAL OBJECTIVES

We have so far only indicated what our instructional objectives should describe. Why do we make instructional objectives? What kinds of instructional objectives are there and how should they be used? These are the three questions we must answer before their value and use are clear.

Instructional objectives are statements of what a student or a group of students are to be like after some period of instruction. They are statements of the kinds of behaviors that we wish to alter as a result of the students' learning experience. Why do we use instructional objectives? We use instructional objectives so that we may determine if learning occurred, how much was learned and what was learned. Further, instructional objectives, when given to students as they should be, tell students what and how much they should learn. They are statements to students of what they ought to be able to do as a result of our instruction.

Instructional objectives also provide us a guide for our instructional procedures and how we will assess the learning of our students. For example, if one of our objectives for a class of eleventh grade students is to be able to "recognize the names of presidents of the United States," this statement would allow us to determine whether or not such learning occurred. (This objective, of course, may not be a particularly worthwhile one.) Either students can recognize the names of presidents or they cannot. We can also find out how many names of presidents are recognized by students and vary our assessment procedures to examine the conditions under which our students recognize the names of presidents. As will be seen, this example was poorly written but our assessment of learning becomes more accurate as we write better objectives. Our objective, poorly written as it is, still tells students what they are to do. They are to recognize the names of presidents. This kind of statement should be an aid to their preparation for our assessment of their learning. However they go about preparing, they will have a statement of exactly what to prepare for rather than worrying about "what the test is going to be like." Lastly, this objective should provide guidance for our instruction. Since we have said we want recognition, our activities in class will be geared toward this behavior rather than some other activities that teach things we will not assess.

Long- and Short-Term Instructional Objectives

Now that we have indicated what instructional objectives are and why they are used, we must differentiate between the two basic forms of instructional objectives, long-term and short-term. Long-term instructional objectives are those objectives we use to describe the kinds of behaviors we wish students to perform after lengthy periods of time such as a semester, a school year or at the end of twelve years of instruction. Short-term instructional objectives are those objectives we use to describe how students will behave after periods of instruction shorter than one semester and more commonly for briefer periods of time such as one class period, one week or one unit of instruction.

Since this book is written for prospective teachers who will be concerned primarily with enhancing their instructional effectiveness on a day to day basis, we shall emphasize short-term instructional objectives and refer to them henceforth as *behavioral objectives*. We shall, then, first describe how you may write correct behavioral objectives to present you with some contrasts in how the two forms of objectives are written.

Behavioral objectives are exactly what the term implies. They are descriptions of behaviors that we expect from students after a period of instruction. Behavioral objectives are also behavioral in the sense that they are written in ways that follow behaviorist prescriptions for describing behaviors. In other words, only those verbs that describe *observable* and *measurable* behaviors can be used in a behavioral objective. Those verbs we think of as "action" verbs make up the pool of verbs we can choose from in writing behavioral objectives.

To demonstrate how the choice of verbs in writing behavioral objectives is all important, we shall digress for a few moments and provide you with some typical examples of verbs that do not allow for observation or measurement as they may appear in some "objectives." Remember the history professor who gave you the objective "Appreciate the Constitution of the United States" and then measured your appreciation with a 200 item, multiple choice test? Or how about the mathematics instructor that wanted you to "understand" some new principles. Weren't you surprised when you found out that "understand" meant "derive"? Many professorial types ask you to be "aware of" some bit of information. Sadly, being "aware of" almost always meant defining. Our all-time favorite is the instructor who wants students to "grasp the significance" of something or other.

What do all these nonaction verbs mean? Let's take a look at "appreciate" as an example. When an instructor tells students to "appreciate" something, what does he/she communicate? For some students "appreciate" means memorize. For others, "appreciate" means recognize and for still others it means to "feel happy when that bit of knowledge is contemplated." There are probably as many interpretations of "appreciate" as there are students who are asked to "appreciate." The problem with verbs such as "appreciate," "understand," "really understand," "know," "really know," "be aware of," and "grasp the significance of" (just once the authors would like to see a significance they could really put their hands on and squeeze) and so forth is that they do not clearly specify what it is that the instructor wants or what the students are to do. Such verbs cause

10

needless confusion and do not help the assessment process nor do they help students learn. The only way to avoid this problem is by using action verbs that allow for the direct observation and measurement of the behavior which the instructor wants.

The first and most important component of a properly written behavioral objective is a verb that specifies the behavior you want in absolutely unambiguous terms. If you plan to assess learning via performance on a multiple choice test, a matching test or a true and false test, why beat around the bush and talk about "appreciate," "be aware of" and so on? If this is the behavior you want, you should unequivocally say so. "The student will recognize" (identify). This tells the student what behavior is expected and helps you plan your instruction and assessment to meet this need. Objectives written with verbs such as "recognize "identify," "describe," "define," "list," "construct," "solve," "write," "draw," "discuss" and so on allow you to say what you mean. If you ask students to list ten learning theorists, you can see exactly how to assess the learning and they see exactly how to prepare.

We are not saying that "appreciation," "awareness," "knowing," "understanding" and the like are not good things to want from students. Perhaps they are. The problem is that such terms are so vague that they will, inevitably, be misunderstood by some students. They are also devilishly difficult to assess. How do we ascertain whether or not material is appreciated? If appreciate means list, describe, define and so on, why not just ask for this specific behavior? All behavioral objectives must be stated with verbs that can be observed and measured. Appreciate, be aware of, grasp the significance of and all the rest just do not allow for ease of observation or measurement.

The second major component of behavioral objectives is the criterion for acceptance of the students' behavior. In other words, if you ask students to list ten cognitive psychologists, how many errors can a student make and still have his/her behavior be deemed acceptable by you? Will eight out of ten be good enough? Can the students misspell some of the names? How many names must be spelled correctly? Must the names appear in some order? Giving an observable and measurable verb in your objective certainly makes it far more worthwhile than if you don't, but your objectives will be better still if you give the criteria for an acceptable behavior. This helps you during the assessment of student learning and it helps students prepare for the assessment.

No matter what you ask students to do, you must say how good is good enough. If you ask for a definition, what must be included in the description? Including the criteria for acceptance of a behavior helps you further clarify your instruction, your assessment and how your students will prepare.

11

The third component of behavioral objectives that you must include is the conditions under which the behavior will be assessed. Think about how differently you might prepare as a student to discuss the Treaty of Versailles in writing on a written examination and orally in front of a foreign diplomacy seminar. If a student is to construct a distillation apparatus, will it be done in class or at home? If a student is to define several new terms, will this be done at home, at school, with reference books, without reference books, individually or in groups? Specifying the conditions under which the behavior will occur also helps you plan your instruction, plan your assessment, and it certainly helps students prepare. Let's take a look at a series of correctly and incorrectly written behavioral objectives. See if you can tell which ones are correctly written and which ones are not. Can you identify those incorrect or missing portions of the incorrectly written objectives?

1. The students will list Maslow's hierarchy of needs in correct order without misspelling any words. This will be done on a written examination in class without reference materials. The students must list all five needs to meet our criterion.
2. The students will really know the difference between phenomenology and existentialism. They will know all six major differences during a written examination in class without reference materials. All six major differences must be fully understood to meet our criteria.
3. The students will correctly say the sound of "ph" 27 out of 30 times they see the letters "ph" on flash cards in class.
4. The students will demonstrate their conceptualizations of the phonetic unit "b" in class on 27 out of 30 flash cards.
5. The students will compare and contrast the concepts of discipline and punishment.
6. The students will grasp the significance of Sir Cyril Burton's improprieties in conducting research.
7. The students will describe the concept of state's rights including all eleven points outlined in class. The description will be done at home on a paper to be turned in the next day. The students must list each of the eleven points and relate each to state's rights for the paper to be acceptable.
8. The students will crystallize their thinking on freedom of speech and write a 2,000 word essay supporting their views to be turned in next week.
9. The students will cursively write the letter "A" 10 times on notebook paper during the first five minutes of class. Neatness must be apparent.
10. The readers will identify each correctly and incorrectly written behavioral objective in this list of ten and identify the missing or incor-

rect components of those behavioral objectives identified as incorrect. The readers will do so wherever they happen to be as they read this and an acceptable behavior shall be a perfect agreement with the writer's responses below.

Now that you've read through all of the objectives above, let's go back and see if your responses are aligned with ours. Objective number one is a well-written objective. It contains a verb that can be observed and measured (list) and it describes the criteria for acceptance as well as the conditions under which the assessment will take place.

There are some problems with number two. The modified verb "really know" is ambiguous. What does "really know" mean? Who really knows? There are attempts made to provide criteria but here the words "know" and "fully understood" cause us to wonder how in the world the assessment will take place. The conditions are specified.

Number three is correctly written. "The students will correctly say" provides specific directions for what will be done. The criteria and conditions are also specified.

Number four starts out impressively but incorrectly. "Demonstrating conceptualizations" sounds nice but it does not communicate to anyone what is expected of the students. The criteria and conditions are spelled out but as you can see they are rather meaningless given the verb forms used for that objective.

Number five starts off well asking for comparisons and contrasts but even though these verbs lead to observable and measurable behaviors, without criteria they do not allow for much of a communication to students for what is to be done. The conditions are also absent. Broad kinds of verbs such as compare, contrast, discuss, write and the like must be accompanied by very carefully stated criteria.

Grasping significances, the verb form used for objective number six, is one of our pet peeves. This objective misses on all three counts; the verb leads to ambiguity, no criteria are spelled out and no conditions for assessment are provided. All in all this is a terrible objective.

Objective number seven contains a reasonable verb form; "describe," qualifies this verb with rather strict criteria and provides for the conditions under which the behavior is to occur. This kind of objective, assuming that an appropriate verb is chosen, depends very much on the clear and concise statement of criteria for acceptance of the behavior. As this objective is written, no conditions for the length of the paper, spelling and so on are given. If these are important considerations for the writer of such an objective, they must be clearly spelled out.

Objective number eight is another example of "doublethink" language that sounds impressive but is not. Chemical solutions crystallize, thoughts do not. The verb form here is ambiguous and gives no inkling of what the writer wants. The criteria are very weak (2,000 word essay) and do not give the reader much information. The conditions are roughly specified but they could be clearer as well.

Objective number nine contains an appropriate verb that leads to observable and measurable behavior. The conditions are also very clear, "during the first five minutes of class," but the criteria are simply terrible. How do we assess apparent neatness? We cannot. Whatever you want in such an objective must be spelled out clearly in the criteria for acceptance.

Objective number ten, besides its obvious educational significance, contains an excellent verb highly likely to lead to observable behaviors. The criteria, perfection, are a little bit overstated but by now you should be striving for that. The conditions are specified by you, the reader.

By now you should be able to list the three major components of behavioral objectives (short-term instructional objectives) and you should be able to identify those that are correctly and incorrectly written while identifying the missing or incorrect components. The use of observable and measurable verb forms, criteria for acceptance of behaviors and the conditions under which the behavior will be assessed are the three dominant characteristics of behavioral objectives. Every behavioral objective must have these three components. (Note: Where the conditions and criteria for many objectives are the same, e.g., those listed at the beginning of this chapter or a list of objectives you may provide students for a week's lesson, you need only state the criteria and conditions once and indicate that these directions will remain constant throughout. This saves you the trouble of writing and rewriting the same statements over and over.)

Long-term instructional objectives differ from behavioral objectives on the basis of the time for meeting the goals and because they seldom specify criteria for acceptance, conditions under which the behaviors are to occur and frequently use ambiguous verbs. This is a lamentable difference but easily traced to its source when we examine who writes them and where they come from. Long-term instructional objectives are typically written by legislators at the federal and state level, legislative committees, administrators of school systems, schools or departments, textbook writers and only infrequently by classroom teachers. They are statements, very appropriate in political tenor, of what groups of students are to be like at the end of long periods of instruction. Statements such as "The students will appreciate the significance of our democratic system of government" frequently are made by the setters of long-term objectives. We will not attempt to justify such poorly written objectives but they are a fact of life. You, the teacher, must take long-term objectives and develop a series of behavioral objectives leading to the goals specified in the long-term objective. You will, no doubt, go through a series of "list," define," and "recite," kinds of behavioral objectives with your students and decide that all these behavioral objectives taken together are what is meant by "appreciate the significance of."

We should point out that long-term objectives serve a different purpose than do behavioral objectives. While behavioral objectives guide you in planning instruction and evaluation and give your students direction, long-term objectives provide only the broadest kinds of goals for large numbers of students in a very ideological sense. It may be quite wonderful for a state government to decide that children should appreciate their government. This is the government's statement of what it wants from students in an ideological sense. It is written to provide you with some general notions about the kind of teaching you will do. It is up to you, as the teacher, to transform such global statements into objectives that will lead to observable and measurable behaviors.

THE RELATIONSHIP BETWEEN BEHAVIORAL OBJECTIVES AND INSTRUCTION

In educational psychology there exists an apparent trichotomy of kinds of learning that students engage in. One of these categories is concept learning, those kinds of changes in behavior that are related to the cognitive domain. The second category is skill learning, those kinds of changes in behavior that are related to the psychomotor domain. The third category is the learning of values, attitudes, beliefs and feelings, those kinds of changes in behavior that are related to the affective domain. These distinctions are given different emphases by different theorists, some contending that all learning is the same, some contending that learning in each domain is clearly distinct from learning in the other domains. These theoretical differences are not important to the goals of this chapter but the very real differences in writing objectives, developing activities to help students meet the objectives and evaluating the students' mastery of the objectives between the three categories of learning cause us to treat them separately. In this section we shall discuss the relationship of behavioral objectives to the development of learning activities and learning material and how student evaluation may be built directly upon correctly written objectives.

The activities a teacher engages in to help students meet the behavioral objective he or she has devised must be built directly upon the objective. Any activities designed to help students reach an objective should meet five criteria. These are:

1. The materials for the learning activities and the learning activities themselves must allow the students to directly perceive the concept that has been set forth in the behavioral objective. Wherever possible, students should have the opportunity to feel, taste, touch, smell, see, hear or read

15

about the concept. If direct contact is not possible the learning activities and materials should relate as closely as possible to previous experiences that the students may have had with the concept. Where direct contact with the concept is not possible, secondary contact through films, audio tapes and reading material should be provided. A mix of both direct and secondary contact is usually a good idea.

2. The kinds of sense receptors that the learning activities and materials have students employ should be as closely related as possible to the concept stated in the objective. For example, if we are going to teach a concept about music, our activities should allow the students to hear the concept. If we are going to teach a concept about the taste of sour, we should do all that we can to see that students actually get to taste a sour substance. Tasting one sour lemon will tell a student a whole lot more about "sour" than five films and several thousand words spoken about "sour."

3. The learning activities should be carefully structured so that the experiences can be easily transformed into verbal learning. In other words, the learning activities should help the children verbalize their experience and relate it in some way to their past experience and previous knowledge. The only way to find out if learning activities are meeting this goal is through the children's oral or written responses.

4. Children should be provided with feedback for their responses during a learning activity. They should have the opportunity to respond to questions or to practice an activity and find out if they are correct or incorrect and exactly what can be done to correct an incorrect response.

5. The student should be an active participant in the learning activity, involved in making overt responses during the activity either verbally or nonverbally.

Meeting these five guidelines does not guarantee that a learning activity will be an unqualified success. However, adhering to these guidelines will insure that your learning activity will be on the right track. Unfortunately there is no substitute for experience in structuring learning activities. Every teacher has some learning activities that are successful and others that are not successful. It seems that only practice allows us to get a feel for the business of structuring learning activities and to maximize the possibilities of having successful learning activities.

EVALUATION

Behavioral objectives and learning activities are two-thirds of the teaching process we will describe here. Evaluation or assessment of student performance is the third component of teaching to which we must address ourselves. To gain maximum benefit from the use of behavioral objectives teachers should use three forms of assessment: *preassessment, formative tests,* and *posttests.* Assessment in the sense that we use it means an evaluation of what behaviors are present in the students at the time that the assessment is conducted. In other words we test children to find out whether some behaviors are present in the students and to what extent they are present. If we want students to recognize the names of Gestalt psychologists, we would assess this by presenting to them a long list of names with some of the names of Gestalt psychologists included. How many they recognize, if any, tells us about that particular behavior (recognition) at that moment in time.

Preassessment is conducted prior to any kind of learning activities to find out how much of the behavior specified in the objective can be performed by the students. If our objective is for students to construct a distillation apparatus in the laboratory, we can ask them to try to do so before any instruction. If they can all do it at an acceptable level, then we really will not have to spend too much time reviewing something they can already do. If we find that they make certain kinds of errors over and over, we can then gear our instruction to remediate these specific errors. Preassessment tells us where students are at prior to our instruction and allows us to obtain a premeasure of what kinds of behavior they can perform. We can later contrast the results of the preassessment to a postassessment to see how effective our teaching methods were.

The second form of evaluation a teacher should use is the formative test, sometimes called the self-test. Formative tests are questions, activities and "noncredit" tests and quizzes given orally or in writing that allow the students to see how they are progressing towards meeting the behavioral objective. These formative tests should be an integral part of the feedback students receive during their learning exercise and should be interspersed throughout the learning activities.

Lastly, the teacher should give a posttest (sometimes called a summative test) at the end of the instructional activities. This, in fact, should be a restatement of the behavioral objective, allowing the teacher to determine if the students met the behavioral objective.

Let us approach the development of writing objectives, developing learning activities and assessing mastery by providing a series of examples and critiques.

CONCEPTS

Behavioral Objective (early elementary): The students will correctly identify all the trees in the schoolyard and distinguish trees from other plants with a 100 percent accuracy rate.

Activity: The teacher first discusses trees and verbally describes some. Then a filmstrip identifying trees of America is viewed by the children.

Following this the teacher and the students walk over parts of the school grounds while the teacher asks, as she points to different objects. "Is this a tree?" The children must respond yes or no and distinguish the trees from the nontrees as they look at and feel them. The teacher will provide prompts and hints where necessary and comment on correctness and incorrectness of student responses. She will also provide correct information if the students are in error.

Evaluation: The teacher's evaluation (assessment of the children's behavior) takes three forms. First, prior to any instruction, she took the children on a tour of the schoolyard and pointed to different objects while asking, "Is this a tree?" and when the children answered yes or no, she followed the answers up with "Why or why not?" This preassessment allowed the teacher to determine how much of the concept (how much of ths material, as it were) the children had mastered prior to any lesson. This also allowed the teacher to gear her instruction to fit her students' specific needs.

The second form of evaluation was formative tests. These took the form of questions to the students during all the exercises, asking about the identification of trees and nontrees. What the teacher did was to restate her behavioral objective frequently throughout the learning activities so that the students could respond to it after various stages of the instruction. In this way both she and the students could see how much progress was being made.

Lastly, the teacher gave a posttest at the end of the instructional period. She again took the students out to the schoolyard, pointed to several objects in the yard and asked, "Is this a tree?" The students had to answer yes or no and provide the reason for why or why not the objects were trees. Her criterion for acceptance was 100 percent accuracy.

Critique: Let us review this hypothetical instance of behavioral objective, learning activity, and evaluation. The objective clearly meets our criteria for an acceptable behavioral objective. It contains a verb (identify) that will lead to behaviors that can be clearly observed and measured. This particular verb form calls for the identification of members of a concept. Either objects are trees or they are not. The conditions are clearly specified as are the criteria for acceptable behaviors.

The activities the teacher had the students engage in to help meet the objective were built directly upon her objective. She wanted identification and the students practiced identification. She met the five criteria we outlined for learning activities above. She met the first criterion as she had the children see trees, hear about them, see a filmstrip about them and actually touch them. They could have tasted and smelled them too, but that probably wasn't our teacher's intent. The second criterion was met by the use of children's visual and tactile sense receptors, they saw and touched trees. Our teacher clearly met the third criterion as the entire schoolyard activity with the children stressed their verbalization. The fourth criterion was met as the teacher gave all the children several opportunities to respond to questions during the learning activity and she provided them with appropriate feedback for their responses. The fifth criterion was met as all the students were actively involved in the learning activity both verbally and nonverbally.

This behavioral objective, through its proper use, led to a good instructional strategy and an assessment of learning that measured exactly what the teacher had in mind. By using behavioral objectives properly, the entire process of teaching can be greatly enhanced.

Behavioral Objective (middle elementary): The students will correctly add two, three digit numbers together. Criteria for acceptance should be correctly solving 17 out of 20 problems in class during a test period without any reference material.

Activity: The teacher first reviews the addition of two, two digit numbers, the lesson the children have just completed. She then demonstrates adding two, three digit numbers together while discussing each step. She then passes out a ditto sheet containing ten sample problems to the children and has them work on these. She wanders through the classroom, stopping at each child's desk rewarding correct behaviors with praise and correcting wrong problems. The children are individually asked what they did and how they did it. The teacher also provides feedback for the verbal responses. After she has talked to each child (this probably took more than one class period) she returns to the board and has the children talk her through a series of problems, always offering feedback. She is careful to call on each child in class at least once. She then assigns some problems to be taken home for homework.

Evaluation: This teacher's evaluation took two forms in a formal sense. She did not give a formal pretest, but since she had just guided the students through the successful learning of solving two, two digit problems, she had, through this experience, a fairly accurate picture of her students' abilities in this area. Formative tests were interspersed throughout her lesson. Each child had the opportunity to work several problems and obtained direct feedback from the teacher as to correctness and incorrectness. To carry this a little further, she could have given the children the correct answers for the homework problems so they could check their work as they did it.

Her posttest consisted of giving the children 20 problems in class, 17 of which they had to solve correctly in order for the teacher to feel that this lesson had been successfully completed.

Critique: This behavioral objective was a good one using a verb (add) that leads to a straightforward assessment of student behavior. The criteria and conditions are also very clearly stated. The activities meet our five criteria. The students directly sense the concept (in early elementary actually touching concrete objects to be added is superior but when two numbers in the hundreds are to be added this becomes unfeasible). All the activities related directly to the objective. Verbal learning was emphasized and the teacher provided for frequent feedback. The students were directly involved in the learning experience.

As an aside we should note that the preparation of behavioral objectives, learning activities and evaluations for cognitively-oriented activities, does not vary from grade level to grade level to a significant degree. As long as behavioral objectives are clearly and concisely stated, learning exercises and methods of evaluation flow directly from them. Of course, as your objectives become increasingly complex, the conditions under which the behavior will be assessed and the criteria for accepting the behavior become increasingly important. We should also note that as the topics you teach become more complex, it is often much easier for teachers to use a series of several brief behavioral objectives rather than a few highly complex ones. Your instruction and evaluation can then integrate a series of objectives. Additional practice in writing and identifying correctly written behavioral objectives is available at the end of this book.

Behavioral Objective (early elementary): The students will hold a pair of scissors correctly and cut along lines drawn on pieces of paper in class. Criteria for acceptance shall be holding the scissors properly and cutting along a 10 inch zig-zag line on a piece of paper without cutting more than a quarter inch away from the line.

Activity: The teacher, bringing a box of blunt-end, "school scissors" with her, holds up a pair of scissors in front of the class and models how they are held (differently for right- and left-handed children). She then describes what scissors are used for and asks the children what scissors may be used for, taking care to let each child have an opportunity to respond. She then demonstrates cutting some paper while describing how the scissors and paper are held.

After this, the teacher passes scissors and paper out to all the children and asks them to practice "just cutting" up the paper. She then goes to each child individually and offers feedback as to how he/she is doing. She praises the children when they hold the scissors correctly and corrects and redemonstrates how to hold them if the children are incorrect. Each child is also asked to describe (verbalize) what he/she is doing and how it should be done. As holding the scissors is very important, she continues to work with the children individually, some moving on to cutting out shapes with paper of different colors while others are still practicing holding and cutting. She provides formative tests by asking each child "Show me how you hold the scissors and the paper." When all the children do this correctly, she is ready to go on to the second part of the learning activity.

Again she goes to the front of the classroom (this may be the same day or at a later date) and reviews the proper way of holding scissors and paper. Then she introduces some examples of paper with designs drawn on the paper (a jack-o-lantern, a "paper doll," a half-moon and so on) and describes how scissors may be used to cut out shapes on paper. She then demonstrates this by cutting out a jack-o-lantern in front of the class. She follows this by passing out several sheets of paper to each child with zig-zag lines drawn on the paper and tells the children that they may start on the jack-o-lantern and other shapes after they can each cut along the zig-zag line on one sheet of paper without getting further away from the line than one-quarter of an inch. (She holds her thumb and index finger at this distance so the children can see what one-quarter inch is.) The children are then told to practice cutting on the lines and as they do one correctly they may go to her "goody box" in the front of the room and get four neat shapes to work on. While the children are practicing she circulates to each individual child offering feedback for his/her work. When a child meets her criteria, she signals that the child may go get the "neat shapes."

Critique: The behavioral objective is clearly stated with an unambiguous verb, clear criteria and a statement of conditions under which the behavior should occur. You should note that statements like "correctly hold" are frequent troublespots with some behaviors. Here, the behavior "correctly hold" must be what the teacher demonstrates. The reason we sometimes say things like "correctly hold," "correctly perform," and so on is because written directions are so complex that they often confuse students more than they help. The activities were such that the students could directly perceive what they were to do. They engaged in actually using scissors and cutting along lines and the teacher went to great lengths to see that verbal transfer would occur. The teacher provided frequent feedback throughout the learning activity and the students were obviously active participants in the exercises.

No formal pretest was given but the teacher structured the activities in a way that allowed students already capable of performing the skill to go on to other activities while she worked with those children who had not yet mastered the skill. Formative tests were interspersed throughout the activity even though they were not formal. Rather, the teacher observed individual children and provided feedback as to their skill performance. The posttest directly assessed whether or not the behavior called for in the behavioral objective had been met. Once again, a well-written objective provided the basis for a good learning activity and appropriate assessment.

Behavioral Objective (early elementary): The students will enjoy reading. Enjoyment shall be defined as students choosing to read when other activities are available and they have no constraints placed on them to choose any particular activity. The criterion shall be each student choosing to read from among many possible activities at least once. This choice shall be made during free-time in class.

Activity: The teacher, after determining what topics interest the children shall read aloud to the class each day a story from one (or more when interests agree) child's area of interest. Further, she shall have the students who expressed interest in certain areas read parts of the stories aloud on the days that their interest is the content of the story. These children shall also be asked to explain what they like about the topic, why they like the topic and if the story was enjoyable. They shall be encouraged to relate anecdotes about their experiences with the content that the story dealt with. For example, one day the story may be about horses which some of the children were particularly interested in.

Further, the availability of "reading time" shall be paired with whatever rewards the teacher uses for especially good behavior from the class. Reading time shall be presented as a treat. As the teacher reads she will be careful to ask frequent questions and evoke responses from children. Praise, attention and other rewards shall be continually paired with reading behavior. The teacher shall always positively reinforce any "free-choice" reading on the part of her students with praise.

The teacher's assessment shall be of an informal nature, taking the form of her observations of the students. Each student will have met the criterion when he/she chooses to read in class as a free-time activity. As this objective may or may not be met with all students, there shall be no time constraints in her observations.

Critique: Critiquing an activity designed to teach a value is far more difficult than critiquing other forms of activities. The behavioral objective was appropriate as the verb form (after qualification) was clear as were the conditions and criteria. However, when we examine the activity to see if it meets our guidelines set out earlier in the chapter, we see that the idea that "reading is enjoyable" can only be indirectly perceived by the students. Our operationalized definition of "reading is enjoyable" can easily be seen but is one step removed from the objective itself. The idea that "reading is enjoyable" cannot be taught directly. (Imagine if you will, the absurdity of preparing a lecture entitled "reading is enjoyable.") Second, the senses that would be used in meeting the behavioral objective are properly engaged in the activity but there is the rather knotty problem of having the children "feel" something. Not only is learning inaccessible to an observer, feeling is every bit as inaccessible. We can see that the behavior we have decided stands for "reading is enjoyable" but we cannot actually see the "enjoyment" part.

The transfer of activities to verbal learning is possible but is not directly taught. Obviously, pairing rewards and treats with reading behavior is getting at the verbalization that "reading is enjoyable" but is doing so in an indirect way. Feedback is present throughout the process but it is limited to praise when reading is present, praise when the children indicate that they are going to read on their own and other less direct comments. Fifth, the students are active participants.

As you can see, we really met only three of the guidelines completely: feedback, appropriate sense usage and active participation. Two of the guidelines, direct perception and transfer of the activities to verbal learning are only partially met. It is true that direct perception of the operational definition of "reading is enjoyable" is possible and that saying "reading is enjoyable" can occur, but these are only indirectly provided for in the instruction. Such an activity based on the behavioral objective written to get at the idea that "reading is enjoyable" may or may not be appropriate as a source of instruction, but values are somewhat more difficult to teach because of the extra step of providing an operational definition of the value.

The evaluation of learning for this activity is probably appropriate. Either the students choose to read during their free time or they do not. That such reading really indicates enjoyment is a matter that can be debated, though.

The reader should note that the objectives, activities and forms of evaluation we have presented in this chapter are, as is all human work, flawed. None of them would be appropriate for all children or for all teachers. Most of the readers could find places to disagree with our activities. The point of this section, though, is to demonstrate how objectives, learning activities and evaluation fit together and the differences between teaching concepts, skills and values.

SUMMARY

In this chapter we defined learning and described its inaccessibility to the teacher. We summarized the value of instructional objectives and indicated their uses. We differentiated between long- and short-term (behavioral) objectives. The three necessary components of behavioral objectives were described as was the way in which they should be used. We outlined how learning activities should result from behavioral objectives and set out five guidelines for any learning activity. Three forms of evaluation were described and examples of their use were provided. Lastly, examples of the use of behavioral objectives-learning activities-evaluation were provided for the reader.

Chapter 3

TASK ANALYSIS

The material in this chapter, task analysis, follows directly the materials discussed in chapter two. After completing this chapter you will (at a 90 percent accuracy rate):

1. Write a statement defining entering behavior.
2. List at least six factors to be considered in entering behavior.
3. Write a statement defining task analysis.
4. Write a statement describing the relationship between task analysis and entering behavior.
5. Write a statement describing the relationship between entering behavior, task analysis and behavioral objectives.
6. Write a statement describing how task analysis proceeds from behavioral objectives.
7. Perform a task analysis for a concept you might teach.
8. Perform a task analysis of a psychomotor skill you might teach.
9. Perform a task analysis for an affective outcome you might teach.
10. Rewrite a behavioral objective for students based on their entering behavior and the task analysis you have performed.
11. Outline the steps you will follow in bringing students from their entry level to the place at which your original behavioral objective was written.

ENTERING BEHAVIOR

Writing correct behavioral objectives is a very big help to any instructor. However, behavioral objectives and the learning exercises that spring from them often are not appropriately written for where the students are. In other words, even the best written behavioral objective may be inappropriate for a student who does not have the background skills and knowledge necessary to meet that objective. Suppose you, a highly literate college student (you must also be very discerning and sharp-witted since you have chosen to read this book) are given the objective "Derive Einstein's special theory of relativity in class tomorrow during a two-hour examination. Your work must be error free to meet acceptable criteria." How many of you (not to mention the writers of this book) could meet this behavioral objective? The odds are very great that almost none of the readers of this book could meet such an objective. We are not in any way reflecting on the ability of the readers, rather we are making the point that your entering behavior, the way you are as you approach the objective today, is not such that you are ready for this objective. In order for this objective (or any objective) to be worthwhile for students, they must be ready to meet it.

Entering behavior is a loosely defined term that describes what a student brings with him/her as the student enters a teaching-learning situation. Entering behavior consists of many kinds of "within-student" variables that effect his/her readiness to learn whatever it is you are planning to teach. We will discuss some of the factors that must be considered in entering behaviors of students. The assessment of entering behavior in a broad sense will be discussed in chapter seven. Here we shall merely identify the factors involved. Then we shall describe how you may determine a student's readiness for the material you plan to teach. We shall be specifically concerned with intellectual and experiential readiness.

For most of us, intelligence is one of the first things we think of when we consider a student entering any teaching/learning setting. No matter how we look at it, some children are more intelligent than others. In any group of thirty children, some will be "bright," some will be "average" and some will be "below average." When thirty such children approach any behavioral objective some will find it very easy to meet and they may be bored with your instruction. Some will find the objective reasonable and they will gain considerably from your learning activities. Some others, of course, will find the objective to be "too hard" and they also may not find your instruction worthwhile and are likely to be bored; not because your instruction is worthless but because it makes little sense to them. Oh, we are well aware that IQ tests and such are at very best very rough measures of intelligence but experience with groups of children over the years makes very clear the differences in ability between different children within the same classroom. Children who are "slow" cannot be relegated to failure. Over the years we have had the statistics of "the normal curve" ingrained in our thinking. Four or five percent of the children make "A's," 10 or 11 percent of the children make "B's," most (about two-thirds) of the children make "C's," 10 or 11 percent make "D's" and the rest fail. That's the way it is with the old normal curve. Some children fail, but that's all right; we can predict it from the normal curve. Only a few children completely master anything we teach, but that's all right too, after all it is very predictable. This kind of thinking leads to energy crises, fuel shortages, dam collapses and other less than admirable catastrophes. We are in business to teach and this means that we must find better approaches to this one facet, entering behavior, than using the normal curve as our excuse for why some kids learn what we teach and others do not.

26

Equally important, if not more important than intelligence, previous experience is a powerful variable in the entering behavior of students. Teaching a child his/her ABC's is far easier if the child has had considerable experience with letters than if he/she has never seen one before. As incredible as it may sound, there are large numbers of children who never see a book, a magazine or even a newspaper in their homes prior to starting school. Compare such a child's possible reaction to instruction in reading to the reaction of another child whose home has constantly been full of books, magazines and newspapers. Think about how differently a child who has learned that reading is a very valuable behavior (after all, he/she has seen his/her parents read all the time) will approach instruction in reading than a child who has no reason to believe reading is worthwhile.

In another light, we are all familiar with children who transfer to a new school and are either ahead or behind their new classmates in terms of what they have learned in school. In any classroom of thirty children, each child will have had different experiences and will approach any topic differently. If we are teaching a class of children how to multiply, some will already be able to perform the task, some will just be getting ready for the task and still others will have gaps in experience that will not allow them to benefit from instruction over new material that they have not met the prerequisites for.

A third factor that affects entering behavior is the health of students. As obvious as it may sound, healthy children are more likely to be ready to learn new things than unhealthy children. Think about yourself for a moment. Haven't you gone to classes on occasion when you were under the weather? How much was your performance affected by illness? Illness may be long- or short-term and mild or severe. The longer and more severe illnesses are, obviously, the more they are likely to inhibit learning.

A fourth variable to consider in a child's entering behavior is nutrition. Children who do not receive proper nutrition are not as likely to benefit from instruction as children who do eat properly. A child who has not eaten in 24 hours could probably care less about the geography of north Texas. Such a child is probably concerned with where his/her next meal is coming from, not with anything being taught in class. Think about yourself again. How much would you care about reading this book and what it says if you had not eaten in 24 hours? Severe malnutrition, of course, has much more serious effects on children leading to possible brain damage and even death.

Psychological health, a highly ambiguous term, is another factor to consider in a child's entering behavior. We might also refer to psychological health as emotional status. Children experiencing psychological or emotional stress are unlikely to benefit from classroom instruction as much as are children not undergoing such stress. A child who comes to school each day after witnessing fight after fight between his/her parents, regardless of how well fed or how bright, cannot possibly give as much to classroom ex-

27

periences as other children. A child in a state of psychological turmoil, for whatever reason, is at a very real disadvantage in school.

Social development, a term referring to how well children have learned to function with other people, is a sixth factor that must be considered in a child's entering behavior. How to play by the rules, how to get along with other children and how to get along with adults other than the parents is a form of social learning that greatly affects a child's performance in school. If children are still learning the social behaviors they must emit in school, they will be at a disadvantage with respect to the formal learning that they are expected to engage in.

The subculture a child comes from is a seventh factor that must be considered in entering behavior. Subcultures within the United States use their own languages (Spanish, Afro-American, Arapaho, etc.), have their own customs and emphasize different kinds of goals for their children. If you and your class are predominately middle-class, white, Anglo-Saxon Protestants, black children, for instance, may be at a disadvantage in your class. Their language may be somewhat different and the past experiences they have had in life will be different from you or the majority of your students.

We could continue to list different factors affecting entering behavior almost endlessly. The eighth and last factor we will list is self-expectancy (which, as you probably know, is related to the expectancies of parents and some vague construct we call self-concept). What children expect from themselves, poor work, good work, average work, excellent work, is reflected almost perfectly in their classroom performance. Once a child learns "I am dumb; I don't do good schoolwork," it is very difficult to keep that child's prophecy of self from coming true.

We have only very briefly skimmed the top of the notion of entering behavior, identifying only a few of the very many separate factors that can be identified as affecting school learning. A student's entering behavior is what a student brings with him/her when entering any learning/teaching setting. The point we want to make is that all children enter learning/teaching situations with unique entering behaviors. As a result of this all children have highly specific needs that must be met in order to maximize learning. A part, and only a part of meeting these needs, is to gear your instruction so that you start teaching where *children* are. If you are going to be about the business of teaching multiplication, you are obviously going to do a better job if you teach addition first to those children who cannot add. Probably you will also do a better job if you teach more complex skills to children who can already multiply.

How do we know what to teach children? How do we know how to gear our instruction to fit the needs of children? How can we analyze what to teach in a way that will result in instruction that most benefits our students? Additionally, how can we find out what children must be able to do in order to obtain the new behavioral objective we have set for them? These questions can be answered by performing a *task analysis* and determining what parts of a task we wish to teach the children can and cannot perform. We shall restrict ourselves to intellectual readiness throughout the remainder of this chapter.

TASK ANALYSIS

Task analysis is a frequently neglected but highly important skill for teachers. Task analysis amounts to the analysis of any task you have for children (adding, multiplying, reading a map, solving molarity problems, analyzing American diplomacy) by breaking the task down into its component parts (component skills) in a hierarchical fashion. Such an analysis is typically done by setting out the task and then working backwards, step by step, listing all the subskills necessary to perform that task.

The best way to show you what task analysis is, is to perform a series of task analyses so that you may see how they were performed.

Example. Solving for an unknown.

$$X + 2 = 5$$

What are the skills which a student must have prior to being able to profit from instruction in solving for unknowns? Let us start backtracking from this task through the various component tasks students must master prior to being ready for this task.

1. The students must perceive that a letter symbol can stand for a number (this opens up the whole discussion of one thing standing for another).
2. The students must perceive that, in specific, X represents a number, the unknown quantity.
3. The students must be able to recognize the symbols in an equation and define the terms they represent (e.g., $+$, $-$, $=$).
4. The students must be able to perform the processess that the signs indicate.
5. The students must be able to correctly "change signs" of numbers (from positive to negative and vice versa) as they are passed across the equals sign.
6. The students must be able to properly place the numbers after they have been brought across the equals sign (e.g., x/y, $x-y$, $x+y$, $x-y$, y/x, etc.).
7. Students must be able to add a positive and negative number together.
8. Students must be able to add two negative numbers together.
9. Students must be able to subtract a positive from a negative number.

29

10. Students must be able to subtract a negative from a positive number.
11. Students must be able to identify and define the concepts of positive and negative numbers.
12. Students must be able to subtract two, one or two digit numbers from each other.
13. Students must be able to add two, one or two digit positive numbers together.
14. The students must be able to perform the process of addition and subtraction with concrete objects.
15. The students must be able to write numbers and symbols.
16. The students must be able to count.
17. The students must have mastered the concept of number and quantity. That is, 3 is so many, 4 is so many, etc.
18. The students must be able to recognize the written symbols for numbers and say their names.
19. The students must be able to say numbers.
20. The students must be able to perceive numbers written on a page or on a blackboard. They must also be able to hear their instruction.

We could probably go on and on adding steps that we may have neglected but the example should serve its purpose. Any objective (task) we wish to teach can be broken into a series of steps much like our example. Such an analysis allows us to review what it is that we are teaching and to identify the major components of the task that the students must be able to perform prior to our teaching for our objective. We can use the steps we have identified in such an analysis to provide us with the steps we will follow in teaching our objective. To digress for a moment, we should point out that such an analysis does not always yield the pattern which our instruction should follow. Obviously if your students have an adequate background as they approach this problem they will probably not need instruction in identifying numbers or counting. However, we have used such an approach in teaching mathematics for remedial students. Our objective was to teach students to solve for an unknown. The students were all college freshmen (freshpeople?) with poor preparation in mathematics. All were taking a course to prepare for taking their first real college math course. As members of a special program, they had to make up several years of work in one semester and as the course started with "solving for an unknown," a lot of backtracking had to be done. To teach for this objective, we started with step 20, literally, and worked our way up, day to day, to step number one. At this point the students were ready for the task set forth in the objective.

Performing a task analysis provides us with considerable insight into what a student must be able to do to perform a new task. A task analysis alone, however, does not tell us which of the component behaviors students can already perform and where we should begin our instruction. To find out where our students are at with respect to our task analysis, we must provide a pretest (remember this from chapter 2?) designed to find out which of the prerequisites the students can perform and which ones of them they cannot perform.

For example:

Locate the numbers of x's equal to the printed number on the left.

1. *3*   (a) xxx, (b) xxxx, (c) xx, (d) xxxxx
2. *5*   (a) xxx, (b) xxxx, (c) xxxxx, (d) xxxxxx
3. Solve the following problems:
   (a) $2+3 =$ (e) $5-3=$
   (b) $3+5 =$ (f) $4-2=$
   (c) $4+7=$ (g) $5-6=$
   (d) $12+8 =$ (h) $14-12=$
4. Add the following numbers together:
   (a) 7 (b) -4 (c) -5
         $\underline{-6}$ $\underline{-2}$ $\underline{+9}$

We could go on and on directing some items at each of the 20 steps identified in our task analysis but this brief example should serve to let you see how our pretest approach works. You may put together a sampling of items on such a test (preferably the test should be "noncredit") in hierarchical fashion so that you may see what each child can do and what each child cannot do. The results from this test allow you to then organize your instruction. You may find that such a pretest will not answer "why" questions. That is, the results will show you what children can and cannot do but it will not tell you why they cannot do it nor exactly what it is they can't do. One good way to get at the "why" and exactly what a student cannot do is to sit down with him/her individually and go through the last step performed correctly and the first step performed incorrectly. Have the student talk his/her way through the process while he/she attempts to perform the task. You should take note of exactly what is done incorrectly and listen to the student's explanation of what was done and why it was done. This process, although time-consuming with large groups of students, will do more to put you in touch with exactly what they can and cannot do and how and what you should teach to remediate the difficulty.

Once you have performed a task analysis and administered and scored a pretest, you may very well need to restate your objective or objectives so that they reflect what will be taught. It may be that "solving for unknown" is at least two weeks away and that you will need to start with "adding two negative numbers." Whatever the result is, you can be assured that the proper use of task analysis and the assessment of entering behavior will enhance your instruction.

THE RELATIONSHIP OF BEHAVIORAL OBJECTIVES, TASK ANALYSIS AND ENTERING BEHAVIOR

Task analysis proceeds directly from behavioral objectives. Any behavioral objective is reduceable into a series of component behaviors or prerequisites. The correct statement of a behavioral objective should allow you to identify exactly what the task is you teach and serves as the starting point for your task analysis. Task analyses cannot be clearly developed unless you have made a clear statement of your objective. How can you analyze that which you have not clearly identified?

Task analysis is related to entering behavior in that you may precisely assess a student's cognitive readiness for a task by performing an analysis of the task and then testing the student over the subtasks you have identified in order to determine where the student is at. Task analysis and pretesting allow you to identify cognitive deficits and readiness only; they do not get at any of the other forms of entering behavior we listed earlier. As we shall see in the assessment chapter, chapter eight, there are other means of getting at these forms of entering behavior.

The relationship of our components of instruction should be: behavioral objective-task analysis pretest of entering behavior, which then leads to a restatement of the behavioral objectives and instruction. This plan for teaching is the beginning of individualized instruction. Individualized instruction is further developed in chapter eight.

TASK ANALYSIS FOR CONCEPTS

As in chapter two, we shall trichotomize the kinds of learning students engage in into concept learning, psychomotor learning and affective learning. We shall provide one example of task analysis for each of these forms of learning.

Task (Behavioral Objective, Twelfth Grade): The students will be able to describe the generation of alternating electrical current. This description must include the function of a magnetic field in generating current, how and why alternation is achieved and a description of what "flow of current" is. The assessment shall take place in class during a written examination.

Task Analysis:
1. Students must be able to describe the operation of a magnetic field on electrons in a conductor passing through the field.
2. Students must be able to define and schematically represent magnetic fields.

3. Students must be able to describe and diagram the formation of dipoles in a magnetized conductor.
4. Students must be able to list and describe methods of obtaining a magnetic field.
5. Students must be able to describe electrical current in terms of electron flow.
6. Students must be able to describe the process of generating direct current.
7. Students must be able to define dipoles.
8. Students must be able to define and describe electrons (this probably also necessitates the definition and description of atomic structure and the properties of conductors.)
9. Students must be able to define conductor and nonconductor.

This beginning of a task analysis demonstrates the process whereby you can take any concept and "backtrack" through all the necessary components a student must have mastered prior to being ready to meet the new objective. In this instance we could continue to backtrack all the way to "be able to read and write" or even further. However, as you will probably have some notion of students' backgrounds (twelfth grade physics students have commonly had two or more years of high school math, general science, biology and chemistry) you may only want to bring your analysis as far back as is feasible in your setting. At some points (no algebra skills, no skills in atomic structure) you probably should see that the students return to or take prerequisite courses. A pretest can easily be developed from out task analysis and we can then see how to structure our instruction to help students achieve our behavioral objective.

TASK ANALYSIS FOR PSYCHOMOTOR SKILLS

A task analysis for psychomotor skills proceeds in exactly the same fashion as does a task analysis for teaching a concept with the addition of "conditioning," "coordination" and other necessary prerequisites that may not necessarily be learned but are rather a part of the state of an organism. In other words, the strength necessary for some psychomotor tasks, the speed necessary for some psychomotor tasks, and so on, are not necessarily learned behavior, they are parts of the "shape" a person is in.

Task (Behavioral Objective, Tenth Grade Typing Class): The students will type an error free paragraph at 30 words per minute during a quiz at the beginning of class.

Task Analysis:
1. The students must be able to place their fingers on the "home keys" and type each letter and symbol on the machine correctly without looking at the key board.

2. The students must be able to type from a copy.
3. The students must be able to strike all "nonhome" keys on the keyboard without looking at the keyboard.
4. The students must be able to strike all "home keys" on the keyboard without looking at the keyboard.
5. The students must be able to identify all "nonhome" keys on the keyboard.
6. The students must be able to identify the "home keys."
7. The students must be able to identify the space bar, shift key, and tab and strike them without looking at the keyboard.
8. The students must be able to correctly "feed in" a sheet of paper.

Again, we have not listed all the possible steps involved in typing a paragraph at 30 words per minute, particularly those that might relate to "building speed." However, the reader should be able to see how such an analysis is performed and how to build evaluation and instruction from this. A large part of many psychomotor skills is conditioning (speed and manual dexterity here) and these are obtained only through practice. Then, too, we should note that some people may never attain certain behavioral objectives for psychomotor skills. Some of us are just not going to be physically capable of performing a correct high-jump, an "iron cross" on gymnastic rings or type 30 words per minute.

TASK ANALYSIS FOR AFFECTIVE OUTCOMES

As we have previously pointed out, affective outcomes are the hardest of all to teach because of the extreme difficulty in specifying the behaviors we want and of assessing an affective outcome. We shall also see that a task analysis of affective outcomes is also extremely difficult.

Task (Behavioral Objective for Ninth Graders): The students will enjoy tumbling. They will demonstrate this enjoyment through attending each class period, being on time for each class period and choosing to tumble during those periods when they have a choice among several activities. Criteria for acceptance shall be meeting all classes on time and choosing, at least once, to tumble when other activities are available.

Task Analysis:
1. Students must be able to perform all the skills necessary in coming to class on time. (This can be taken all the way back to telling time, following directions and so forth.)
2. Students must be able to choose and participate in tumbling.
3. Students must be able to identify "tumbling."
4. Students must be able to do all the things necessary to choose between activities.
5. Students must be able to "enjoy."

This very brief task analysis should serve to demonstrate the extreme difficulty in analyzing affective outcomes. Where an internal state such as "enjoy" is our objective, we cannot analyze its components because of its inaccessibility to us.

REVISITING BEHAVIORAL OBJECTIVES AND OUTLINING TEACHING

The process of rewriting behavioral objectives and outlining your teaching should be a direct result of your task analysis and the pretesting of your students. Your new objective becomes a statement of that first subtask that the students cannot perform. You then teach for that objective and, as mastery is achieved, set new objectives following the steps in your task analysis. You are then engaged in stating the components of the task students cannot perform as behavioral objectives, teaching and evaluating and, progressing, step by step, until you and your students reach the original objective.

SUMMARY

In this chapter we defined entering behavior, described its possible effects on student learning and delineated several factors influencing entering behavior. We then described task analysis and discussed the relationship of task analysis-behavioral objectives and entering behavior. Lastly, we provided examples of task analysis for concept learning, psychomotor learning and affective learning. New objectives and a plan for teaching should follow directly the task analysis and assessment of entering behavior for any behavioral objective.

Chapter 4
SYMBOLIC ACTIVITY: THINKING

The material in this chapter differs rather clearly from the focus of the material in the chapter on operant and respondent conditioning. While attempting to maintain the already established emphasis on change in behavior as our way of knowing that learning has occurred, this chapter will discuss a series of "internal"—inside the head—events which may be presumed to occur in the interval of time between presentation of some stimulus and the appearance of an observable response. Most commonly, this process is called thinking. The process assumes the existence of a storage of past experience in a form commonly called memory. Thinking is presumed to involve not only present stimulus events, but a context from prior experiences (memory) which influences the manner in which the present stimulus setting is interpreted.

The process suggested above, in addition to providing teachers with some sense of the effects of prior experience, is also useful as a teaching tool in that our knowledge of how people think (deal with information) leads to systematic methods for putting teaching material together for instructional purposes. The task analysis techniques acquired in chapter three should be combined here with the way in which the subject matter is organized for maximum learning by students.

After completing this chapter, you will be able to:

1. Write a statement defining thinking.
2. Write a statement defining memory and forgetting.
3. Write a statement defining a concept.
4. Write a statement defining a rule.
5. Write a statement defining a problem.
6. List at least two ways in which concepts may be taught.
7. Task analyze a concept learning task appropriately, establish a behavioral objective for teaching the concept and present a teaching strategy for meeting the objective.
8. Identify a problem, task analyze it into the appropriate rules and concepts, prepare behavioral objectives and a teaching strategy which will teach students to deal effectively with, or to solve, the problem
9. List at least four ways for improving the efficiency of human learning.

We will not spend much time with the word, "thinking," but since it is so much a part of our vocabularies, in this chapter we will define it as a set of symbolic activities of an "internal" nature that substitute for observable behavior. Instances might include such items as the activity implied when instructed: "Do the next five problems in your head."

It seems clear to us that the definition provided covers a great many activities. Hence, in this chapter we will spend most of our time dealing with activities such as remembering, concept learning, problem solving and the like which represent aspects of thinking. Consider the instruction given above. What is implied when you are told "Do the problems in your head?" Descriptively, it seems that you are to provide an internal representation of the "problem," and perform some sort of operations (probably in a sequence), which implies a "memory storage" for both the operations and the sequence. Finally, it also implies that at some point the problems are "solved" and that particular train of thinking terminates. How do we acquire the skills to think? Some preliminary considerations are in order to give us a perspective for examining the rest of the chapter.

The paragraph above alludes to a crucial variable. We can solve the problems "in our heads" if the task is a meaningful one. By meaningful we simply refer to past experience which organizes and classifies information for use. Take the simple instruction "solve the anagram, 'tihgl,' without using paper and pencil." What do you need to know to perform the task? At the very least you must know (from past experience) that an anagram is a set of scrambled letters which can be recombined to form a word. While these five letters are easily solved into the appropriate word, other combinations such as "tlgog" might not be. Why the difference? One of the most powerful variables in predicting anagram solution time is frequency of the word in English usage. Thus an anagram formed from a word which appears with great frequency in English would be more quickly (or certainly) solved than one which appears less frequently. In addition to knowing what an anagram is, you must *know* (have stored in memory) the English word. If the correct combination of letters was one you had never seen before, how would you know it to be correct? Typically people solving anagrams describe the procedure as something like this: "I looked at the letters they sort of flowed into a word that I knew." Not very informative! The task clearly suggests the internal process (thinking) though is not very useful in describing the nature of the process. Fortunately other ways exist for getting somewhat more precisely at the nature of thought.

MEMORY

To restate, solving problems, in our heads or not, requires that we understand the problem—that it is meaningful to us, which in turn means that we have some sort of relevant prior experience with the task. We remember it. Furthermore, problem solution ordinarily implies a sequence of operations. While the exact physiological basis of memory is not known, we are pretty sure that information (memory) is stored in the central nervous system (the brain and the brain stem). Furthermore, there is good evidence that information is not stored randomly. Memory specialists are just beginning to trace out the elaborate mechanisms of memory storage. Tentatively we think of information as being stored in categories. We will talk later in the chapter about concepts which appear to be a major type of category. Equal to the importance of categories of stored information is the interrelations which are developed between the categories. Thus, if we ask you to tell us what the word "flag" makes you think of, we are likely to get from you words such as country, red, white, blue, and proud. It is unlikely that the word made you think of such concepts as grease, psychology, or malted milk. If you are trying to remember someone's name, and you almost, but not quite can, a helpful strategy is to try to think of the person's appearance, the last activities you engaged in with him/her, etc. These activities may serve as cues which get you to the correct category in memory.

In addition to the need to have a category system and a set of relations among the categories we must also have some system of placing new information into the categories. When you learn new information, you add it to your existing information; only occasionally does new information totally replace old. Changing clothing styles may illustrate this. When you see one of your fellow students wearing, as an instance, a down filled jacket which you and others like, then the jacket becomes a part of the category "style." Had you seen one of your stodgy professors wearing the jacket (and no one else) it is unlikely that the down filled jacket would have become part of *student* "style." To some extent, then, *who* wears the article of clothing determines whether or not the new article is placed into the category "clothing in style." We want to point out that the conceptual category "clothing in style" is a very complex one. Our example above provides only limited explanation for how information is added to existing categories.

Summarizing then, cognitive functioning can be considered to involve categories, sets of relationships among the categories and some system for assigning new information into categories. The fact that new information is added implies that memory (and cognitive functioning) are dynamic, that is constantly changing. Formal education does that by providing a systematic long-term program for developing an increasingly elaborate level of cognitive functioning by adding new information to the cognitive structures children bring to a school setting.

Where are we now? Before proceeding further, let's recap the previous material in the chapter. We began with the notion of symbolic activity, commonly called thinking. In order to deal with the internal processing implied by the term, we have discussed memory, a system for long-term storage of information. Furthermore, we have developed a description of a cognitive structure which gives us an intuitive notion of how information processing psychologists believe symbolic activity occurs. While the model of cognitive structure is crude, it permits the development of instructional strategies which, in the final analysis, make up what we call education.

Before beginning a study of concepts from an instructional point of view, it may be worthwhile to point out that concepts such as dog, verb, matter or metaphor all are abstractions. The word "dog," for example, is a label which includes a wide variety of furry, four-legged animals; at the same time the concept "dog" excludes other furry animals (cats, cows, etc.). A concept, then, abstracts into one category the qualities that make all dogs, "dogs," while at the same time excluding all nondogs. It is understandable then that a two- or three-year-old child riding in the country may "make a mistake" and call a horse by the category name "dog." This evidence shows that the child has not learned adequately the bases for labeling an animal a dog or else putting it into some other category

Similarly, in a school setting, when a teacher discusses a concept in science or mathematics or reading the learner is attempting to store in memory the abstract qualities of the concept for future use. So if a teacher states that he/she is teaching the concept "greater than" in mathematics, there is the implication that an internal, "inside the head," category is being acquired by the learner. Once this category is correctly acquired and stored, the learner should be able to use the concept in many situations—he/she should be able to talk about numbers as "greater than" other numbers, but should also be able to talk about a container as having a "greater than" capacity than another container. The learner probably also has stored in the same memory category the sign ">" to symbolize the words greater than. A very important advantage of concepts stored in memory is that they are versatile—they can be used in a wide variety of situations because they are meaningfully understood.

In contrast to the notion of concepts described above, most of us remember some labels we learned (were required to memorize, in fact) which do not have the generality implied by conceptual learning. We refer, of course, to "rote" learning in which criterion for successful learning is the repetition (usually) of a definition or a formula or even a table. The writers recall, painfully, learning (memorizing) a list of definitions for parts of speech: verb, noun, adjective, adverb, etc. A noun was defined for one of us as "the name of a person, place, or thing." While the definition is still recalled, we also remember the painful discovery that memory for the definition did not control our behavior to the extent that we could accurately underline all of the nouns in a series of sentences. Merely having a rote definition failed to permit us to perform effectively. At one time most of you "learned" to solve simultaneous equations in two unknowns. How many could do so now? If you cannot, then you have pretty good evidence that you learned a method by rote—and did not learn an adequate concept of such solution. If you had a clear conceptual understanding of the process, you would still be able to solve them.

How does one teach concepts meaningfully and not by rote? This is a major topic for this chapter. Briefly, though, the task grows out of much of what is implied in previous chapters in this book. You must know what you want to teach—have your objective clearly in mind. At the same time you need to understand the entering level of your students—what do they already know about the objective. The evidence clearly indicates that only when the learner knows something about a newly introduced concept can he/she deal with it meaningfully. If the concept is brand new, the teacher has much work to do. However, most concepts can be related to some aspect of the learner's prior experience—frequently by use of analogy or example. To the extent that a new concept is tied to some prior experience of the learner, the concept is taught "meaningfully" and will not only be understood, but remembered.

CONCEPT LEARNING

Concepts are the basic units of instruction. They are the set of categories which permit us to organize the huge number of objects and infinite bits of information that comprise the world of experience. The organization and classification of information, coupled with its retention in memory, permits us to use combinations of concepts to devise rules (relationships) and use that information to solve problems. A teacher must not only have a clear sense of the conceptual structure and interrelations of his/her subject matter, but must also be able to combine that information with information about the students in his/her classes. On this basis he/she develops strategies for solving instructional problems—problems which may range from simple, daily occurrences such as planning the sequence of activities through a day or a class period, to dealing with complex difficulties where traditional or ordinary instructional techniques fail. Recall from chapter three that the task analyses you performed resulted in a set of behavioral objectives. These objectives made clear the precise nature of the teaching task, whether the task was essentially cognitive, psychomotor or affective. A major goal of this section is to provide you with information about the way in which humans classify (categorize) information, how they acquire that information and how it is used to solve problems.

Writing behavioral objectives and carrying out task analyses are not end points of teacher behavior. Instead they are means of identifying specific concepts, rules and problems for which instruction must be prepared. Thus, part of the task of teaching a concept, for example, requires determining the entering behavior of students with respect to knowledge of and ability to use the concept.

What is a concept? At its simplest level, a concept is a category into which objects (things) are classified on the basis of some set of common characteristics. Consider the concept "bird." What goes into this category? Obviously, canaries, robins, eagles, buzzards, ostriches—but not bats or bees or fruitflies. Even more clearly, elephants, fish and mice do not belong in the category. What determines the classification? For the concept "bird" a number of *dimensions* determine concept membership. Among these are laying eggs with hard shells, presence of a horny beak, etc. Note that flying, an obvious characteristic of many birds, is not a sure dimension for classification of organisms into the concept "bird" even though that is one of the common things we learn very early in our lives about birds. The dimensions listed above for the category "bird" are *relevant* dimensions to use in deciding whether or not an organism is a bird. Size and color are obviously dimensions *irrelevant* to the concept. Robin, canary, etc., are *positive instances* (examples) of the concept, while a bat, a bumblebee, a whale or a squirrel are *negative instances*. The use of such positive and negative instances is a highly effective way of helping students to acquire a concept. Their use can be of particular value in clarifying the distinctions between relevant and irrelevant dimensions.

Two further comments about these sorts of concepts: (1) a concept such as bird (or fish, dog, marsupial, etc.) is frequently called a concrete concept because ordinarily we can identify examples (instances) of it by direct observation; furthermore, (2) concepts may be linked with other concepts. Thus, a canary is a bird; it is also a vertebrate (has a backbone), and an animal. Concepts can be organized systematically. The plant and animal taxonomies learned in most zoology and botany courses are instances of complex organizations of concrete concepts.

The second major type of concept is the abstract, or defined, concept. In arithmetic, we make use of the concept, place value. Thus, in the number 247 (base ten), we have learned that the number consists of seven "ones," four "tens" and two "hundreds." Place value is an abstraction because we recognize (finally!) that the number 22 consists of two "ones" and two "tens," and placement is the key dimension. Our system of counting requires understanding of place value. We can estimate the degree to which students understand the concept by giving them problems in arithmetic which require use of the concept. In effect, place value, (and other abstract concepts) is a rule, i.e., "the first number to the left of the decimal is the ones' place." Note that this rule involves the relationship of several other concepts—left, decimal, first, etc.

What about the concept, justice? It, too, is a defined or abstract concept. In the same manner as a concrete concept, justice is defined in terms of a particular set of *relevant dimensions.* What do you think they are? Dimensions which are *irrelevant,* such as courtrooms, blackrobed judges, lawyers, etc., must be dispensed with in order to clarify the nature of the concept. (Note that one form of the word justice is a concrete concept or category of which the Chief Justice of the United States Supreme Court is a positive instance.) The abstract concept, justice, frequently would be seen as involving such dimensions as equity or fairness and impartiality. The dimensions used to define the concept are themselves abstract concepts. How many of you have said to a teacher, parent, or friend, "but it's not fair!"? The statement implies that a particular act is a *negative instance* of justice. For abstract concepts such as those we have listed, positive and negative instances may be the best (if not the only) way to teach the concepts appropriately. Our dictionary defines justice as "administration of law, according to the rules of law, or equity"; and "the principle of rectitude and just dealing of men with each other." Asking even secondary students to learn the rules from the dictionary certainly does not insure the ability to correctly classify a set of acts into positive and negative instances of the concept, "justice." If sufficient positive and negative instances are provided, students may learn to infer the appropriate dimensions for the concept in a way meaningful to them.

TASK ANALYSIS OF A CONCRETE CONCEPT

A partially completed task analysis of a concrete concept may be useful in suggesting the implications of concept learning for teaching. Suppose that you wished to teach fifth grade students the concept "parallelogram." Let's begin with the definition from our dictionary. A parallelogram is a four-sided figure with opposite sides parallel and opposite angles equal. In the margin at right, draw a parallelogram (you know how!!) and a rectangle and a square. Does the definition distinguish among them? Surprisingly, perhaps, it does not. Strictly speaking all three are parallelograms. However, very commonly we wish to treat a parallelogram as a concept different from a square or rectangle or other polygon. Assuming we decide to do this, what differentiates the parallelogram from the other figures? Something about the angle; right? Suppose we added a statement about the angles—and note that the statement will include discussion about the *opposite* angle. Such a statement might take the form "opposite pairs of

43

angles are equal with one pair consisting of angles less than 90 degrees and the other pair greater than 90 degrees." Would it be essential to add that the four angles sum to 360 degrees?

What have we learned so far? First, a dictionary (or any verbal) definition may not include enough information to guide one's behavior, even though it may be "correct." Second, the three drawings in the margin provided us with one positive and two negative instances of the concept. Thus, the square and rectangle are negative instances of the concept "parallelogram" while the parallelogram is, obviously, a positive instance. Examination of the positive and negative instances enabled us to realize that an addition to the dictionary definition was necessary in order to differentiate parallelograms from the other figures. Finally, it is probably possible to teach the concept without words simply by showing the children a carefully constructed series of positive and negative instances and cueing them as to which are parallelograms and which are not. Why would we want a verbal definition? For two reasons: (1) so that we can communicate about "things" with other persons; and (2) so that we can get maximum generalization. It is impossible to show a child every conceivable parallelogram shape, but the definition, if "understood" and remembered will correctly classify any object as a parallelogram or not a parallelogram.

Having discovered the relevant dimensions of the concept, we are now in a position to begin our teaching effort. Since we are teaching fifth graders, some of whom might be familiar with the concept, we need a pretest. A simple and effective pretest would consist of 20 figures consisting of say, four parallelograms of different sizes and angles and sixteen other polygons. Set your criterion at 100 percent accuracy. Assuming that a large number of the children fail to meet criterion, we now find it necessary to set an objective so that we can proceed with the task analysis. For the moment, let us use the following objective: On completion of instruction, each student will be able (a) both in class and on the playground to point to positive instances of parallelograms presented among other geometric forms with 100 percent accuracy, and (b) in class each student will be able to recite a definition of the concept which includes the relevant dimensions and, in addition, write that definition on a test. All relevant dimensions should be present in appropriate relationship. A further, related objective might be that "students should be able to draw parallelograms clearly distinguishable from squares, hexagons, etc. If that objective is desired, criteria for performance would be necessary.

Back to the task! We will now define a parallelogram as: a four-sided figure with opposite sides parallel and opposite angles equal, with one pair of opposite angles each less than 90 degrees, and the other pair each greater than 90 degrees.

What does the student need to know in order to differentiate a parallelogram from other polygons? Even a very preliminary task analysis suggests the following:

1. The student must be able to perceive or measure opposite sides which are parallel.
2. The student must be able to perceive or measure opposite angles which are equal to each other and greater or less than 90 degrees.
3. The students must know the concepts: opposite, equal, parallel, degree, angle. Note that if any of these concepts are unfamiliar to the students, task analysis and instruction in each must take place.
4. The students must be able to understand the concepts "equal to," "less than" and "greater than."

Obviously this task analysis could be extended indefinitely—students must have the concept of "number," "four" and "one" as instances. However, by the time a teacher begins to deal with this concept he/she should have a good sense of the entering behavior of the class with respect to these concepts. On the other hand, if an instructional sequence based on the task analysis suggested above fails, examination of presumably already known concepts, such as number would be warranted in an effort to find out where the plan went astray.

Depending on the class, then, more or possibly even fewer steps would be necessary. A reasonable plan of attack would be to identify the relevant concepts to be learned, assess student entering behavior with respect to each and as necessary develop a task analysis which will permit development of a teaching strategy for each concept to be learned.

Following instruction, a posttest, growing out of the objective specified above should be administered. Remember to give both types of items— identification of positive instances as well as the definition. All of us "know" some definitions which are not functionally useful—that is they do not lead to exhibition of behavior appropriate to the definition.

TEACHING ABSTRACT CONCEPTS

Teaching abstract concepts such as the concept of "justice" mentioned earlier poses some additional difficulties. As mentioned above, it is possible to teach a concrete concept simply by pointing to positive and negative instances. Abstract (or defined) concepts do not have that quality, hence we must rely more heavily on the definition of the concept. All of us, we again remind you, may be able to provide the definition in response to teacher request, without being able to use the concept effectively in applica-

45

tion. A little thought will review that "justice" is particularly difficult to adequately define. Once more, our dictionary states that justice (as the abstraction) is "The maintenance or administration of that which is just; also, merited reward or punishment; or administration of the law, according to the rules of law, or equity." Most of us can think of instances where the rules of law are appropriately followed, but equity is not observed. Consider this case: a teacher tells his English class that any student tardy for class more than three times in a six-week period will receive a letter grade reduction. Two students each are late four times and the teacher reduces their grades according to the rule. It turns out that one student was late the fourth time because he helped a student who had fallen and severely cut his head. First, is the punishment just? Second, was the rule applied equitably? Questions might be raised about both. Consequently, the verbal definitions fail to precisely define the situation, and with abstract concepts there are no easy positive and negative instances to point to. It is for these reasons that there is such lack of clarity even among adults, much less children, about the meaning of concepts such as beauty, freedom, courtesy, etc., as well as such relationships as cousin or aunt. Note that even in the deceptively simple word, "cousin," you cannot point to positive or negative instances *until* you know the definition (or rule) for categorizing. Simply stated, a cousin is the child of one's aunt or uncle. One must know the relationship before using the concept.

In teaching abstract concepts the same task analysis process must be followed. As suggested above, the task analysis would start, typically, with the definition, or rule, which specifies the dimensions which make up the concept. Since positive and negative instances are difficult to identify, it is particularly important that each concept in the definition also be clearly known. Thus, the task analysis of all concepts is crucial. Following the acquisition of the definition, and with it definitions of all the concepts implied in the definition, it is still necessary to try out the concepts on situations. It may have occurred to you already that when you try out a concept such as justice, inevitably you find that you and some of your students will hold values different enough from each other to make it very difficult to come to agreement about whether a particular situation is "just." Kohlberg's seven stages of moral development provide a rather clear developmental pattern of increasingly complex conceptions of words such as justice, which might be a valuable reading for you to understand the complexity of this task.

RULES

As noted in the prior section, concepts are the basic units of instruction. More complex forms of learning occur when concepts are linked together. This linkage may occur in two ways, one simple, the other more complex. The first we described in the section on concepts. Concepts may be linked simply in a subordinate-superordinate way. We can think of a robin as a bird, as a vertebrate, as an animal as a living thing. Living thing is a superordinate concept with respect to vertebrate, bird, etc., because it includes all instances in the concepts below it. Concrete concepts are often particularly easy to link in this way.

On the other hand, all of us are familiar with a more formal sort of linkage among concepts. This takes the form of a specified relationship among a set of concepts. Our common term for this relationship is, of course, rule. The circumference of a circle is equal to pi times diameter $(C = \pi D)$. This rule is made up of six concepts; circle, circumference, equal, pi (a constant), diameter, and the multiplicative relation between pi and D. Thus teaching the rule for finding the circumference of a circle involves a task analysis and pretesting sufficient to discover whether or not a group of students knows each concept individually—and in turn all of the concepts subordinate to the ones in question. For example, what concepts does one have to know to have an acceptable concept of circle?

Mathematics and the sciences appear to many learners to consist largely of rules. It is not so apparent that other areas of our lives are rulebound also. What is "good behavior" in a classroom? What is "appropriate behavior" at a party? What is "appropriate speech" in the classroom, on a date or in a term paper? All of these behaviors are rule governed. The rules in some cases are less well specified, but nonetheless in force. Many a term paper has been returned "marked down" for inappropriate or perhaps over simple use of language!

A feature of particular importance in rule learning is the distinction between a rule as a capability to perform a particular operation under the appropriate conditions as opposed to the capability to recite or verbalize the rule. How many of us learned a set of formulae in physics or chemistry or axioms in geometry which permitted us to pass particular sorts of tests, but not to solve problems? In the writers' experience this was a frequent occurrence. Conventional evaluation systems such as poorly constructed objective tests or recall questions demanding rote recitation of a rule without application foster verbalization without understanding—so often characterized today as regurgitation of knowledge. Just as the crucial test of acquisition of a concept is categorizing new information appropriately, so the application of a rule to a new situation is the crucial test of rule learning. The verbalization is simply a convenient tool for reminding us of the rule's availability in memory should it be necessary for use. Consider this question for your own rule learning: You have read a chapter on task analysis and the prior material in this chapter on concept learning. From this you may have learned to task analyze a concept. You may verbalize the process as: break the concept definition down into smaller units (perhaps subordinate concepts) and define any relationships among the parts. Provide a set of positive and negative instances of the concept and practice using it in a variety of situations. However you verbalize the process, it takes the form of rules which, presumably, guide your behavior. The key question is simply, *does* the rule guide your behavior? Take a sheet of paper and task analyze the concept "metaphor." Can you? The test of your task analysis knowledge is its value in turning the task analysis components into a teaching strategy which would, in this case, teach the concept "metaphor" to a group of children who do not know the concept initially. Try it! When you can make it work you have demonstrated rule governed behavior in a task of considerable importance to teachers. (Of course you can, if you wish, use another concept on which to perform the task analysis.)

LEARNING HIERARCHIES

Much of our learning takes the initial form of a verbalization—sets of words linked together which define a concept or a rule. Learners at any age may be able to recite a verbal chain by rote; the value of a chain cannot be denied as a possible cue for behavior. One of the tasks of a teacher is to see that the verbal chain level of learning is extended; probably first to the level of concept learning. If a learner can both define a concept *and* provide new positive and negative instances of it, we can reasonably assume that he/she "understands" the concept, i.e., can put the verbal chain into practice. A still more complex level of learning is, of course, the rule. Once more teachers must make sure that learners have opportunities to *use* rules in the settings for which they are appropriate—not simply give a verbalization of the rule. In a sense then, verbalization, concept learning and rule learning can be seen as three steps in a hierarchy of increasingly complex learning tasks. An even more complex form of learning, called problem solving, is at the top of the hierarchy. This will be the topic of the next section.

PROBLEM SOLVING

In this section the term problem solving will be used in two ways. First, consistent with our treatment of concept and rule learning on the preceding pages, we will define problem solving as the top level in the hierarchy of learning just proposed. In that sense problem solving is the discovery of the combination of previously known information (rules) which produces a solution to a "problem situation" in which one is required to respond although no single past response is appropriate. In addition, we will treat it as a process, as in the sense expressed by the statement "he taught the students to problem solve." In both cases problem solving refers to finding new solutions to novel problems. The term should be very clearly differentiated from the sort of common usage such as "do the ten problems at the end of the chapter." This instruction is most typically one demanding the routine use of already learned rules. Instead of problem solving as we consider it here, "doing the problems at the end of the chapter" is more closely akin to drill.

Problem solving as the top of the learning hierarchy appears to require the following steps: (1) recognition of a difficulty or dilemma, (2) recall of previously learned rules which are appropriate to the dilemma, (3) selection of the appropriate combination or recombination of known rules and finally (4) the recognition of the solution (following verification) as a higher order rule which can be remembered for future occasions. An example of problem solving may clarify the distinction. Most of us who operate automobiles can change a tire. We know how to block the wheels, jack the car up, remove the wheel, replace with the spare, etc. When we have a flat tire then, we do not (typically) have a problem. We simply apply already known rules. Suppose though, that you were "fifty miles from anywhere," and you discovered that you had a flat tire *and* you also discovered that your jack was missing or broken. No neighbors close, an infrequently traveled road, and you need to be somewhere else in a hurry. You have a problem! Once one defines the problem as finding a substitute for the jack (as opposed to walking the fifty miles, or praying for aid) the problem becomes focused on "jack substitutes," or else repair of the existing jack. If the latter is impossible, then a substitute must be found. How can it? One might remember from previous experience (perhaps in a course in physics) that a jack is simply a highly efficient lever. Given that clue, one might then think of a definition of a lever. In our experience the concept that comes to mind is a long rod and a fulcrum. That recall may be sufficient to solve the problem. A reasonably solid fence post and a rock may provide an inefficient, but adequate solution to the broken jack problem. In an experience one of us had, numerous rocks and considerable time were required, but solution (change of the tire) was accomplished. Note that the solution to the problem involved the recall of already known information, the recognition that the jack was a lever and the search for a different form of lever. Without the prior information solution would have been impossible.

As a process, problem solving is conceived of somewhat differently. Dewey in 1910 formulated a series of steps in problem solving which are still valid: (1) define the problem; (2) generate alternative solutions to the problem; (3) evaluate the alternatives; (4) choose one alternative and try it out; and (5) assess the effectiveness of the solution. If the alternative chosen does not solve the problem, then the process begins again either by redefining the problem or by considering and testing another alternative.

Prior to task analysis of the two aspects of problem solving described above, we should point out to you that different types of problems raise the need for different sorts of teaching strategies. A major difference in types of problems is contained in the distinction between formal and informal problems. Formal problems are most simply defined as those for which there is one, clear unambiguous solution. Some positive instances may make the definition clear. Suppose that you are asked to solve an anagram from a sequence of letters. If the anagram has only one solution, then the problem is solved when you find that single solution. On the other hand, consider the problem of making a vocational choice. Obviously, no simple, clear-cut solution is appropriate. The "right" vocation for you depends upon a number of variables—furthermore, you may find that the vocation right for you at age 25 is not appropriate at age 35. Thus, vocational choice is an informal problem; solutions vary both between individuals and even within individuals at different times. The typical "problems" given in school mathematics or science books are usually examples of simple formal problems. Occasionally problems in English or social sciences may fit the informal definition. Consider the task "Examine the text of the attached poem. Choose the lines which *in your judgment* best exemplify the central theme of the poem. Defend your choice." To the extent that readers of the poem will differ in their judgment of which lines exemplify the theme of the poem, the answer is as variable as is the number of students responding to the question. A teacher scoring the question would have to rely on an evaluation of the defense of the choice, and even here the ability to clearly call a defense inadequate, much less wrong, is debatable.

Task Analysis. Let's consider a fairly typical problem setting. Suppose that in an English class you provide students with a short story of about six pages length. They are then instructed to read the story and to summarize the plot in not more than five sentences and furthermore they are asked to make up a clever title for the story. Note that this problem has both a formal and an informal component. The instruction to summarize the story is pretty largely a formal task. The instruction to generate a clever title is more of an informal task since there are presumably a fairly large number of clever titles, of which the student need provide only one. Task analysis would then proceed separately for the two types of problem.

The first instruction to "read the story" should invoke a host of (we hope) already learned rules for dealing with prose, since teaching reading is not, presumably, the focus of this assignment. However, given that the students can read the story they must, at a minimum, know the meaning of the concepts "summary" and "plot," as well as have knowledge of how to construct new sentences which convey the plot in a very brief series of statements. Implied in the instruction is a rule to "summarize the major points of the story" in order to meet the length constraint. Each of these concepts and/or rules requires further task analysis if they are not already a part of the student's habitual patterns of response.

In addition to the task analysis for the plot, the student must also engage in a separate task analysis dealing with the instruction to provide a clever title for the story. We would assume that this task generates an activity much more like that described under problem solving as a process. In order to solve the problem, the student needs to generate alternative story titles (presumably the instruction provides sufficient definition of the problem); then he/she must evaluate the alternatives against a criterion of "clever" which, incidentally, must fit not only the student's but also the teacher's concept of cleverness. The student must choose an alternative which best meets the criterion and deliver the title to the teacher. The success or failure of the solution (ordinarily verification by the teacher) provides the final steps in the problem solving process. A favorable comment or grade by the teacher would likely validate the process by which the clever title was produced. Furthermore, it is likely to reinforce the student for engaging in that sort of behavior.

The example of "cleverness" described above comes close to getting at one additional concept related to problem solving. This concept "creativity" may be considered to be a special form of problem solving in which the task requires drawing together concepts and rules so diverse in nature that their productive combination brings from the viewer or hearer of a creative product a sense of "effective surprise." This is the type of reaction one occasionally has after reading a poem, seeing a particular piece of art work, etc. There is little doubt that the "giftedness" which is presumably implicit in people who display creative problem solving is in substantial measure a function of hard work in whatever medium the creativity takes its form. Yet the special conditions which cause some individuals to display such behavior remain undiscovered.

Talented behavior, in contrast to creative behavior, is at present seen as more genetically linked, in the sense that an individual may be a talented singer, athlete, etc. In these instances talent clearly refers to a genetic inheritance which, with training, results in displays of (usually) physical performances of unusual skill or beauty. The search for appropriate means to identify as well as to train talented young people should be pursued as vigorously as current programs to provide special programs for the creative or gifted child.

MEMORY

The discussion of problem solving and creativity above have implied that much of creative behavior involves the search for concepts and rules which linked together in new ways result in products or responses we call creative. A rather obvious requirement of this activity, then, is a storage of information—in short, a memory. Recent psychological research has revealed considerable information about the topic. At present, the physiological basis for memory is unclear. We *do* know that information we regard as "in memory" is stored in the central nervous system (CNS). Furthermore, by examination of the brains of persons who have suffered accident or disease (tumor) as well as precise experiments in single neuron brain stimulation, we have learned something about the localization of memory in particular portions of the brain. Functionally, however, we have gained considerable information.

Long-Term Memory (LTM). Our present conceptualization of memory includes two major functions. The first, LTM, is, as the name implies, the repository of those things we mean when we are asked to "remember" something. Such information that we remember is stored in some sort of categorical fashion—perhaps in units something like the concepts we discussed earlier in this chapter. We know that once an item is entered in LTM, it is virtually remembered for life—providing, of course, that we can get access to the item. Think about the well-known phenomenon of the elderly person who can remember his/her childhood of 60 or 70 years ago, but cannot recall the current day of the week, or the name of a visitor whom he sees daily. This example suggests the reality of LTM, while it raises an as yet unsolved problem about why recent information is forgotten so quickly (or at least is unavailable for recall).

Short-Term Memory (STM). As the name implies, STM is of very brief duration, usually of not over 15 to 20 seconds. Consider this example: Suppose you are looking up the telephone number of someone you have never called before. You find the name in the book, examine the number, close the book and begin to dial. At that point a friend asks you two questions: Can he/she borrow your notes from your Chemistry class. You say yes, and the friend asks Where are the notes? There is a very high probability that no matter how brief your answer to that last question, you will have to look back in the phone book for the number. On the other hand, frequently used telephone numbers are stored in LTM so well that with appropriate prompting you may be able to remember numbers you thought you had forgotten years ago. STM is a sort of working memory which allows us to keep track of events (such as a strange telephone number) long enough to carry out the act of calling, but the information is not placed in LTM. Names of persons we meet but do not expect to meet again are also used only in STM unless a special effort is made to get the name into LTM. Ordinarily this can be accomplished by consciously repeating the name, using it in conversation and associating it with some previously learned and remembered information, such as "Jane Doe works with my friend in a department store downtown."

52

Organization of Memory. While there is much we do not know about memory, the evidence is clear that information stored in LTM is organized systematically. Even at the level of simple word association such as sky-blue, the occurrence of word responses such as cloud, dark, sunny, etc., as opposed to violet or crank, or hither suggests that words are in some way organized in memory. As implied previously, a model such as the following describes the current status of memory organization: information is stored in categories (perhaps in conceptual networks); the categories are inter-related in some manner so that remembering an item in one category can elicit an item from another. Think of the process you go through trying to remember the name of a forgotten item. Such behavior appears to represent an attempt to make a linkage between categories. New information is or-dinarily stored in LTM according to some as yet undefined set of rules, although crudely we can say that new information is stored with (or near) related information. These three elements: categories of information, inter-relationships among categories, and rules for classifying new information permit us to make use of a vast accumulation of past experience, and perhaps more importantly, to respond to new situations in a meaningful manner.

Memory Use. The most basic use a teacher can make of memory is to treat it as the repository of past experience for the learner. As implied in the section above, a child brings to any new learning experience a substantial fund of prior experiences. To the extent that new information is in-corporated into existing categories the learner is more likely to both under-stand (see relationships) the new and, in addition, remember the new, that is enter in LTM. How does a teacher make material meaningful? Of a myriad of possible ways, here are a few: use language consistent with the learner's past experience (to teach a child that the center of the earth is in a state of ig-neous fusion as opposed to the center consists of rocks so hot that they have melted is to result in no new learning); use examples which are familiar to the learner (that is, part of his LTM); provide definitions, then ask the child to recall examples consistent with the definition; program the experience of the learner with new material so that he uses the new material a number of times in a number of different ways so as to insure that the information enters LTM, etc. The more flexible the category systems become, the greater the opportunity for problem solving and creative behavior to occur. Much as we might wish it were otherwise, creative efforts and successful problem solving come as a function of effective use of prior information stored in memory as opposed to sudden "new" insights. The statement that genius consists of 90 percent perspiration and 10 percent inspiration is not far off the mark.

IMPLICATIONS FOR EDUCATIONAL PRACTICE

The practical teaching implications of this chapter are numerous. The following statements should be useful in guiding a teacher's behavior as he/she attempts to help children learn and remember information, processes, etc., once they *have* been learned. As will be noted for each section, some techniques suggested are more valuable for improving learning than for retention.

1. Meaningfulness. Perhaps foremost in any set of rules for improving *both* learning and retention is the necessity for making new material meaningful to the learner. As noted above, meaningful material is related to prior experience, and hence already learned to some degree. Little learned in school is *totally* new to the learner. On the other hand, a teacher may provide a substantial guide to a learner by pointing out the similarities of "new" material to that which the learner already knows; the relevancy of "new" to "old" learning material may not be obvious to the learner. The psychological evidence for this variable is very substantial—yet it seems to be widely overlooked in education. Well-understood (meaningful) material is remembered for extraordinarily long periods of time, probably in part because well-understood material gets frequent use.

2. Conceptual structure. A major vehicle for systematically providing for meaningfulness is through the use first of all, of concepts, followed by combinations of concepts into rules and into problem-solving strategies. Wherever possible concepts rather than verbal chains should be taught. The learner should be required to develop "new" positive and negative instances of each concept as well as to complete tasks, exercises, etc., which require the organization of individual concepts into clusters, rules, etc. Such activities again will improve both learning (response acquisition) and retention.

3. Affective components. It almost (but not quite!) goes without saying that the conditions under which material is to be learned effect both response acquisition and retention. If learning activities are carried out in a classroom in which there is a high level of emotional turmoil, the learner is likely to divide his time and energies between the learning tasks of education and the task of maintaining a sense of self-worth in the classroom. One of the purposes of chapter seven is to provide you with techniques which will provide opportunity for the learner to focus his attention on the educational tasks of the classroom rather than on matters of a "disciplinary" nature. A somewhat different affective component is that of the learner's attitude toward a particular subject matter. The "I hate math" syndrome is a serious problem only when the attitude diverts the learner's attention from the task, focusing instead on avoidance behaviors.

4. Active vs. passive learning. The best way to learn and remember

new information is to *use* it! A prominent virtue of assignments to students which require them to "do" problems, write themes, construct an apparatus, search for information in the library, etc., is that the student is actively involved in the process of learning and storing new information, and at the same time relating it to already known material. As a very specific instance, there is pretty good evidence that reading *and* taking notes over a difficult chapter in a book produces learning superior to reading and rereading the same material several times. The act of taking notes involves the learner in actively deciding what things should be a part of the notes, what can be ignored. Reading and rereading does not require that sort of active decision making.

5. "Practice" schedules. Occasionally school tasks include components (some meaningful and some not) which *must* be memorized in order to efficiently perform some other task. Thus in Chemistry it may be convenient to require learners to memorize the symbols for twenty or thirty of the common elements so that these may be used in formula development and in problems. At the elementary level, the wide value of the "multiplication tables" may make drill in their use advisable. The first requisite is *meaningfulness*. Before any task is provided for memorization, both the nature of the task and the reason for the necessity for memorization should be provided to the learner. Given that, psychological evidence suggests that with highly structured material such as a list of formuli, definitions, arithmetic combinations, etc., where the task is very clearly specified, students should be given what are called spaced practice schedules. In other words, the teacher should arrange for relatively short practice periods, perhaps 5-10 minutes in length, interspersed with other activities. In a self-contained room, a teacher requiring memorization of the "multiplication tables through ten" might provide 5-10 minute practice periods 4 or 5 times per day until criterion is reached. Massing the practice (long 30-40 minute practice periods) of this sort of information will result in fatigue and loss of interest.

On the other hand less well structured memorization tasks such as those necessary in "figuring out" a process for an experiment or a project probably should be carried out with a fairly extensive "practice" period of 30 minutes or more in order that the learner can (perhaps through trial and error) attempt various strategies and evaluate them all within the same basic time period.

6. Mnemonics. A further aid to memory (retention) is the mnemonic device. While these can range in complexity and scope, simple ones have already been suggested in this chapter. In music, remembering the "notes" of the staff is significantly improved through use of the mnemonics FACE and *E*very *G*ood *B*oy *D*oes *F*ine. Similarly, one can develop his own

mnemonics or use such associative devices as the following: "one is a bun, two is a shoe, . . ." and so on through ten (or more where each item of a list to be learned is linked associatively in some bizarre way with an item in the mnemonic.

7. Overlearning. Most of us know that recalling a list we have learned to a criterion of one error-free trial through the list is likely not to be perfectly recalled after the passage of time. One device to overcome this is to tally the number of trials to get through the memory task one time perfectly. If the learner will then practice (overlearn) the task an equal number of additional trials (or even half as many), recall of the task will be significantly increased. However, the drudgery of such a task warrants its use only under conditions where memory is of crucial importance.

HOW TO STUDY

Much of the direct educational import of this chapter is summarized in a systematic program for study devised by Frank Robinson in a book *Effective Study*. A brief presentation of the technique follows, with suggestions for the implications of each segment for aspects of this chapter. The method is applicable to the study of prose material (as in chapters in a textbook) as well as to understanding the purpose and outcome of a laboratory experiment or even the learning of a long poem.

Step 1. *Survey.* The purpose of this first step is to familiarize the learner with the objectives of the material to be learned, to get a sense of what the task is about—in a word to make the learning task *meaningful*. This can be accomplished by looking at a book chapter, by examining the title, section headings, summary passages, etc., with the idea of finding the relevance of the new task to one's past experience. The same procedure would be used for learning a long poetry piece.

Step 2. *Question.* The second step has the function of making the learner actively involve himself/herself with the material to be learned. The learner should ask such questions as What is the author trying to accomplish? Why is this material in this course? How does this relate to what I already know? and any other questions which actively engage the learner's attention to the task *and* to material he already knows. Hence, this step once more makes the learning task more meaningful and involves the learner more actively in the task.

Step 3. *Read.* In studying a chapter of a book, one proceeds to process a section of the material—material for which he/she already has surveyed and for each section developed a question getting at the writer's intent. Thus the topic of this section could be turned into a question: "How should students study?" Note how this question focuses attention on the very process we are discussing here. The material is read to answer the question.

Step 4. *Recite*. As soon as a section is read, and before going on to the next section, the reader should attempt to answer the question raised prior to reading. She/he is thus actively involved in extracting meaning from the passage and (not so incidentally) relating that new material to what he already knows. Thus the recitation process has a primary function of improving meaningfulness.

Following step 4, the remainder of the learning task is completed, for each portion cycling through the Question, Read, Recite process.

Step 5. *Review*. The final (and most clearly valuable) feature of the process is Review. On completion of a chapter in a book, one then reviews it *not* by rereading, but by taking each section and asking oneself again the question and then reciting to oneself the answer. If this task is accomplished, the section need not be reread. For questions which the learner cannot answer, that particular section is reread and the recitation process used again. Thus review time is spent only on material which requires study, that is, on material not previously learned or remembered. At the same time the review process provides an additional learning trial (practice) over the entire chapter.

To make use of our suggestion of the use of mnemonics, the writers point out to you that this study method is commonly called the SQ3R method—*S*urvey, *Q*uestion, *R*ead, *R*ecite and *R*eview.

CHAPTER SUMMARY

The goal of this chapter has been to present a brief overview of a rapidly growing field—information processing in humans. While we are accustomed to using such terms as "thinking," "problem solving," etc., the term "information processing" is more inclusive covering not only those two topics, but also the nature of memory and strategies for both learning and remembering.

The chapter begins with discussion of thinking and suggests our present understanding of how it is organized. It then deals with how information to be learned is organized into categories (concepts) and suggests that the rules (relationships) we use are specific linkages of concepts. These concepts and rules form the basis for problem solving.

Implied in discussion of both the learning of concepts, rules and problem solving skills *and* their recall, is the crucial variable of meaningfulness. A number of techniques are suggested to facilitate "meaningful" learning as well as recall.

Chapter 5
THE INDIVIDUALIZATION
OF INSTRUCTION

In chapter two we described the preparation of behavioral objectives for cognitive, psychomotor and affective learning. We then described how behavioral objectives should result in learning activities and briefly described the assessment of the behavioral objectives. In chapter three we described entering behavior of students and how entering behavior is related to the tasks we wish students to complete; meeting our objectives. Chapter four explained how we may go about teaching concepts, principles, rules and problem solving skills. Of primary concern to teachers is the relationship of where students are at to what it is we plan to teach. A determination of this relationship can be made via a task analysis of the concept, psychomotor task or affective goal we plan to teach and then using a series of items developed from this analysis to determine where students fall on the hierarchy of skills necessary to perform the task. We indicated that at this point we must rewrite our behavioral objectives so that they are the next logical step for students to take in their learning.

In essence, the above is an outline of teaching what can be pictured as a flow chart. Such a chart appears in Table 5.1. This kind of process in instruction is appropriate for entire classes of children but it is most effective if administered in a way that allows each individual child to pass through the procedure in his/her own way.

TABLE 5.1
A Flow Chart for Teaching

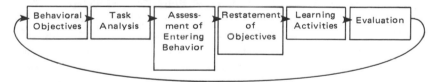

In this chapter you will be introduced to the steps you can take to individualize instruction. At the end of this chapter you will be able to:

1. Write a statement describing the Diagnostic-Prescriptive Teaching method.

2. Outline the four steps in the Diagnostic-Prescriptive Teaching method (DPT).
3. Outline your role in the DPT process.
4. Outline the role your students must play in DPT.
5. Describe the process of "making prescriptions."
6. Describe the way in which a classroom should be physically arranged to allow the best use of DPT.
7. Describe the logistic problems involved in the exchange and storage of DPT materials.
8. Describe your role as a tutor.
9. Describe the process of peer tutoring.
10. Describe the importance of observation, providing hints, prompts and help in general and, keeping track of what all the students are doing.
11. Describe two forms of keeping track of student progress.

DIAGNOSTIC-PRESCRIPTIVE TEACHING

There are many ways of individualizing instruction ranging from the age old tutoring approach which private music teachers still use to the often technologically spectacular computer assisted approach to instruction. In this chapter we shall describe the Diagnostic-Prescriptive Teaching (DPT) approach. We choose this approach because it most nearly coincides with our outline for instruction with groups as per the discussions in chapters two, three and four. You will see that the tasks you mastered in chapters two, three and four will fit very nicely into the DPT approach.

DPT is exactly what the terms connote. It is a highly structured approach to individualized instruction that is dependent on teacher direction although it can be modified to allow considerable student freedom. Essentially DPT is a teaching process built around an assessment of what children can do on entering a new learning situation, setting objectives for the children based on their entry level, prescribing learning activities for the students so that they can meet the objectives and then assessing their mastery of the objectives after the learning activity. The term diagnosis is used to describe the process of determining where the child is located on the hierarchy of skills he/she should develop and selecting the necessary objective for the child. DPT is finding out what students need to learn (diagnosis) and choosing activities (prescription) designed to meet this goal.

DPT is an individual approach. In other words, the diagnosis and prescription are made for each student on an individual basis. This is done in recognition of the fact that each student has different needs and different optimal ways of meeting these needs. For example, if we are teaching a unit in solving for an unknown, some children will start with adding and sub-

60

tracting, others with the actual process of solving for an unknown and perhaps others working on still more complex tasks.

Inherent in DPT or any other form of individualized instruction is the fact that each child will best master the objectives at his/her own rate of progress with experiences that may be different from experiences that will benefit others. In truth, individualization means that each child will be learning what he/she is ready to learn at his/her own pace and in the manner (tutoring, reading, watching films, constructing, etc.) in which he/she benefits most from instruction.

Each child will have a different entry level for instruction. Each child will learn material at a different rate at which he/she can best learn the material in order to gain our objectives and each child will have the best ways of learning different materials. DPT is designed to meet these three facts. We won't deceive you. Without commercial programs, DPT or any other individualized program is more difficult for first year teachers than teaching through the "everybody on the same page, everybody covers the same material in the same way at the same rate" approach. The benefits of DPT, however, are such that the investment of teacher time is well worth the effort.

All this may sound a little confusing to you but before you make a decision about individualized instruction one way or the other, let us outline a DPT approach. We shall follow the outline with suggestions and guidelines we have found to be valuable for teachers implementing individualized instruction.

PROGRAM COMPONENTS AND TEACHER FUNCTIONS

There are four components or steps involved in DPT: devising the behavioral objectives for your overall lesson, diagnosing each child's needs, prescribing the activities that each child will engage in to meet the objectives and evaluating the students after their activities have been completed in order to see whether or not the objectives were met. These steps are basically the same as those we have outlined for a group approach to instruction. In using DPT to individualize instruction, your role changes. There are six major functions a teacher must perform in DPT: organizing the program, performing individual diagnoses, making individual prescriptions on the basis of your diagnoses, tutoring individual students during their learning activities, evaluating students after their activities and keeping records of what each child has done and is to do next.

ORGANIZING THE PROGRAM

Organizing a DPT program consists of developing objectives for the students, explaining the program, giving directions as necessary and managing the classroom behavior of students. As we will devote an entire chapter to managing classroom behavior and as we have already devoted another to developing objectives, our comments here shall be directed to some of your tasks which are peculiar to DPT.

DPT programs may be used with a commercially prepared program or without a commercially prepared program. If you have a commercially prepared DPT program available, you will not need to spend time devising objectives, since this will have been done for you in the program. However, since many teachers do not have access to commercially prepared materials, they must devise their own objectives. How is this done?

To devise your own objectives, identify the goals of your unit of instruction (for one month, one semester, etc.). Transform these major goals into behavioral objectives as per our discussion in chapter two. Once you have set out the behavioral objectives for your unit of instruction, perform task analyses on each. Each step in the hierarchy you develop in each analysis becomes a separate behavioral objective. You may need to continue this process until you have reached the assumed entry level of students for your units. That is, move backwards step by step making each step in the analysis an objective until you get back to the beginning of the unit. You may wish to go a few steps further than the assumed entry level (where the text materials start or where you think students should start) because some of your students' entering behaviors may not be at the level you are assuming as the starting point.

This process takes work and it requires considerable effort on the part of the teacher. However, you only have to do it once for each unit and you may very well use these objectives and the analyses you performed for more than one year. You will also make this time back because when your DPT program gets going, your need for extra preparation decreases, you have already accomplished the majority of it. After completing this "backtracking" process, you will have a long list of objectives through which the students can progress a step at a time to meet the overall unit goals.

Explaining how DPT works amounts to providing the class with a summary of the students' roles as well as your own role. We will describe the students' roles somewhat later. Giving directions is always a part of teaching and differs here only in the fact that you are going to give directions for how to use the materials. Classroom management poses no special problem in a DPT setting and the techniques described in chapter seven can be used here.

PERFORMING INDIVIDUAL DIAGNOSES

The diagnosis process should probably start as a group assessment, that is, the original diagnostic test can be given to all of your students at one time and each may be scored individually to determine each student's entry level. After each student is off on his/her own program, the diagnoses are performed individually. The diagnoses are nothing more than a determination of what the students can or cannot do with respect to the next objective or objectives they are to meet. This kind of test is constructed in exactly the manner we described in chapter three. You may wish to give a very thorough test to begin with and, after your students have gotten going in their individual programs, move to a much less formal approach where only a few items appear on a diagnostic test. Your diagnostic test actually allows you to place each child on your skills hierarchy devised from the task analysis, finding out exactly what the child can and cannot do.

MAKING INDIVIDUAL PRESCRIPTIONS FOR STUDENTS

On the basis of your original objectives, and the task analysis directed diagnosis, you should be able to choose either (a) new objectives and learning activities designed to meet these objectives or (b) activities designed to meet the original objective. This process should be very straightforward. Your diagnostic test will tell you what the students can and cannot do. You simply pick out the first objective that hasn't been met in the hierarchy you have developed and start from there.

Okay, so finding the place to start isn't difficult but where do the activities (the "lessons" for us old timers) that the students are supposed to participate in come from? If you have a commercial program available, this is not a problem; the activities have been developed and matched to the objectives throughout the program. If you are devising your own, you have work on your hands. Depending on how ambitious you are, what kinds of resources you have to work with, the age of your students, their particular needs and the content of your teaching units, you may want to follow the directions we outlined in chapter two for developing learning activities to produce activities in several different forms, e.g., readings, tapes, etc. Remember, one of the ideas behind the individualization of instruction is to let children work with lessons in those media that they benefit the most from.

Even if tape cassette recorders, video tapes, filmstrips and the like are not available, having different written or participation-oriented lessons will benefit your students. Prior to beginning your unit of instruction and after you have defined your objectives that make up the entire unit, you should develop your lessons. The lessons (learning activities) should follow logically from the objectives as per our discussion in chapter two. It is a good idea to go through available workbooks, supplemental activities books and your text materials to select activities for reproduction with ditto or mimeograph stencils. Your colleagues are also a good source of activities. We know teachers who, over a ten to twelve year period of time, have compiled tremendous learning activities resources which they add to and adjust every year.

Part of becoming a good teacher is to develop a supply of resources that may be used over and over. After all, some things never change. We also recommend that you invest in workbooks and supplemental texts. Another good source of activities is your university library, the city library or the library of the college/university nearest your teaching location. It takes time to develop activities but the process is far easier if you ask for and look for those that have already been developed. You will, of course, develop your own and compile them over the years. One last note about help with teaching activities is appropriate. We and our colleagues at colleges and universities all across the country welcome visits and phone calls from our former students who are now teaching. Believe it or not, we are actually good sources of learning activities as well as resource persons for all kinds of questions you may have. If we don't have the answers we probably know somebody that does. Keep in touch.

TUTORING INDIVIDUAL STUDENTS

After you have performed a preliminary diagnosis for all your students, prescribed the activities they are to engage in and helped them locate the materials and start on them, your role changes. You are now in an observation, monitoring and helping role. As each class hour passes, children will have questions about the materials. When they raise their hands you will stop by their work areas and answer or at least try to answer the questions. Other students will need help or individual instruction from you to work through the material. You will sit down with them and provide the instruction or help they need.

This may seem difficult but it isn't too bad. Some children will need little if any help on certain days while others are working together on some task and can help each other. If three or four children are working on the same activities, you can work with them together and increase your time effectiveness. You should also consider *peer tutoring* which has been demonstrated to be a very good teaching technique. In peer tutoring you just have a child who can perform the task sit down and help the child who cannot. It doesn't if the tutor is only one lesson or several ahead of the child he/she is to tutor. Research results reveal that as long as the tutor has mastered the material he/she is to teach, this tutoring will benefit the other child.

EVALUATION OF STUDENTS

The evaluation of students in a DPT program is essentially the same as the outline we suggested in chapter two. After the learning activities have been completed, use any form of activity, paper and pencil tests, oral questioning, performing another activity, constructing an object, etc., that requires that the student perform that behavior stated in the objective to the criterion you specified and under the conditions you specified. If the criteria are met, fine, go on to the next objective and activity for the child. If not, assign other learning activities, individual tutoring or peer tutoring to give the child a review. In DPT the prescription should provide the children with all the activities, materials and so forth they need to meet objectives and they should be able to work at their own pace. This means that once the program is in operation, children will be at all levels of completion with some entering new units before others have gotten half-way through the previous one.

KEEPING RECORDS

Keeping records in a DPT program is important. You must be able to determine exactly what objective each child is working on, which objectives each child has finished, which objectives each child must proceed to and keep track of which activities children have completed for the various objectives. This sounds like a very difficult task but it can be greatly simplified by keeping a master list of children's names with places for you to check off activities and objectives met. A typical chart that will allow you to do this is pictured in Table 5.2.

TABLE 5.2

A Master List of Student Progress

Name	Objectives and Activities					
	1	2	3	4	5	6
Cindy	A-1 √	B-1 √	C-1 √	D-1 √	E-1	
Ralph	A-1, A-2 √	B-1 √	C-1 √	D-1 √	E-2	
Albert	A-1 √	B-2, B-3 √	C-1, C-2 √	D-1 √	E-1 √	F-1
Sarah	A-2 √	B-1 √	C-2 √	D-2		
Joe Bob	A-2, A-3 √	B-1 √	C-3 √	D-2, D-3 √		

Note: Check marks are placed by completed objectives. Activities for each objective are referred to by letter and number. Ralph, for example, completed activities A-1 and A-2 to meet objective number one. Each child is working on that first objective where there is no checkmark.

Such a chart can be kept on notebook paper but it is a good idea to place it on a large sheet which the children can check to see what they are to be doing each day.

THE STUDENTS' ROLES

The students' roles should be posted in a couple of places in your classroom for easy reference. The roles are really seven behaviors. (1) The students must take the diagnostic tests. (2) The students must have their diagnostic tests checked by you (or you may develop self-checking procedures). (3) The students need to confer with you to obtain their next activity (your prescription). (4) The students must locate and go to work on their new activities. You may wish to give these out or label them so that the students can be told which materials to get. For example, "Bill, go get activity E-2 from the cabinet on the blue paper and work on it this period." (5) The students must finish the learning activities. (6) The students should have the teacher look over the completed activities. (7) The students should take a summative test to find out if the objectives have been met.

This whole process is not difficult but it does take a couple of days of getting used to. Once the children get the hang of it, it works very smoothly. Color coding the materials children are to obtain and clearly labeling them are big helps.

PHYSICALLY ARRANGING THE CLASSROOM

To facilitate DPT, the classroom can be organized in any way that allows different children to do different things at the same time. You will probably want to scatter clusters of desks or tables around the room and centrally locate the cabinet that you keep the learning materials, diagnostic tests and so forth, in. Ideally, there should be partitions to separate children working on different kinds of activities. Your resources (study carrels, tables, tape machines, bookcases and so on) will do more to determine the structure of your room than anything else. A good arrangement is one that eliminates traffic through areas where children are working. Regardless of what you have available there should be four kinds of areas: (1) easily accessible storage areas for the tests and objectives, (2) quiet study areas, (3) activity areas where noisy things can be done and, (4) an easily accessible storage area for the learning materials.

LOGISTIC PROBLEMS

Who is going to be responsible for getting what and putting what back where it belongs? This simple question can cause real headaches if you have not thought ahead enough to make these decisions before you start. If the children are to be responsible for checking out and replacing materials, fine. However, you will need to check over your storage area daily to reorder those things put in the wrong place. This is going to happen. Children are children. If misplacement becomes a severe problem, use the correct checking-out and replacing of materials as part of a behavior contract or proclamation.

OBSERVATION

DPT is a program that will gain optimal results only if you are on the ball. As you get to know your students you will pick up their behaviors which indicate "help is needed," "clarification is needed," "I'm stuck," "I have the wrong materials," and so forth. Your role in part becomes that of a very attentive observer ready to step in and offer help at a moment's notice. You don't interfere with students who do not need help but you are constantly watching for the times you should step in. You may consider that you have become a consultant in addition to a teacher.

Your observation will result in stopping by a student's work area and offering assistance, working with him/her for a few moments or just offering hints, prompts and encouragement to help a student get over a tough spot in his/her learning activity. If you have taken laboratory courses, you can use the behavior of the lab instructor as they circulated around the room as a model for how you will circulate around the classroom.

Your observation will also allow you to keep tabs on the students. You will see who is doing what, what kind of progress each child is making, who is goofing off and who is just plain stuck. It will never be too hard to keep track of who is doing what in DPT as your whole program revolves around objectives. Your chart will tell you what everybody should be doing; your observations will tell you what they are doing.

TEACHER-STUDENT CONFERENCES

One of the things that makes DPT an especially nice approach is the fact that you will have the opportunity to confer with each individual child alone. In such a conference you will want to review the work the student has completed. Not only will you want to canvass the work but you should also try to have the student talk about what he/she liked or did not like, what was easy, what was hard, what kinds of difficulties were encountered and how the student *felt* about what was done.

The conferences can also be used as a source for additional data to allow you to determine what and how much was learned. What does the student remember of the learning activities? Can the student *generalize* knowledge gained in the activities to other areas? Does the student indilate that the learned materials meant something to him/her other than "just something to do"?

A third component of the conference can be having the child evaluate his/her own progress. Does the child think he/she is doing well? Is the child bored with the material? Does the child believe that the material is of any benefit? Are there any alternative activities the child can suggest?

Fourth, you should include just *plain talking* in the conferences. When other matters are settled there should always be time to talk about the fair, the circus, a school play, anything that the child especially wants to talk about. You may be surprised to find that you will learn more about your students in the few moments a week you "just talk" than at any other time.

How often should conferences be held? We suggest that you set aside at least 10 to 15 minutes a week for each child. This can and should be done more often if you can arrange it. The students of many of the teachers we have observed come to look forward to the conferences as the most enjoyable time of the week. Don't be surprised if you find them to be the most enjoyable school activity of the week as well.

KEEPING TRACK OF STUDENT PROGRESS

In addition to the large chart we described earlier, it is a good idea to keep individual objective/activity lists for each child in a folder. This folder can also contain notes you make during and after the conferences, samples of student work or any other information you may find to be of value for student evaluation. The record keeping work isn't bad, jotting down the students' activities and the objectives that have been met. Other materials will be filed by you as you see fit.

SUMMARY

In this brief chapter we described the Diagnostic-Prescriptive Teaching (DPT) approach to individualized instruction and outlined the roles you and your students play in such an instructional format. You should have noted the great degree of similarity between DPT and the group instruction procedures we described earlier. The DPT process can be outlined as diagnosis-prescription-learning activity-assessment and rediagnosis.

DPT, or any other individualized approach is harder work than teaching for the average but it is also far more rewarding. No matter how we slice it, hard work is absolutely necessary on your part to implement the program. You must remember, though, the longer you do it, the easier it gets. Lastly, your sources for help (activities, objectives, materials, etc.) are most important to you. Start setting up your supply lines now!

Chapter 6
AN INTRODUCTION TO
THE OPERANT WAY OF THINGS

After completing this chapter you will be able to meet the following objectives at a 90 percent accuracy rate. The conditions under which you meet them will be of your own choosing. The specific criteria are spelled out in the chapter.

1. Write a statement defining operant theory.
2. Write a statement defining the term "stimulus."
3. Write a statement defining the term "neutral stimulus."
4. Write a statement defining the following terms:
   a. reinforcing stimulus
   b. positive reinforcer
   c. negative reinforcer
   d. primary reinforcer
   e. secondary reinforcer
5. Write a statement that delineates between the terms "reward" and "reinforcer."
6. Write a statement defining the following terms:
   a. escape behavior
   b. avoidance behavior
7. Write a statement defining the term "punishing stimulus."
8. Write a statement that delineates between how the term "punishment" is defined in lay language and how "punishment" is defined by operant psychologists.
9. Write a statement defining the term "eliciting stimulus."
10. Write a statement defining the term "discriminative stimulus."
11. Write a statement defining the term "shaping."
12. Write a statement defining the term "stimulus generalization."
13. Write a statement defining the term "response generalization."
14. Write a statement defining the term "stimulus discrimination."
15. Write a statement defining the term "schedule of reinforcement."
16. Write a statement defining the term "extinction."
17. Write a statement defining the term "spontaneous recovery."
18. Write a statement defining the term "internalized reinforcement."
19. Provide an example of each of the terms you defined in objectives 2-18.

OPERANT THEORY

As any student of human behavior becomes aware after coming in contact with any group of psychologists, there are several different theoretical positions which different psychologists adhere to. The argument of which is the best, which is the most nearly correct or which one has the best evidence to support it, is an argument that continues endlessly among psychologists. In this chapter we present an introduction to one of the major theories in psychology, operant theory. We introduce you here to operant theory rather than psychoanalytic theory, Gestalt theory, existentialistic psychology or cognitive psychology because operant theory best lends itself to application in the classroom in many situations that you will find yourself in, especially the analysis of student behavior and the control of classroom behavior (often called discipline). We do not pretend that other theoretical frames of reference will not work for you or other teachers but we do believe that the available evidence to date indicates that a mastery of the basics of operant theory coupled with the techniques we describe later in classroom management, will allow you to sample of our techniques directly in a successful way to allow you to analyze student behavior in fruitful ways.

Operant theory is a branch of the behaviorist school of thought that can be traced back to the British Empiricists. Operant theory has always been closely associated with B. F. Skinner, its founder. Although he did write a series of articles in the early 1930s that began to outline his new theory, the first formal statement and outline of his theory is usually identified as his 1938 book, *Behavior of Organisms*. At the time that Skinner's first major work appeared, there were several competing behaviorist theories (e.g., those of Hull, Guthrie, Tolman) but only Skinner's (with several substantial changes developed by Skinner and other luminary figures in psychology) has stood the test of time and remains a viable theoretical frame of reference for behaviorists. This is not to say that there are no other behavioristically-oriented theories in use today but the newer ones (post 1940) are either based in whole or in part on the work of Skinner (e.g., Staat's Social Behaviorism, Bandura's Social Learning Theory, and so on).

Our task is not to trace the development of operant theory from its origins to the present nor is it to compare and contrast it to other theories, current and historical. Rather, our task is to briefly introduce you to the operant way of things.

JARGON

One of the biggest problems facing any student beginning a review of operant theory is the terminology, jargon, that is used in operant theory.

Many of the terms used in operant theory have very specific, highly restricted meanings that are quite different from the way these terms are used by the general population or even other psychologists. Hence, as we outline operant theory it is necessary for us to introduce terms, define them and demonstrate how these terms (we could use the word concepts) fit into a theory of behavior. Although it is not much fun to memorize a series of terms and the concepts they refer to, to successfully deal with this chapter you must commit the terms to memory. (For some help in doing this you may refer to chapter four.)

BASIC NOTIONS

Operant theory evolved from the cause and effect, British Empiricist school of thought. It is based on the notion (in admittedly simplified form) that organisms (including people) perform those behaviors which result in satisfying or pleasing outcomes and do not perform those behaviors which result in unpleasant or unsatisfying outcomes. This hedonistic sounding premise (quite similar to the ideas of Alexander Bain in the 1850s) forms the basis for operant theory. In short, we would define operant theory as that theory that accounts for behaviors through the consequences of an organism's behaviors. In other words, in operant theory behavior is governed by the consequences of behavior. Some consequences of behavior cause the behavior to be strengthened, some consequences cause the behavior to be weakened. What these consequences of behavior are, how they affect behavior and how we may utilize them are the questions that the remainder of this chapter addresses.

STIMULI

Any theory that emphasizes the consequences of behavior (what happens when an organism *operates* on the environment) is emphasizing the environment and its interaction with organisms. Operant theory is a theory describing what effect the environment has on organisms. We must define environment and all of the components of environment in order to begin to answer our questions about how the consequences of behavior affect organisms.

For us to define environment it is first necessary to describe what the environment is composed of, stimuli. A stimulus is anything that an organism can perceive through any of its sense modalities. A stimulus may be very large (a dump truck) or very small (one of the lug nuts on the wheel of the dump truck). Some psychologists argue that stimuli are irreduceable elements in the environment that may be perceived by an organism and call things like dump trucks groups or series of stimuli. For our purpose, stimuli

71

are defined by their effect on behavior rather than any notions about the irreduceability of stimuli, hence we may perceive one faint dot of light as a stimulus or an entire dump truck as one stimulus.

Stimuli may be external to organisms, the sounds of traffic, the air temperature and so on or they may be internal, the feeling of contractions in the stomach, a tickle in the throat, the sound of your heartbeat, etc. Stimuli may be perceived through only one sense modality (music as auditory only, looking at a painting as visual only, putting your hands in a bag and trying to feel what is inside—tactile only) or they may be perceived by a combination of sense modalities. We can hear, see, feel, taste and smell dump trucks, hamburgers and many other objects. Stimuli may be animate, other persons and lower organisms, or they may be inanimate, concrete blocks and cheesecakes. However, it is not the size, shape or color of stimuli that matter nor through which sense modality we perceive them but rather the effect they have that is important. Our environment is made up of five distinct kinds of stimuli, each having different kinds of effects on behavior.

NEUTRAL STIMULI

Neutral stimuli are those stimuli we perceive that have no effect on our behaviors. In fact, most of the stimuli we encounter fall into the category of neutral stimuli. The color of the walls in your classroom is probably perceived by you and if it has no effect on your behavior it is a neutral stimulus. The color and style of your instructor's clothing are probably neutral. The sounds of traffic outside the building are also probably neutral. If you will look around you as you read this you will probably see (or hear or feel) many stimuli that you were aware of, if only vaguely, that have no discernible effect on your behavior. As we shall see, neutral stimuli do form the pool of stimuli from which many secondary reinforcers, secondary punishers, conditioned eliciting and discriminative stimuli are formed.

REINFORCING STIMULI

Reinforcing stimuli are those stimuli that strengthen behavior, increase the frequency of behavior or increase the probability of occurrence of a behavior in the future after the reinforcing event. Reinforcing stimuli are also referred to as reinforcers, a more manageable term than reinforcing stimuli. Reinforcers are not synonymous with rewards. Rewards are things that we apply to a person's behavior (we shall cease talking about organisms, all sorts of living animals, and restrict ourselves to persons as most of you will not have classrooms full of dogs, cats or planaria) in an attempt to strengthen behavior. As you know, rewards sometimes work and sometimes don't. Reinforcers by definition, are stimuli that *do* strengthen behavior. Anytime you hear the statement "I tried reinforcement and it didn't strengthen the behavior," or similar statements, the person uttering that statement is wrong. Reinforcers are not defined by what they look like, taste like, feel like or what we think they *should do* to someone's behavior. Reinforcers are defined only by what they do to behavior. If a stimulus strengthens a behavior it is a reinforcer. This is the only consideration necessary. If you kick someone in the seat of the pants and this kick (decidedly a stimulus if the person perceives it) makes that individual's behavior occur more frequently in the future, then that kick was a reinforcer.

In order to see how reinforcers operate, it is necessary for us to categorize reinforcing stimuli into two forms: positive reinforcers and negative reinforcers. A positive reinforcer is a stimulus that, on being applied after a behavior, strengthens the behavior it immediately follows (behavior + stimulus ———➤ strengthened behavior). If the consequence of a behavior is a positive reinforcer, the behavior is strengthened. Positive in the sense we use it, does not refer to a "positive" behavior (good behavior), a "positive" feeling on the part of the person (thinking of the stimulus as a good consequence) or anything else other than the fact that positive reinforcers are stimuli that strengthen behaviors they follow. Positive reinforcers are defined (identified) by the effect they have on behavior. Any stimuli from a kick in the pants to an M&M *can be* positive reinforcers but they are not necessarily positive reinforcers. If a stimulus strengthens a behavior it follows then it is a positive reinforcer.

Negative reinforcers are stimuli that, when removed by a behavior that follows the application of the stimulus, strengthen the behavior that allows the removal (stimulus + behavior ———➤ behavior that removes stimulus is strengthened). Negative reinforcers are usually considered to be aversive (uncomfortable, irritating, noxious, etc.) to a person and it is the removal of this aversive stimulus which results in the strengthening of the behavior that brought about the removal. For example, suppose a fly is buzzing around your head. If this stimulus (the "buzz" primarily) is irritating to you, you will probably seek to get away from or escape from this stimulus. You may perform several behaviors to remove this noxious stimulus. Whatever behavior you finally emit that removes the stimulus (e.g., swatting at it with your hand) will be strengthened and will be more likely to occur in the future during similar circumstances. The whole business is very much like hitting yourself on the head with a hammer because it feels so good when you stop.

Negative reinforcers are defined by the effect they have on behaviors. While most of us would look on them as being aversive to the person that is trying to remove or escape them, this aversiveness is not crucial to the definition, or the effect that negative reinforcers have on behavior. An example that deals with "perceived aversiveness" may help to clarify our

73

point. Suppose you want to reward a small child for a particularly good behavior. In order to do this you run up to the child, in front of his/her peers, and give the child a big hug and a kiss. You fully expect this kiss and hug to operate as a positive reinforcer, strengthening the behavior that it followed. However, as all humans are unique and as many stimuli are defined for us by the context they appear in, let us suppose that the kiss and hug are not positive reinforcers but are, instead, noxious to the child. (Remember how uncomfortable you used to feel when you were small and an adult hugged you in front of your friends?) This noxious stimulus, then, is something that the child would like to escape or have removed. Suppose that the child says "Don't do that in front of my friends" and as a result of this behavior (his/her statement) you stop the hugging and kissing routine. If the child's behavior (the statement he/she made) is strengthened then you have negatively reinforced the child. You had no way of knowing in advance whether the stimuli would be positive reinforcers or negative reinforcers. Kisses and hugs *seem* as though they ought to be positively reinforcing. It is the person's perception of the stimuli that is important as the stimuli are encountered, not what we mean to do or the way we perceive the stimuli.

Another way to categorize reinforcers is by identifying them as primary or secondary reinforcers. A *primary reinforcer* is a stimulus that is reinforcing to us because of the biological nature of our bodies. In other words, primary reinforcers are those stimuli that are innately reinforcing to us because we need them for individual or racial survival. We need not learn primary reinforcers. We are born in such a way that certain stimuli strengthen our behaviors because we must have these stimuli to remain alive. Primary reinforcers include food, water, air, climatic comfort, rest, affection (this may be disputed by some psychologists but the evidence drawn from studies of orphanages in the aftermaths of wars seems to indicate that affection is necessary for survival among infants if not among adults) and sexual stimulation. These stimuli are necessary to our biological survival and we are evidently designed (the term designed may connote too much purpose in our existence but each to his/her own) in a way that those behaviors that obtain food, water, air, etc., are quickly learned without having to learn anything about these primary reinforcers.

We need never have encountered Polish sausage, for instance, for it to function as a positive reinforcer if we are hungry. We need never have encountered Wildroot Cola for it to function as a positive reinforcer if we are thirsty. Our biological nature insures that primary reinforcers are reinforcing because we must have them. It is probably appropriate to point out, at this time, the fact that our experiences with life can reorganize the *potency* of reinforcers. (More about potency later.) For example, some young people suffer from a condition known as aneroxia nervosa which amounts to a rejection, almost totally, of eating. It isn't that food is not a primary reinforcer for such people but rather that other reinforcers are more important (more potent) or outweigh the strength of food.

There usually is not much written about primary (innate, unlearned) negative reinforcers. There is no doubt, though, that many stimuli are noxious to us because of our biological natures and that escape from or removal of these noxious stimuli can result in negative reinforcement. A South Floridian, for example, may never have experienced extremely cold weather. If we were to take such a person and transplant him/her to Nebraska in January, we would no doubt find that escape from or removal of the cold would result in a negatively reinforcing series of events. We could go on and on citing various stimuli that are either innately positively reinforcing or negatively reinforcing but we believe that you should by now have seen what is meant by primary reinforcers.

Secondary reinforcers (learned reinforcers) are those stimuli that have little or no reinforcing value in and of themselves. They have reinforcing properties for us because we have learned they are reinforcing. Some examples of secondary reinforcers are money, poker chips, credit cards, new clothing, smiles, music, paintings, the "feel" of fur and on and on. Secondary reinforcers are commonly formed from neutral stimuli through a process we call associative pairing. In associative pairing a neutral stimulus is either paired with or exchanged for a primary reinforcer. The process can be represented this way for direct pairing:

behavior + primary positive reinforcer --→ strengthened behavior

+

neutral stimulus

Then, after several trials

behavior + formerly neutral stimulus --→ strengthened behavior
(now a secondary reinforcer)

The process can be represented this way for exchange:

behavior + neutral stimulus + exchange for primary rein --→
strengthened behavior

Then, after several trials

behavior + formerly neutral stimulus --→ strengthened behavior

75

This associative pairing process results in neutral stimuli literally acquiring some of the reinforcing qualities of the primary reinforcing stimuli they were associated with. Smiles, for example, have no innately reinforcing properties but as we know they do have the ability (please excuse the anthropomorphism) to strengthen our behaviors on occasion; they do function as positive reinforcers.

Let us use the example of a hypothetical infant who has just come home from the hospital three or four days after arriving in our world. Our infant cannot read or write, our speech makes no sense to him/her and facial expressions, including smiles, have no meaning at all. Now, let us consistently pair smiles from the parents with every feeding, with hugging and cuddling (affection) and with all the primary reinforcers the child obtains. Let us also withhold smiles, for a while, on other occasions. After we pair smiles over and over with all this infant's primary reinforcers, we should not be at all surprised to find that smiles by themselves will serve as stimuli that can be used to strengthen behaviors. Smiles have obtained, through direct association with primary reinforcers some of the reinforcing properties of the primary reinforcers. This is the process through which many neutral stimuli come to have reinforcing properties, e.g., tones of voice, particular places, particular words, looks, etc.

One of the best examples of the learning of a secondary reinforcer through exchange can be seen in the formation of money as a secondary reinforcer. Money, in and of itself, has no innately reinforcing value. Money cannot provide nourishment (it can be eaten but somehow does not have the same properties as a steak). You can't drink money. Money cannot provide affection (at least not directly). Money, by itself, is nothing more than paper and metal. We would all agree, though, that money, enough money, can serve as a very powerful source of reinforcement for many of us. How something as biologically worthless as paper and metal can come to have reinforcing properties should reveal to us how secondary reinforcers can be formed through exchange.

Let us suppose that a hypothetical visitor to our planet has landed on the outskirts of any large town. Our visitor, with all his amazing gadgetry, stayed in orbit for several weeks preparing for his visit prior to landing in the United States. During our visitor's preparation time, he observed as carefully as possible life on Earth and determined that those pieces of paper and bits of metal we carry about with us are important. Based on his observations, he reproduced several hundred of the green pieces of paper and a few of the metal discs (as our visitor was so proficient in duplicating Earth materials, his money is perfect and indistinguishable from the real thing). So, upon landing at the edge of a large American city, our visitor is dressed inconspicuously and he has a large amount of money. Our visitor, however, has no idea as to the worth of money. The galactic tourist starts walking up a sidewalk observing the comings, goings and doings of the folk he sees. After a few hours, our friend becomes hungry, thirsty and tired. Now our alien has already determined that he can eat and drink Earth food and, as he really wants to find out about our culture, he continues walking until he arrives at a place where he can see many people eating. He observes for a while and then nervously enters the establishment. The Earth residents are standing in lines in front of a long counter and people in blue uniforms are dispensing what appears to be food wrapped in paper to them. Standing in lines is a universal problem and our visitor steps behind the last person in the shortest line. After several moments he finds himself at the counter. Through his observations in the restaurant he has noted that each person exchanges some of the green rectangular paper or metal discs for the food. He has prepared for this and has four of the pieces of green paper in hand. The person behind the counter nods to him and says "Serve you, sir?" This seems to our alien to be a strange request but since he is hungry he manages to verbalize the same sounds he heard many people ahead of him make as they were at the counter: "A big Mac, fries and a pie." The counter attendant scurries away at once and returns with a paper bag obviously containing many edible goodies. "That'll be one dollar and fifty cents." Without waiting for a reply, the attendant plucks two of the paper rectangles from our alien, returns two discs of silver and says "Next!"

The alien seats himself and proceeds to consume the food, neglecting to remove the paper wrappers first. At any rate, his hunger is satisfied. What we have just described is the exchange of a neutral stimulus (two pieces of paper) for a primary reinforcer: food. According to operant theory, the paper rectangles should be beginning to acquire some of the reinforcing value of the primary reinforcers.

To make a long story short, our friend eventually exchanges money for drink at an establishment nearby and has the secondary reinforcing value of money strengthened. He also learns much about our culture in Mama Possum's Bar, Grill and Go Go Room but that is another textbook. Later he takes a room at a motel for rest, purchases breakfast and in general comes to feel quite proficient in surviving our culture. Money has come to be a secondary reinforcer for him.

To summarize, reinforcers are stimuli that strengthen behavior, increase their frequency of occurrence or increase their likelihood of appearing in the future in similar circumstances. Positive reinforcers occur after behaviors and strengthen the behaviors they follow. Negative reinforcers occur prior to behaviors and result in strengthening those behaviors that seem to remove them or allow escape from them. Primary (innate, unlearned) reinforcers are stimuli that are reinforcing to us because of our biological nature. We must obtain primary reinforcing stimuli in order to stay alive. Secondary reinforcers are learned through the pairing with or exchange of neutral stimuli for primary reinforcers. We determine whether stimuli are reinforcers solely by their effect on behavior. If their application strengthens behaviors, they are reinforcers. If their application does not strengthen behavior, they are not reinforcers.

Potency

In our discussion of reinforcers we alluded to the fact that different reinforcers have different strengths. That is, some reinforcers strengthen behaviors to a very great extent while others only very slightly strengthen behaviors. We refer to the relative strength of reinforcers as the *potency* of reinforcers. The greater an effect a reinforcer has, the more potent it is. The weaker an effect a reinforcer has on behavior the less potent it is. As we shall see later in this chapter, potency may also refer to the strength of a punishing stimulus.

It would be very nice if we could characterize reinforcers by how potent they are with respect to each other. That way we could always refer to our list of reinforcers and choose the most potent in order to change the way in which people behave. Would that it were so! Each of us, every human, has an absolutely unique set of reinforcers with unique potencies for each reinforcer. For some of us butterfly, coin, or stamp collections are highly potent reinforcers. Others of us perceive such things as neutral stimuli or even punishing stimuli.

Even more confusing is the fact that the same stimuli have different potencies at different times. How potent a reinforcer is food for you when you have just finished a sumptuous seven course meal? Food would probably be a much more potent reinforcer if you had not eaten in two days. The same kind of change of potency can occur for any reinforcer. Overall, the potency of a reinforcer is a function of the current state of the organism (the person) and the environment around him/her. We can only be sure that a reinforcer is relatively potent when it, in fact, potently affects behavior.

ESCAPE AND AVOIDANCE

When we discussed negative reinforcement we frequently mentioned the terms escape and avoidance. In operant theory we occasionally talk about escape behavior and avoidance behavior, usually with reference to negative reinforcement but sometimes with reference to punishment. Escape behavior is quite literally the escape of a person from a noxious stimulus. In other words, escape behavior consists of a person who encounters a noxious stimulus and then performs a behavior that allows escape from the noxious stimulus. This series of events results in the negative reinforcement of the behavior that allowed escape.

We all engage in escape behaviors from time to time. Many of us have been to social functions that we found aversive or unpleasant. We escaped these stimuli (social functions) by developing a convenient headache, stomachache or thinking of an "appointment" we had to meet. Whatever successful behavior we chose was negatively reinforced by allowing us to escape from the situation. Another example of escape behavior can be seen when meter readers walk across back yards. If a vicious dog starts after the meter reader, snarling and snapping all the while, the meter reader is likely to perceive this dog as a noxious stimulus. Jumping over a fence, climbing a tree or running from the dog may allow escape. If any of these behaviors allow escape then the successful behavior will be negatively reinforced and will be more likely to occur under similar circumstances in the future.

Avoidance behavior amounts to a person's perception of an oncoming aversive stimulus and emitting a behavior that postpones or avoids the noxious stimulus. Avoidance behavior can be conceived as of a form of escape because the organism must perceive that the noxious stimulus is coming. Hence, avoidance of a noxious stimulus is negatively reinforcing because it allows escape from the perception of the coming noxious stimulus. For example, let us suppose that you wake up tomorrow morning and remember that there is a major examination scheduled in your first class of the day. This somewhat noxious stimulus (the examination) becomes even more noxious as you realize that you forgot to study for the test. You now perceive a highly noxious stimulus, one that you would like to avoid. As you become more and more desperate you finally call your instructor and tell him/her that your grandmother has just passed away and that you will have to miss the examination. You also ask if you can make it up at a later date. Much to your surprise your instructor turns out to be a very sympathetic person and informs you that, yes, you may take the exam at a later date. You are relieved and very powerfully negatively reinforced. From this experience it is more likely that your grandmother will pass away in similar circumstances in the future.

The discussion of escape and avoidance behavior has been presented in order to help you see how many of our behaviors are negatively reinforced and to help you begin to analyze your own behaviors and the behavior of your future students.

PUNISHMENT

We have thus far discussed two of the kinds of stimuli which the environment is made up of, neutral stimuli and reinforcing stimuli. A third form of stimulus we must consider is the punishing stimulus. A punishing stimulus is a stimulus that, when applied after a behavior, causes the behavior it follows to be weakened, to lower its frequency of occurrence or to decrease its likelihood of appearance under similar circumstances in the future. A punishing stimulus has exactly the opposite effect that a positive reinforcer does on behavior.

Punishing stimuli are generally considered to be aversive to the organism that encounters it, but this is not necessarily a criterion. The only criterion for a punishing stimulus (punishment) is that it weakens the behavior it follows. A punishing stimulus (punishment) is defined as a stimulus that weakens behavior. It does not matter what the stimulus looks like, feels like, tastes like or anything else. All that matters is that the stimulus weakens behavior. Our intent in applying a stimulus to another person also does not matter. Intent obviously does not guarantee effect.

If you ever hear a statement like "I tried punishment but it didn't work," you have heard an incorrect statement. Punishment always works. If a behavior weakens as a result of a stimulus applied after it, we have punishment. If we apply a stimulus after a behavior and it does not weaken the behavior then we have not applied a punishing stimulus.

All of us can remember instances when a teacher "punished" a child for some particular behavior and then was terribly disappointed when the behavior was not weakened. This is an example of the lay use of the word punishment. Lay people refer to punishment as an attempt to weaken behavior or as an attempt to make people feel bad. An operant psychologist would not consider a spanking to be a punishment unless the behavior was weakened by this stimulus. The lay definition of punishment is inaccurate for our purposes because it deals with the intent of the person administering the stimulus.

Punishers are not ordinarily classed into learned and unlearned categories although such a categorization could be performed. Unlearned punishers would be those stimuli that weaken our behaviors because of our biological nature. Generally, any kind of painful stimulus meets this criterion, at least prior to other learning. Learned punishers are those stimuli that have acquired some of the punishing value of unlearned punishers through being paired with the unlearned punishing stimuli. This associative pairing process is identical to the one described for the learning of secondary reinforcers:

behavior + unlearned punishing stimulus --►weakens behavior

\+

neutral stimulus

Then, after
several trials

behavior + formerly neutral stimulus--►weakens behavior
(now a learned punisher)

Learned punishers are abundant in our environment. Think about how dirty looks, certain phrases, flashing lights or a police car coming up behind you and other stimuli weaken your behaviors.

Potency, a term we introduced in our discussion of reinforcers is also important as we think about punishers. Each person has an absolutely unique set of stimuli that are punishing, at different levels of potency for him or her. The potency of punishers is also determined to some extent by the situation the person finds himself/herself in. A "dirty look" given you by your opponent in a game of chess may not be punishing at all but this same "look" may be a rather potent punisher if this person "catches you" whispering in church.

In addition to the problem that some punishers are determined by overall situations, we have the problem of several stimuli, reinforcers and punishers, "competing" for effect on behavior. In other words, some of our behaviors may result in both punishing and reinforcing outcomes. We go to work in a driving rainstorm and as a result we get very wet and feel good about being at work. The wet feeling may be a punisher while getting to work may be a reinforcer. If getting to work is more reinforcing than getting wet is punishing, we go to work. If getting wet is more punishing than getting to work is reinforcing, we stay home. This kind of "competition" of stimuli can be seen in children who misbehave in class to get attention (a potent reinforcer) even though they realize that a spanking (a stimulus that may be a punisher) will be the consequence of the misbehavior. If the attention is more potent than the spanking, they will misbehave. However, if the punisher is stronger than the reinforcer, they will not misbehave.

Not only is there a problem with competing stimuli that occur at about the same time, there is also the problem of short- and long-term consequences for a behavior. All of us have had the experience of needing to study for a test the night before its administration but participating in other activities instead. At that time, participating in other activities (going to a party, playing cards, etc.) was extremely reinforcing. However, the long-term consequence of that behavior, getting a test back with an F on the front of it, was extremely punishing. Generally speaking, when an activity has both long- and short-term consequences, we tend to be more affected by the short-term consequence, given that the long- and short-term consequences are of comparable potency.

This "competition" between long- and short-term consequences explains at least partially why many people seem to behave in illogical ways. People living in a shack may, for instance, spend all their money on a color television set (a short-term reinforcer) even though they will not be able to purchase enough clothes at the end of the month (a long-term reinforcer) or they will not save money to purchase a better home (a long-term reinforcer). We can rearrange this sequence of events and begin to explain why some people throw garbage out windows rather than walk down six flights of steps to place it in a garbage receptacle. Walking down six flights of stairs and out into the rain or snow with a parcel of garbage is not particularly

81

reinforcing. In fact the effort and the consequent wetness may be seen as a punishing outcome (a short-term punisher). Throwing that trash out the window is far less aversive at that moment and it also gets rid of the garbage. However, the long-term consequences of this behavior, a clean apartment house without rats, roaches, bad smells and the like, are reinforcing but are so far removed from the current behavior that many persons choose to avoid the short-term punisher but gain for themselves a loss of a long-term reinforcer.

Pervading the whole issue of long- and short-term consequences is the relative potency of the consequences. People, for example, who perceive a college education as a highly reinforcing long-term consequence may work many more hours than necessary and forego all sorts of short-term reinforcers in order to save the money to go to college. Other people who say they want to go to college find the short-term reinforcers so powerful that they cannot pass them up and consequently give up on the long-term consequence, affording a college education.

The whole business of figuring out punishers and reinforcers in any person's life is extremely complex. All of us have unique sets of reinforcers and punishers with variable potencies depending on a variety of situations. We all also perceive long- and short-term consequences differently. Reinforcers and punishers govern much of our lives and a thorough analysis of a person's behaviors (to be discussed in our classroom management chapter) will allow us to manipulate variables in the person's environment to bring about change.

One last point needs to be made concerning punishers and reinforcers before we close up the topic. The perceptive reader may have noticed some real similarities between punishers and negative reinforcers. Remember, negative reinforcers strengthen those behaviors that allow removal of the stimuli while punishing stimuli weaken those behaviors they follow. It is possible for a stimulus to be both a negative reinforcer and a punisher at the same time, weakening the behavior it follows and strengthening the behavior that allows escape from it. This can be represented this way:

behavior-stimulus-behavior

if

behavior is weakened-stimulus-this behavior strengthened by escape from stimulus we have a stimulus operating as both a punisher and a negative reinforcer.

We may see an example of this when a child has performed some behavior, dipping another child's pigtails into an inkwell, and as a result received a spanking. If the spanking weakened the "pigtail dipping behavior," it was a punisher. During the spanking, let us suppose that the

82

child cried very hard. If the child perceived that the crying allowed escape from the spanking and if this crying behavior was then strengthened, negative reinforcement had occurred. We commonly do not analyze stimuli in such a complex way. Usually we are concerned with only one effect, reinforcing or punishing, but it is reasonable for you to consider that a stimulus may have more than one effect on occasion.

ELICITING STIMULI

When most people think about behaviorism or conditioning, they think about Pavlov and his classical (respondent) conditioning of reflexes. Classical conditioning is a part of human learning although we do not believe it is a major portion of the learning we engage in. However, as we want to sample all the stimuli that are a part of our environment, we must spend some time with eliciting stimuli, those stimuli that *elicit* reflexes. (Note: The term "evoke" is used for operant behavior and the term "elicit" is used for respondent behavior. When we bring forth a reflex we say that we have *elicited it* or that the person elicited the reflex. When we bring forth a voluntary behavior, we say that we have *evoked* it or that the person *emitted* the response. You should try to be careful not to mix up how you use *elicit* and *evoke*. *Elicit* refers to involuntary behaviors, reflexes. *Evoke* and *emit* refer to voluntary behaviors, nonreflexive responses.)

Eliciting stimuli are unlearned stimuli that when applied to a person bring forth an involuntary behavior, a reflex. Many authors use the word response for both operant and respondent behaviors but as this practice can lead to confusion we shall refer to respondent behaviors as reflexes and operant behaviors as responses. There are many kinds of stimuli that elicit reflexes: an ice cube slipped down the back, a puff of wind on the eye, a rubber hammer tapped on your top knee when your legs are crossed and so on. As reflexes are innate, involuntary behaviors, we have no control over them. Given the proper stimulus we will elicit a reflex.

As you might imagine, neutral stimuli can come to have some of the properties of eliciting stimuli through the same sort of association process we have described for secondary reinforcers and learning learned punishers. This is the classical (respondent) conditioning that Pavlov's name is associated with. We can represent it this way:

eliciting stimulus →reflex

+

neutral stimulus

Then, after
several trials

formerly neutral stimulus→ reflex
(now a conditioned eliciting stimulus)

Within the terminology of classical conditioning, eliciting stimuli are referred to as unconditioned stimuli (UCS), unconditioned reflexes are referred to as unconditioned reflexes (UCR), learned eliciting stimuli are referred to as conditioned stimuli (CS), and the reflex elicited by the CS is referred to as a conditioned reflex (CR). All the CSs, CRs and so sorth frequently give students problems so we shall consistently refer to them as eliciting stimuli or conditioned eliciting stimuli.

An example of the classical conditioning of a reflex should help you to see how the process works. Suppose we are performing an experiment with undergraduate educational psychology students as our subjects. We have brought one of them in and strapped her to our experimental apparatus. Our purpose is to see if we can condition a reflex. Our student sits on a chair facing an apparatus that can blow puffs of wind directly into her eyes. The puff is strong enough to elicit the reflex of eye-blinking but not so strong that it causes more than a very slight discomfort.

We try out the apparatus a few times and see that it works as planned. Every time we push a button a puff of air hits her eye and she reflexively blinks. Now, let us introduce a small light bulb above the aperture through which the wind passes. For the next several times we turn on the puff of wind we shall also turn on the light about one second before the puff of wind. After these trials we shall then only flash on the light without the wind. If she blinks now when the light comes on without the puff of air, we have classically conditioned a reflex.

To get ahead of ourselves a little bit, if we just kept turning on the light over and over without the wind, our subject would stop blinking in reflex to it after a few trials. This cessation of the appearance of a reflex to a conditioned eliciting stimulus is known as extinction. To go one step further, if we sent our student home and asked her to return the next day, we could see if another interesting phenomena known as *spontaneous recovery* would occur.

When she returns the next day we place her in exactly the same situation she was in before. Now, rather than start the process with a puff of wind, we shall only turn on the light. If she reflexively blinks at the appearance of the light, we will have observed spontaneous recovery, the return of a formerly extinct reflex. We shall return to extinction and spontaneous recovery with respect to operant behavior later in this chapter. We described it here for respondent behaviors because the processes are somewhat different in the two kinds of conditioning.

DISCRIMINATIVE STIMULI

The last form of stimuli that make up the environment are discriminative stimuli. Discriminative stimuli are those stimuli that, quite literally, tell us what to do. More formally discriminative stimuli are those stimuli in whose presence we have been reinforced for performing certain behaviors in the past and as we encounter them now and in the future, we perform those behaviors we have been reinforced for performing in their presence. Whew! Put another way, a discriminative stimulus is a stimulus in whose presence we have learned how to respond because of our previous experience with it. We should note that most psychologists refer to discriminative stimuli with respect to being reinforced in their presence. Discriminative stimuli may also be formed by punishing certain behaviors in their presence. This results in a person learning what not to do in the presence of a discriminative stimulus.

We can refer to the learning of discriminative stimuli as a form of the associative pairing process we have heard so much about already. We can represent it this way:

organism   perceives stimulus "a"

behavior 2 + reinforcement

Then, after several trials

organism perceives stimulus "a" --►behavior 2

or

organism   perceives stimulus "b"

performs behavior "y," is punished

Then, after several trials

organism perceives stimulus "b," inhibits behavior "y"

Discriminative stimuli are associated with behaviors that have either led to reinforcement or punishment in their presence in the past. Discriminative stimuli do not "force" an organism to respond the way that an eliciting stimulus elicits a reflex. Rather, it is just a sign, as it were, that certain behaviors are more likely to result in reinforcement than others.

A classic example of a discriminative stimulus is a driver's behavior at a traffic light. When an average driver is approaching a traffic light, we commonly think of him/her having two alternatives. He/she could stop or just keep going. If the light is red, the driver stops. If the light is green, the driver keeps right on. Why? The lights do not "force" the driver to behave in this way. They don't somehow exert a "mind control" influence on the driver and make him/her stop. The driver could go on red and stop on green if he/she wished. Discriminative stimuli, of which a traffic light is one example, are only stimuli in whose presence a person has been reinforced for performing some behaviors in the past. Stopping at a red light must be the result of a person's experience with red traffic lights. Probably there has been a combination of positive and negative reinforcement for stopping behavior in the presence of red traffic lights in the past. When a person first learns to drive, positive reinforcement in the form of praise from a driving teacher no doubt strengthened stopping behavior. Negative reinforcement, through the escape or avoidance of noxious stimuli can be seen when we consider the consequences of "running" a red light: traffic citations, accidents, and the angry reaction of other drivers. It takes only a few encounters with such consequences for correct stopping behavior to be very potently negatively reinforced by allowing the driver to avoid the noxious stimuli. It is little wonder, then, that as a driver pulls up to a red light, with such a powerful history of reinforcement for stopping behavior, that the driver stops. The same logic can be applied to green lights as well.

Discriminative stimuli are all around us in the environment and they "control" nearly all of our behavior. We have learned how to behave in classrooms, service stations, theaters, at the breakfast table and on and on. In fact we could characterize the majority of human behavior as responses to discriminative stimuli.

DISCRIMINATION AND GENERALIZATION

We have now described all five kinds of stimuli that make up the environment: neutral, reinforcing, punishing, eliciting, and discriminative. These stimuli account for our behaviors but it is necessary to understand some of the processes we undergo in encountering such stimuli. Although we can explain the maintenance of behaviors via reinforcers and punishers, we have not yet accounted for where behaviors come from in the first place. We shall do this when we discuss shaping in the next section. And, although we can explain why we behave the way we do in situations we have previously encountered (by referring to discriminative stimuli) we have not accounted for how it is that people "know how" to behave in new situations, that is, how behaviors are emitted in the presence of new discriminative stimuli. In this section we shall explain how people behave appropriately in new situations by discussing stimulus generalization and stimulus discrimination.

Stimulus generalization refers to the fact that people tend to generalize responses learned in the presence of one stimulus to similar stimuli. In other words, those behaviors that are likely to occur in the presence of one discriminative stimulus are also likely to occur in the presence of similar discriminative stimuli. In general, the more similar a new stimulus is to a previously learned discriminative stimulus, the more likely stimulus generalization is to occur. This phenomenon accounts for how it is that we can enter a classroom we have never before encountered and behave appropriately. We behave in the presence of a new classroom (a new discriminative stimulus) the same way we behaved in situations we perceived to be highly similar to the old one.

Stimulus generalization is important because it reduces the complexity of the environment and reduces the amount of learning we must engage in. Without stimulus generalization we would have to start from the beginning to learn how to act in the presence of every new stimulus we encounter. Obviously this does not occur and so our observation of stimulus generalization must be a reasonable one.

Stimulus generalization, however, does not always occur. We are all aware of the phenomena of a class of children who are as quiet as mice and as well behaved as could be imagined in one room that, when moving across the hall, become loud, disruptive and unmanageable. Why doesn't such a class generalize between the two stimuli? Although the children probably do generalize in part, the difference in their behavior can be described by referring to stimulus discrimination. Stimulus discrimination quite simply refers to the fact that we can perceive differences between different discriminative stimuli and behave appropriately in the presence of each. Although there may be many similarities between the classroom that results in quiet and the classroom that results in chaos, students perceive the differences and behave in those ways most likely to gain reinforcement in the different situations. Stimulus generalization accounts for how we behave in new situations but stimulus discrimination describes how, once a person encounters a new discriminative stimulus, he or she delineates it from other discriminative stimuli and behaves differently in the presence of each.

Lastly, it is necessary to point out the phenomenon of response generalization. In the presence of any discriminative stimulus some behaviors will be reinforced. These behaviors then become stronger in the presence of that discriminative stimulus. Response generalization refers to the fact that not only do the reinforced responses become stronger but also responses that are similar to them. For example, once a child has been consistently reinforced for saying "Hi" in the presence of his/her parents, this behavior is more likely to occur in the future but so are similar responses— responses like "Bye."

SHAPING

Shaping is a process whereby new behaviors are formed and fixed into a person's repertoire of behaviors. Shaping amounts to the reinforcement of successive approximations of a goal behavior from the person's entering behavior until the goal behavior has been performed correctly. Suppose we wish to teach an 18-month-old child to say the words "Mickey Mouse." The child, at the beginning of our process, is able to say "M's," "ou's," "i's" and all the component sounds of "Mickey Mouse." We could work without any kind of visual cue but suppose we have a picture of Mickey Mouse to work with. We could start, much as one of the writers starts with his daughter, by pointing to different objects and pictures and asking "What (who) is this?" As our toddler responds (she has already learned that playing this game is highly reinforcing as it leads to lots of smiles, hugs, kisses and positive comments) we then move our finger from object to object until we reach the unknown, Mickey Mouse. We then say "This is Mickey Mouse." Then we point back to the picture of Mickey Mouse and ask "Who is this?" The first response (the entering behavior) we did get was Mah-kah," which, for an 18-month-old, is not a bad approximation. We then reinforced the response with praise and say "yes, that's Mickey Mouse."

We have completed the first step in the shaping of a new behavior. Now we go back to some other objects and work our way to the picture of Mickey Mouse. When we reach it we ask, "Who is this?" In shaping we must now withhold our reinforcement until we obtain a better approximation of the goal behavior. So, "Mah-kah" is not quite good enough. We stay with Mickey Mouse (perhaps offering prompts) until we get a slightly better approximation, "Mih-kah." As soon as we get this, we reinforce it.

As 18-month-olds do not have the longest of attention spans, we stop playing our game to take it up later in the afternoon. When we resume we are looking for still a better approximation of the goal behavior. This time we wait until we hear "Mika-Ma." This same process goes on and on, always moving up the criteria for reinforcement a step at a time until we reach the goal behavior, saying Mickey Mouse.

Shaping is the forming of behavior from its entry point to the behavior in final form through the reinforcement of successive approximations of the goal behavior. Making the sounds of two words is one example but others can be seen in behaviors as diverse as learning to ride a bicycle or adding two numbers together. Shaping occurs formally in the sense that we can use the process to "teach" children or it may occur informally when children learn behaviors through experience without instruction. Shaping accounts for how many, but not all, behaviors are learned and fixed into our repertoires of behavior.

EXTINCTION AND SPONTANEOUS RECOVERY

We have spent a great deal of time talking about the learning and maintenance of behavior but gave only passing mention to the "unlearning" of behavior with respect to classically conditioned reflexes. That behaviors are unlearned is, of course, obvious. Extinction is the term we use to refer to the unlearning of behaviors. When a behavior has been unlearned we say that it is extinct or that it has been extinguished.

Extinction occurs in two ways for operant behavior. (We have already discussed extinction for classical conditioning.) The first way to extinguish an operant behavior is to remove the reinforcing consequences for that response. Assuming that money is a major source of reinforcement for you, how long would you continue to go to work if you were informed that you would never again be paid for working? The odds are that you would stop fairly soon. Or suppose that you play poker and that winning "hands" is the reinforcer that maintains your behavior. If you never win another hand, sooner or later your poker playing would become extinct. There are numerous problems involved in doing something that appears to be as simple as removing the reinforcers for a behavior. In our chapter on classroom management we shall discuss the methodological problems of extinguishing behaviors.

The second way to extinguish behaviors is to replace the reinforcing consequences of a behavior with punishing consequences or to add a punishing consequence that has greater potency than the reinforcing consequence. This will extinguish behaviors. For example, suppose that you have always been reinforced for raising your hand in class. In a new class you perform this behavior a few times and each time you do, your instructor calls on you (the reinforcer) but then always sarcastically "puts you down" (a punisher). If the sarcasm is more potent than being called on, your hand raising behavior will soon be extinct.

Spontaneous recovery, a phenomenon noted for respondent behaviors, also occurs for operant behaviors. The term refers to the return of a behavior that has been extinct. If you have ever quit smoking (extinction) and then started smoking again, you have experienced spontaneous recovery. Spontaneous recovery may occur for any extinct operant behavior.

SCHEDULES OF REINFORCEMENT

In operant psychology much is made of when and how often organisms are reinforced for their behaviors. As we are not about the business of writing a guide for experimental psychology, we shall only note a few phenomena about when people are reinforced and what the implications are for teaching. A schedule of reinforcement is exactly what the words imply, a schedule whereby a person obtains (or is given) reinforcement for a behavior. The best way to teach new behaviors is to use a constant schedule of reinforcement, one reinforcement for each appearance of the behavior. When the behavior appears to be firmly fixed in a person's repertoire of behaviors, it is wise to move to a more variable schedule of reinforcement, one that will help the behavior become more resistant to extinction. The change from constant to variable reinforcement of a behavior is called "schedule stretching."

Why stretch a schedule of reinforcement? How can we stretch a schedule of reinforcement? The kind of schedule of reinforcement a behavior has been maintained on has a direct relationship to how impervious the behavior is to extinction. Simply, the more variable and infrequent reinforcement is, while still maintaining the behavior, the more resistant to extinction the behavior is. Let us compare two hypothetical behaviors to exemplify this point. Response "A" has always been reinforced each time it has occurred, one response, one reinforcement. Response "B," on the other hand, has been maintained on a highly infrequent schedule of reinforcement, one reinforcer for every 120 responses. So, when we remove reinforcement altogether, we find that after five response A's, the person has missed five reinforcers. It takes 600 response B's, however, for the person to miss five reinforcers. Since removing reinforcement for a response will extinguish it, it will take far longer to extinguish response B than it will response A. If we want a behavior to be relatively impervious to extinction, we should attempt to maintain that behavior on a schedule of reinforcement that provides relatively infrequent instances of reinforcement.

To stretch a schedule of reinforcement is a relatively simple matter once a behavior is learned on a constant reinforcement schedule. Simply start skipping a reinforcer for the behavior once in a while and very gradually reduce the number of times you reinforce the behavior. You may move from one-one ratio to a two-one ratio and so on until you are adequately maintaining the behavior on a relatively infrequent schedule of reinforcement. You must be careful to do this so gradually that the behavior is not weakened.

In a more pragmatic sense, you will, as a teacher, want to maintain many good behaviors on infrequent schedules of reinforcement just because of the logistic difficulties involved in reinforcing every time it occurs. You will not have time to do this and the schedule stretching approach allows you to maintain behavior without worry about not having the time or opportunity to reinforce each one. Reinforcement once in a while will maintain the behaviors you want.

INTERNALIZED REINFORCEMENT

The last topic we will deal with in this chapter is internalized reinforcement. Internalized reinforcers allow us to see how it is that people perform many behaviors without any perceptible evidence of external reinforcement for the behaviors. Internalized reinforcement can be visualized in two ways:

self-reinforcement and the reinforcing value of some behaviors in and of themselves.

Self-reinforcement is quite literally the reinforcement of the self for some behaviors. We all perform behaviors occasionally that go unnoticed or unreinforced by others and then we "pat ourselves on the back" (self-reinforcement). This patting on the back which can extend to buying ourselves a treat or taking a break, are self-reinforcers, a way of maintaining our behaviors in the absence of external reinforcement. We may, for example, get too much change back in a checkout counter and return the change. If anything we may only get a dirty look drom the checkout person. As we leave, however, we congratulate ourselves for being so honest.

Another way to look at internalized reinforcement is to look at some behaviors we perform because the behaviors are reinforcing in and of themselves. Some people play tennis, ski, play chess or whatever because these behaviors are highly reinforcing. They become reinforcing by being paired, over and over, with all sorts of other reinforcers until the behaviors themselves have acquired reinforcing value. After this occurs, the behaviors are much like any secondary reinforcers. For one of the writers, driving golfballs is a highly reinforcing behavior. For another, running is highly reinforcing. These behaviors are reinforcing because they have acquired reinforcing value through previous association with other reinforcers.

SUMMARY

Operant theory is a cause and effect theory of human behavior stressing the observable events in human life, behavior. It is a theory that accounts for human behavior as a result of human-environment interaction. The environment, made up of five kinds of stimuli (neutral, reinforcing, punishing, eliciting, and discriminative) interacts with the human based on the human's previous history and its current physical status.

Those phenomena that cannot be directly accounted for through an examination of these five stimuli are accounted for through various internal processes: stimulus generalization, stimulus discrimination, and internalized reinforcement as well as through external factors, schedules of reinforcement and the potency of reinforcers. Behaviors are learned through shaping and are extinguished by removing reinforcement or through punishment. Operant theory is limited in that it can only deal with that which is observable.

Chapter 7

CLASSROOM MANAGEMENT AND
BEHAVIOR ANALYSIS

Upon finishing this chapter you will be able to:

1. Write a statement describing what impact teacher behavior has on student behavior.
2. Write a statement describing how you may change a student's behavior by changing your own.
3. Upon reading about a "problem behavior," you will be able to define that behavior or a portion of it in observable terms.
4. Write a statement describing a frequency count and list its disadvantages.
5. Write a statement describing time interval assessment and list its advantages and disadvantages.
6. Write a statement describing "on-the-count" assessment and list its advantages and disadvantages.
7. Write a statement describing (a) concomittant assessment, (b) simultaneous assessment, and (c) consecutive assessment.
8. Upon being given data, you will be able to reduce it to a graph format.
9. Upon seeing a graph of behavior you will interpret it correctly.
10. Upon being given a graph of teacher and student behaviors, you will analyze the effects of teacher behavior on student behavior.
11. Say what a "baseline," "treatment condition" and "return to baseline" are. Provide an example of such a triad.
12. Say why an ABA design is commonly used in behavior change procedures.
13. Write a statement describing the usefulness of a "return to baseline condition" for teachers not conducting an experiment.
14. Write a statement describing "time-out" and describe an appropriate time-out room and the procedures to be used in placing a person in time-out.
15. Write a statement defining group contingencies. Provide one example of group contingent reinforcement.
16. Write a statement describing the Premack Principle and describe an example of the Premack Principle in use.
17. Write a statement describing what "assigning responsibility" is and why it is used. Provide a hypothetical example of this technique.

18. Write a statement describing what a behavior contract is. List three differences between a behavior contract and the other techniques described in this chapter.
19. List all the necessary components of a behavior contract.
20. Describe the procedure for initiating and implementing a behavior contract with a class of students.
21. Write a statement describing the relationship of reinforcement potency to behavior contracts.
22. Say what a proclamation is and compare and contrast it to a contract.
23. Write a statement telling what individual contracting is and what the necessary components of an individual contract are.
24. Describe how you might devise an individual contract with a hypothetical student.

THE ANALYSIS OF BEHAVIOR

Teaching is more than a mastery of subject material, an ability to write good behavior objectives, task analyses, assessments of entering behavior and structuring learning activities. Teaching is also the ability to deal with the behavior of your students in a way that will result in the best possible classroom atmosphere for learning. The sort of procedures used to deal effectively with student behavior are frequently referred to as discipline. However, there are a good many misconceptions about what discipline is and what it is not. Prior to talking about the analysis of behavior it is necessary for us to define what we mean when we say the word "discipline."

Discipline is not simply punishment although it has come to have that connotation in lay usage. Statements like: "That kid needs disciplining," are inaccurate because the speaker is actually talking about spanking, hitting or otherwise hurting a child which may not even weaken the "target" behavior. On the other hand, discipline is not simply the reinforcement of "good" behaviors while ignoring those behaviors that are "bad." Discipline is a combination of reinforcement, punishment, encouragement, counseling and the setting of conditions that allow teachers to control behavior. Discipline is, in fact, all those things that teachers do to help students become self-directed.

There is, naturally, more to discipline than us telling you "Okay, you know what discipline is now. Go out and discipline your kids." Discipline, the controlling of student behaviors, is best approached through a systematic, scientific approach to the analysis of human behavior. Put another way, we cannot effectively impose discipline on our students unless we can "understand" why they do what they do" that is the major topic in the first part of this chapter.

As you read through this chapter you may get the notion that classroom management supersedes everything else. Not so. We are purposely restricting ourselves in this chapter to your nondidactic roles, those duties you perform in addition to disseminating knowledge, supervising practice, evaluating students, and so on. Discipline does not occur in a vacuum. It is a part of your total role as a teacher. All of the procedures we describe deal only with a very small portion of your behaviors and an equally small portion of your students' behaviors. Most of your time will be spent in "real teaching." Very little of your students' time will be spent in misbehaving.

Misbehavior does occur. You, as the teacher, are responsible for controlling this misbehavior so that it will not interfere with your major, nondiscipline duties. Even the worst class we have ever observed still had students behaving in appropriate ways 60 percent of the time. Discipline is a part of your overall teaching behavior that should complement the other things you do. Frankly, even though many teachers complain longly and loudly about discipline, teachers seldom spend more than a very small portion of their time engaged in classroom management. We suppose it seems so important because a few instances of misbehavior are truly irritating and in great contrast to the way students usually behave.

We hope that you sense that discipline is only a component of your overall teaching behaviors and that it should not interfere with your other duties. In this chapter we seldom mention other things you do, choosing to emphasize the management of behavior. We don't do this to show that there isn't more to teaching than discipline. The artificial dichotomy we set up between discipline and other teaching duties is set up for the convenience of presenting material. In practice you will seldom be able to clearly separate discipline from your other duties.

TEACHER BEHAVIOR

To have gotten this far in the book you must also by now have met all the objectives in the previous chapters and are aware of how it is that the consequences of behavior govern behaviors. Behaviors that are reinforced are strengthened and will be more likely to occur in the future. Behaviors that are punished are weakened and will be less likely to occur in the future. A knowledge of these facts is all very well and good if we are working with white rats and can control what is reinforcing (starving a rat to three- fourths of its free-feeding weight will make sure that food pellets are highly reinforcing) and what is punishing (placing a rat on a wire grid and pumping a powerful electric current through the grid will hurt the rat and be a powerful punisher). The problem is that humans are infinitely more complex than white rats and that we cannot ethically even think of such a thing as starving a student to three-fourths of his/her free-feeding weight, let alone wiring up our students to shock them when they do the wrong thing.

Dealing with humans is far more difficult because we must work with far more subtle stimuli and becasue each student's history of reinforcement will be unique. Given such difficulties, the task may seem insurmountable but it is not. It is possible to analyze student and teacher behaviors to determine what consequences are causing behaviors to appear or what other consequences are causing some behaviors not to appear.

Teachers are commonly very powerful sources of reinforcement for many children. All of us have had the experience of working especially hard to please certain teachers and all of us have tried to figure out what "bugged" another teacher we did not like in order to irritate him/her. Teacher behavior is a very important source of consequences of student behavior. How we react to student behavior is an immediate consequence and is easily visible to the student.

For example, let us take a look at Ms. Ped Antic. Ms. Ped Antic is a new teacher, just out of college, teaching ninth grade general science. She is fairly well satisfied with how things are going but is a little bit worried about Bill. Bill, an honor student throughout his first eight years in school, poses an interesting problem. He is obviously very intelligent. He reads very well and does well on his assignments. Bill, however, is always complaining to Ms. Ped Antic about how hard her course is and how much he must work. She always informs him that he is doing very well and that he is a very bright student, fully capable of doing excellent work on all his assignments. Reassurance doesn't seem to do any good, though, for Bill's complaining and whining increase nearly every day. No matter how much time Ms. Antic spends with Bill, he continues to tell her how worried he is about flunking and how hard all those assignments are. What could Ms. Ped Antic do about this problem?

A poor self-concept you say? Maybe, maybe not. Not enough personal esteem, you guess? Maybe. Could Bill be a compulsive "overachiever" on the brink of a nervous breakdown? Maybe so. Could the material really be too hard for Bill? That, too, is a possibility. Let's check things out. Poor self-concept? Ms. Ped Antic checks with her colleagues and finds that Bill does well in all his courses and that he doesn't complain in those settings. He also participates in several student government activities and volunteers to go to mathematics contests, spelling bees and science contests. Nope, we can probably rule out a "poor self-concept" for someone who seems to have so little fear of failure in other settings. Personal esteem? Again, probably not. Bill is very well aware of his accomplishments in other classes and in extracurricular affairs and, if questioned, will launch into an hour-long monologue about what he has accomplished. A chronic overachiever? A quick look at Bill's cumulative folder indicates that his intelligence quotient (not necessarily a good measure) is in the gifted range. No, he certainly is not overachieving. And, since Bill made excellent grades in Science 2 the year before and won a statewide science contest, the material isn't too hard for him. What is it then?

Let's go back to what Ms. Ped Antic does after Bill's complaining behavior. In other words, what is the consequence of Bill's complaining behavior? Why, Ms. Ped Antic always reassures, flatters and gives him all the time and attention he needs. Could these consequences possibly be positive reinforcers for Bill's behavior? That is, could attention and flattery alone be enough to maintain Bill's complaining behavior?

There is only one way to find out. As Ms. Ped Antic reviews her Ed. Psych. one weekend, she stumbles across some old operant "junk" and decides to modify Bill's behavior. Deciding that Bill may really "need" the attention (maybe he doesn't get enough at home or maybe his self-concept really is a bit weak) she decides to never give Bill any more attention for complaining (removing a reinforcing consequence) but only to give him attention for appropriate behavior (turning in his homework, leading group discussions and so on). She will also keep a list of how often Bill's complaining behavior occurs during this process so that she can check the results of her strategy.

Two weeks pass, and lo and behold, Bill's complaining behavior has really dropped off. Ms. Ped Antic found it very hard to ignore the complaining. In fact when she first started ignoring it, he seemed to complain more often and more loudly, but she always left the area, turned her head or acted as though she did not hear him. Further, providing reinforcement for Bill's appropriate attention getting behavior wasn't too bad. Ms. Ped Antic is pleased and seriously considering rewriting her evaluation of the Ed. Psych. course.

In this instance, at least, teacher behavior controlled an irritating student behavior and by changing teacher behavior, student behavior was changed. When teacher behavior functions as the consequence for a student behavior, and this consequence may be reinforcing or punishing, then a change in teacher behavior will result in a change in the student's behavior. Frequently, in order to change student behavior it is only necessary to change our behavior.

As you might imagine, it is difficult to determine the effects of teacher behavior on student behavior, or for that matter, to determine why student behavior is maintained at all. Such determinations may frequently be made intuitively by experienced persons we recognize as "good teachers." Most of us, however, do not have the capacity to make such intuitive judgments. For us, then, it is necessary to learn some very basic things about the study of behavior based on a scientific regimen generated by psychologists and educators who are engaged each day in the analysis of behavior.

97

GATHERING DATA

Prior to doing anything else, it is necessary for us to examine some basic points about the observation of human behavior. One of your students is disruptive, you say, what does disruptive mean? Does disruptive mean screaming and shouting? Does disruptive mean telling jokes? Does disruptive mean hitting other children or throwing objects? As you can see, the word "disruptive," although in common usage and thought to be rather clever by some of the lesser lights in education, does not mean very much. Does this problem sound familiar? It should. In chapter two where we hammered away at the need for using verbs that would allow a teacher to observe and measure behaviors, we noted this same problem. Any behavior we wish to change among students must be so carefully, so unambiguously defined that there can be no mistake about when the behavior has occurred and when it has not occurred.

The first major point to be made in our discussion of behavioral analysis is that whatever behaviors we study must be very clearly and carefully defined. If we are having troubles with a child who we believe to be "disruptive," we must state precisely what this disruption is in nonambiguous, precise verb forms that allow us to directly observe, measure and replicate what we have observed. Is the disruptive kid throwing spitballs at your head? This may be disruptive but everyone is going to know exactly what you are talking about if you say that "he is throwing spitballs," whereas if you say he is "disruptive," who knows what he is doing?

The same kinds of guidelines we used for describing behavior at the end of a teaching unit, written in the objectives, can be used in defining other student behaviors. If a child is getting out of his or her desk, say so. Don't say anything about the child being troublesome, meddlesome, having a "bad attitude," being disruptive, etc., etc., ad nauseum. As you know, only clearly stated verb forms allow you to observe and measure the behavior, let alone communicate intelligently what is happening.

Wait a minute. Wait a minute, here. Won't *I know* what is going on with my students? Won't I decide whether or not they are disruptive, disrespectful, etc.? Of course you will. We are about the business of trying to make your life and future profession easier. We're not trying to sell you a worthless bill of goods just because we like to sit up late at night and write books which you can be required to read. You derive several real benefits from *formally defining your students' behaviors.* (1) There will be absolutely *no doubt* as to the effectiveness of your behavior change procedure. No matter what we think, it is very hard to tell the difference between 50 instances of inappropriate talking behavior and 40 such instances. This kind of change, although still leaving the talking behavior at a relatively high level, is significant but it can and does go unnoticed by teachers who do not accurately define what they are looking for. (2) You can share the results of your procedure with other professionals knowing that there is no way for them to misunderstand what was done. (3) You can train paraprofessionals (teacher's aides), parents, counselors, other students, or any available other warm bodies, to keep track of the behavior for you so that you can be freed for other duties. (4) If you choose to use some of the techniques outlined later in this chapter, you and the student can come to an absolute agreement of what behavior is under consideration. (5) You will have that "good feeling" inside knowing that you are not just verbalizing euphemisms about "disruption," "aggression," "disrespectful," etc., etc.

Now that we have finished our justification for why we should always clearly define behaviors in observable and measurable terms, we will start describing how we may measure these behaviors. The most simple way of keeping track of a person's behaviors is by keeping a *frequency count* of his/her behavior. A frequency count is nothing more than a tally of how often the defined behavior occurred while someone was observing the person. For example, suppose we are observing how often Bill is "out of his seat" during third period as defined by the loss of buttock-seat contact. A tally of this would be a frequency count and would look like this:

Bill's out of seat behavior ~~IIII~~ III

That's all there is to a frequency count. A teacher can frequently keep such a count while doing many other things merely by making a note to oneself when the behavior is perceived. A plastic "click-counter" of the sort that can be purchased at dime stores for one dollar (personally we'd rather buy one at a dollar store for a dime but times have changed) works beautifully for keeping a frequency count. We should like to point out, though, that the most accurate observations are performed by people who don't have to do three or four things at once, a person that can be instructed to watch a student and keep a frequency count of the student's behaviors. We will come back to where to get such an observer later.

There is one very severe and frequently fatal drawback to frequency counts. Frequency counts cannot be used to discriminate among behaviors that are not equivalent. That is, in a frequency count we cannot tell the difference between a behavior that lasts five seconds and one that lasts five minutes; both are counted as one behavior. Hence, frequency counts are only useful for behaviors that are of brief duration wherein each behavior is equivalent to each other behavior. Where a behavior is studied that can last for varying durations, talking, being out-of-seat, etc., other observation techniques are more useful. For many behaviors such as hitting, name- calling, foot tapping and the like, a frequency count is a good method of gathering data. Incidentally, so that we don't forget that kids do good things once in a while, frequency counts are really good for keeping track of how many pages were read by a child, how many problems were worked during a class period and so on. We can work at increasing student behaviors just as well as we can work at eliminating undesirable student behaviors.

A *time-interval assessment* is an assessment of behavior wherein a tally of behaviors is kept during specified intervals of time. In other words, we may want to break up an hour long class period into 12, five minute blocks of time and keep a tally of behaviors in three or four of these. Other than the time constraints it is identical to a simple frequency count. A time-interval assessment has two major advantages over a simple frequency count. (1) It does not require that the entire period be spent observing behaviors while still providing a reasonable sampling of the behaviors you are interested in. You would assume, for example, that if you kept a behavior tally during three, five minute blocks of time that your data would comprise about one-fourth of the total behaviors occurring during that hour. (2) To some extent, a time-interval assessment reduces the problem of behaviors occurring at different durations. By checking at different times, you will catch behaviors continuing from a previous time interval, during the current time interval and some that just begin at the end of the time interval. There are two drawbacks of the time-interval assessment. (1) Some amount of observation time is given up. However, as you continue to observe over several days you should obtain a good representation of the overall behavior. (2) You must randomly choose the time intervals and keep accurate track of the time. This may be difficult for you logistically.

An *on-the-count* assessment is the most useful form of gathering behavioral data in most classroom settings. However, it is almost mandatory that an independent observer be used to gather the data as the technique requires too much concentration for you to be able to teach and gather data at the same time. An on-the-count assessment is a tally of behaviors kept at previously determined times interspersed throughout the observation period. Most frequently an interval of ten seconds between observations is used. The technique requires that the observer have a prepared tally sheet such as the one pictured in Table 7.1 where he/she can watch the clock or a watch with a sweep second hand for ten seconds, observe the student(s), jot down whether or not the behavior(s) were occurring and again watch the clock.

This procedure may seem difficult but it is not. If the behavior is well defined, about one-half hour of practice will result in quick and accurate tallies of behavior at the times you choose. You could choose longer intervals of time between observations, thirty seconds, one minute and so on, but we have found that teacher aides, parents and other students can master the ten second interval easily and this short time between observations doesn't allow the observer's attention to be distracted. Some teachers have

TABLE 7.1

A Prepared Tally Sheet for On-the-Count Assessment

Time	Behavior (√ for yes, blank for no)
1:00:00	
1:00:10	
1:00:20	
1:00:30	
1:00:40	
1:00:50	
1:01:00	
1:01:10	

Note: The observer is instructed to place a checkmark by those times at which the behavior was occurring. Other times are left blank. A tally sheet for actual use would be much longer than this example.

even equipped their observers with a tape recording playing a "beep" every ten seconds so that they may hear it via earphone and not have to look over at a clock at all.

The on-the-count assessment eliminates any problem with behaviors of varying durations. If Dana is talking at 10:10:10, still talking at 10:10:20 and still talking at 10:10:30, this talking behavior is counted three times rather than just once as in a simple frequency count. A behavior that lasts five minutes is counted thirty times and carries much more weight than a behavior that lasts only ten or twelve seconds. Some behavior, of course, is not observed but the sample you get by checking at ten second intervals will be highly representative of the behavioral overall. The obvious drawback is the need for an independent observer who has an available clock, watch or tape recording and a prepared tally sheet. However, the benefits of a time interval assessment far outweigh its disadvantages.

We have discussed three ways of gathering behavioral data for students. As you can see, the on-the-count method of assessment is by far the most accurate and will give you the most meaningful data. Where do you get observers? The first people to try are your colleagues. As you will find out, teachers frequently spend considerable amounts of time talking with each other about their respective problems. Other teachers are a source of well-educated and situationally knowledgeable people. You may get a colleague to help you during his/her free period or even during the lunch hour. You will, of course, want to reciprocate. If you have a teacher's aide, this person can readily be trained to do what you want and still feel that he/she is well within the job description of a teacher's aide. At some schools the guidance counselor may help you by gathering data or assigning one of his/her staff to perform that service for you. Many schools have parent-volunteer programs where parents work in the schools on a volunteer basis. Parents are an excellent source of help and you should try them. It is a good idea, though, not to use a parent who has a child in your classroom. On occasions some students from other classes or other grades may serve very well as your observers. Care should be taken to choose a student who does not have friends or acquaintances in the class he/she is to observe.

Don't all these observers confound the issue? Won't students behave differently if they know there is an observer in the classroom? Surprisingly after a day or two the observer becomes part of the furniture and is ignored. The presence of an observer does not affect classroom behavior. You must be very careful, though, to instruct your observers to avoid any interactions with students and to sit in a place that is not frequented by the students. We realize that observers may not always be available, but we feel that their presence is well worth the efforts to find them.

BEHAVIOR ANALYSIS

Generally, behavior analysis amounts to the observations designed to gather data that can be evaluated so that the teacher can determine what environmental factors are contributing to the maintenance of extinction of student behavior. We will be primarily concerned with the relationship between teacher and student but will also investigate student-peer interactions.

At the beginning of this chapter we presented the example of Ms. Ped Antic and how her behavior controlled Bill's behavior. Her analysis was an informal one. Although not stated at the outset of this chapter because of its ambiguity, we would like to have you think like Ms. Antic by the end of this chapter, i.e., we want you to think about what impact your behavior has on the behavior of other persons. One way to go about this is to present you with three formal methods of analyzing behavior and by presenting you with examples of behavior analysis.

To determine the effect of teacher behavior on student behavior, it is necessary to observe the behavior of both the student and the teacher. One way to do this is with the *concomitant method* of observation. Simply, the concomitant method requires two observers, one to observe the student, the other to observe the teacher. The observers may perform simple frequency counts, interval assessments or on-the-count assessments. If a concomitant method is chosen, it is probably most beneficial to have the observers use the on-the-count assessment. This way you will have a tally of the student's behavior and the teacher's behavior at intervals throughout the observation time. Synchronization of observers is important but very difficult. The question you want answered is, what do I do when or after the student performs the behavior I want to extinguish? Data drawn from such an observation procedure may allow this or it may not, depending on the quality of the response definitions and the synchronization of the observers.

For example, suppose your student, Jane, persists in drumming her fingers on her desk, rubbing a pencil across the spiral binding of her notebook or twanging her ruler on her desk. These three behaviors have been defined by you as noise-making and you have one observer tallying her noise-making behavior at ten second intervals through your class period. You have done this because you don't like these behaviors, because the behaviors disrupt the class and because you want to extinguish these behaviors. How you will extinguish the behaviors will be decided after you determine whether or not *your behavior* is maintaining her behavior. That is, are your reactions to her noise-making behaviors functioning as positive reinforcers?

To answer this question you have another person observing you at ten second intervals throughout the same class period. Speaking to Jane, looking at Jane, calling Jane down, shouting at Jane, reacting to the noise, commenting on Jane's behavior to other students have all been defined by you as "attending behavior." So, you now have one person tallying Jane's noise-making behaviors and another tallying your reactions to Jane's behavior. Two or three class hours of such data gathering should allow you to decide if you are maintaining Jane's behavior. Table 7.2 presents such a tally sheet for these days, picturing some of those instances where Jane made noise and what your reaction was.

Of the 21 times Jane made noise, you reacted to her with attention 18 times. (We will assume that if we pictured all the observational data that we would have the same kind of result.) This does not "prove" that you are maintaining her behaviors but it certainly indicates good reason to suspect that it might be the case.

A *simultaneous assessment* is very much like the concomitant except that one observer is trying to observe both student and teacher behavior simultaneously. This can be an effective form of gathering data if the observer is highly proficient but we suggest that it should be used as a last resort because of the difficulty in obtaining accurate data if the observer is not highly trained. The data, of course, would appear similar to those pictured in Table 7.2.

The best method of gathering teacher-student behavior is probably the *consecutive method*. In the consecutive method, only one observer is employed but he/she takes turns at ten second intervals checking your behavior and the student's behavior. A prepared form such as the one pictured in Table 7.3 is necessary. This technique allows the gathering of data from both the teacher and the student by one observer without the problems of synchronization or trying to have one observer do two things at once.

TABLE 7.2

A Tally of Jane's Noisemaking Behavior

Jane's Noisemaking Behavior	Teacher's Attending Behavior
10:00:00	yes
10:00:10	yes
10:00:20	yes
10:00:30	
10:24:00	yes
10:24:10	yes
10:24:20	yes
10:24:30	yes
10:24:40	yes
10:35:00	yes
10:35:10	yes
10:35:20	yes
10:35:30	yes
10:35:40	yes
10:35:50	yes
Day 2	
10:05:10	yes
10:05:20	
10:05:30	yes
10:05:40	yes
10:05:50	yes
10:06:00	

For example, suppose Ed has an irritating practice of muttering or mumbling in class just loud enough for you to hear it, but never loud enough for you to hear what is being said. Because you believe that this

TABLE 7.3
An Observation Form for Consecutive Observations

Time	Student Behavior	Time	Teacher Behavior
2:00:00		2:00:10	
2:00:20		2:00:30	
2:00:40		2:00:50	
2:01:00		2:01:10	
2:01:20		2:01:30	

Note: The observer is instructed to alternately observe student and teacher behavior at 10 second intervals. If the defined behaviors occur, a checkmark (√) is placed by that time interval.

behavior is disruptive you would like to extinguish it. Is your behavior, your reaction to the mumbling, controlling Ed's behavior?

To find out, you instruct your observer to tally Ed's mumbling behavior at twenty second intervals throughout the class hour. You have defined mumbling as any verbal sound coming from Ed that is not in response to a question from you but is, in fact, an audible noise directed at no one in particular. Additionally, the observer will check your attending behavior, defined as any glance, statement, reaction, etc., to Ed at twenty second intervals so that an observation of your behaviors is always sandwiched in between observations of Ed's behaviors. Table 7.4 pictures the results of such an assessment showing selected intervals in which Ed mumbled. Ed mumbled 23 times and you attended to it 17 times. Again this is not "proof" that your behavior is maintaining his behavior but it should cause you to wonder about what might happen if you changed your behavior.

DATA INTERPRETATION

While we have just briefly skimmed the notion of behavior analysis, we should point out that tally sheets of data are often confusing and hard to interpret, particularly when several behaviors are being observed. We have not discussed the procedure, but after some practice, an observer could tally as many as twelve different behaviors for both students and teachers at ten second intervals merely by placing an abbreviation in the time slot rather than a check mark placed by a time when only one behavior is considered. Concise definitions of behavior allow this.

By converting tally sheets into behavioral graphs we can greatly aid our

105

TABLE 7.4
Ed's Mumbling Behavior; Teacher's Attending Behavior

Ed	Teacher
11:00:00 √	11:00:10 √
11:00:20 √	11:00:30 √
11:00:40 √	11:00:50 √

Day 2

Ed	Teacher
11:10:00 √	11:10:10 √
11:10:20 √	11:10:30 √
11:10:40 √	11:10:50
11:11:00 √	11:11:10
11:11:20 √	11:11:30 √
11:11:40 √	11:11:50 √
11:12:00 √	11:12:10 √

Day 3

Ed	Teacher
11:20:00 √	11:20:10 √
11:20:20 √	11:20:30 √
11:20:40 √	11:20:50 √
11:21:00 √	11:21:10 √
11:21:20 √	11:21:30 √
11:21:40 √	11:21:50 √
11:22:00 √	11:22:10
11:42:00 √	11:42:10 √
11:42:20 √	11:42:30
11:42:40 √	11:42:50
11:43:00 √	11:43:10 √
11:43:20 √	11:43:30
11:43:40 √	11:43:50 √

interpretation of what's happening in the classroom. For example, compare Table 7.4 to Table 7.5, both representing the same information.

Table 7.4 is a tally sheet of one day's partial observations. Table 7.5 is a graph representing that data as well as the rest of the observational data taken over fifteen days. As you can see, fifteen tally sheets leave much to be desired in terms of your interpretation of the data while one graph can picture fifteen days' worth of behavior easily and clearly.

TABLE 7.5

A Behavioral Graph of Ed's Mumbling Behavior Across 15 Days

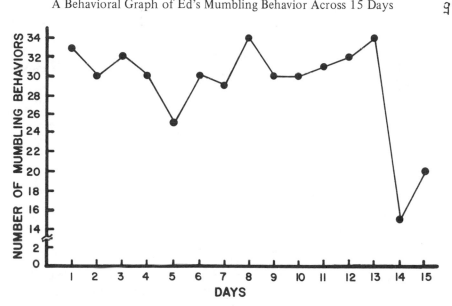

Preparing a behavioral graph is really very easy. Place days (or whatever time interval you think is most reasonable) across the horizontal axis as per the illustration in Table 7.5. Then place the number of behaviors from bottom to top on the vertical axis in the same way as we picture it in Table 7.5. Plot the total number of observed behaviors from each day's tally sheet at the coordinates where it belongs. For example, if there were fifteen of the behaviors you were recording on day 3, place a dot or an X at the joint where a line drawn up from day 3 and across from 15 behaviors intersect. This is pictured in Table 7.6. You will, of course, want to erase the lines you use to plot the data.

When you have plotted all your "data points," connect them with a line (see Table 7.6). Such a graph of behavior allows you to quickly and easily see what is happening with the behaviors you observe across several days. At this point you should turn to the back of the book and find exercise number one for chapter five and complete it. Exercise number two is a graph that you are to interpret. For our purposes, an interpretation is nothing more than a verbalization of what you see.

If you are performing an analysis of the effect of teacher behavior on student behavior you may picture both teacher and student behaviors on the same graph if you wish. Use an X for student data points and a Y for teacher data points. Make the connecting lines for student behavior solid

TABLE 7.6
Preparing a Behavioral Graph

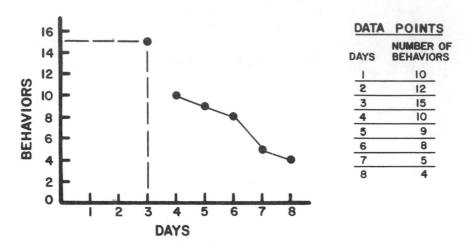

DATA POINTS	
DAYS	NUMBER OF BEHAVIORS
1	10
2	12
3	15
4	10
5	9
6	8
7	5
8	4

and the connecting lines for teacher behavior broken. An example of this is pictured in Table 7.7. Exercise number three should be completed at this point followed by your interpretation of the graph pictured in exercise number four.

TABLE 7.7
Teacher and Student Behavior

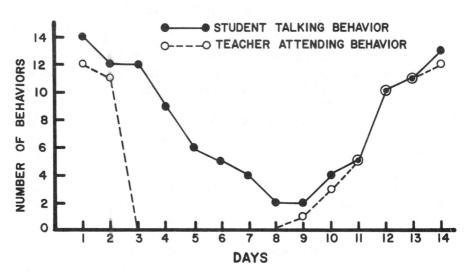

BEHAVIOR ANALYSIS AND INTERVENTION

At this point you should be able to operationally define the behavior you wish to observe, instruct raters in how they are to observe and record behaviors, and picture the results in a graph. These skills are the beginning of the analysis of behavior. Getting a "feel" for what is going on is necessary but it is only a beginning. After you have taken data for a reasonable length of time (perhaps five, one hour periods is a reasonable length of time) it is necessary for you to institute a plan of attack to change the behavior, a treatment.

The treatment part of any behavioral analysis technique amounts to your systematic variation of the environment (you and other students are parts of the environment) in order to attempt to change the "target behavior." The treatment should be the result of your observations of baseline behavior and your inferences about what is controlling the target behavior.

For example, in our previous discussion of Jane's noise-making behavior, we suspected that teacher attention (as we had operationally defined it) was maintaining the behavior. Our treatment may then consist of (1) ignoring all of Jane's noise-making behavior and (2) paying careful attention (10-12 times per hour) to Jane's appropriate behavior (appropriate defined as nonnoise-making classroom activity oriented behaviors). If our treatment works, we should notice a change in Jane's noise-making behaviors. The results of such a treatment are pictured in Table 7.8.

You can see that Jane's noise-making behavior did drop off after the teacher stopped attending it and instead attended to appropriate behaviors.

Obviously, not all treatments are going to be effective. Some treatments are ineffectual because they are not implemented properly by the teacher. In the previous example, if the teacher had been unable to control his/her attending behaviors, the treatment could not have been effective. Once you decide on a treatment, you must adhere to it consistently and perform the changes correctly. An inconsistent treatment is probably worse than no treatment at all.

A second reason that treatments do not work is because the teacher has "guessed wrong" and changed something in the environment that was not controlling the behavior. This will be evident to you after about 8 to 10 class hours of treatment observation. If you do not obtain a change in the target behavior, you should first determine if the treatment was correctly and consistently implemented and then consider alternatives. Where a change in your behavior is the treatment, use the consecutive form of observation to determine whether or not your behavior has been correctly and consistently changed in the way you wanted. If you can establish that the treatment was

109

properly implemented and carried out but that the target behavior did not change, alter the treatment.

Regardless of what many of our colleagues say, successful treatments are found through a combination of inference from baseline data, trial and error and luck. You should stay with a treatment long enough to give it a chance (we recommend ten class hours) before you decide to scrap it and try something else. Even then, if you have gotten only slight changes in the target behavior, you should consider adding to your treatment rather than dropping what you are doing and changing entirely. In our example of Jane, we could have found that her noise-making behavior dropped off slightly. If this were so, we might consider that it could be a combination of teacher and peer attention that is maintaining her behavior. If this was our assumption we could go to a time-out procedure to be described later or we could solicit the help of the class by getting them to ignore her noise-making behavior. You should never give up a treatment and decide to "live with" an inappropriate behavior. Sooner or later you will hit on the combination of consequences you can manipulate to change a person's behavior. You might (a) send home a copy of the daily tally sheet to the child's parents with a note explaining the problem, (b) have the child come to the front of the room and make noise constantly for thirty minutes until the reinforcing value of peer attention has lost its value, (c) lead the class in a round of applause for the child's noise-making behavior each time it occurs, (d) set up a group contingency to be described later, or (e) go to a contract or proclamation approach described in the last portion of this chapter. *Something will work.*

A return to baseline condition, a withdrawal of treatment conditions so that you are, in effect, returning the environment to how it was prior to your intervention, is commonly used by researchers in behavioral analysis. It is used to determine if, in fact, it was the treatment that caused the target behavior to change and not some extraneous variables such as a change in the weather (kids tend to behave better on lousy days than on beautiful spring days), changes at home (Mother and Father have reconciled and the child no longer needs as much attention from outside the home) and so on. Theoretically the target behavior should return to its baseline levels during a return to baseline condition.

We do not recommend that you use a return to baseline because once you are successful at changing a target behavior you should have no reason to cause it to go back to its baseline levels unless you are conducting an experiment. In other words, why mess with a good thing? This base-line-treatment return-to-baseline procedure is commonly referred to as an ABA design.

110

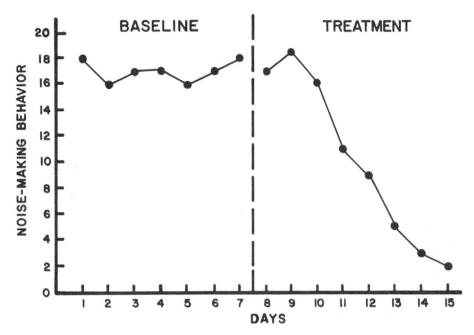

TABLE 7.8

Jane's Noise-Making Behavior—Baseline and Treatment

TECHNIQUES IN BEHAVIOR CHANGE

There are many common techniques that have been demonstrated to be reasonably effective in behavior change. Many are designed to get at the fact that attention is the most common reinforcer that maintains inappropriate behaviors. Teacher behavior can be controlled by you in ways we have previously described. Peer attention, which may be an even more potent source of reinforcement than teacher attention, is more difficult to control. In this section we will describe four techniques that are applicable in classroom settings and that have been proven to be effective if properly utilized.

TIME-OUT

If your best inference from analyzing behavioral data is that your student(s) behavior is being maintained by peer reactions (hooting, clapping, laughing, attention, etc.) your obvious choice of a treatment to reduce this target behavior should be one that gets at removing this reinforcement, the peer reactions. One method of doing this is with a time-out procedure.

111

Basically, a time-out procedure consists of removing a student from the environment that is providing reinforcers and placing him/her in a non-threatening but nonreinforcing environment until the target behavior has ceased to occur. This technique is designed to take the student away from reinforcers that cannot otherwise be controlled.

There are some guidelines for using this procedure *that you must very carefully attend to* or the procedure will be worthless. (1) Do not attempt to remove a child from his/her environment if it will involve a struggle. Fighting with you, screaming and carrying-on are nonproductive outcomes and are behaviors that are highly likely to be reinforced by peer attention. You should make no comment to the child other than "Please come with me," or a similar statement. Anything else can be perceived by the child as a reinforcer, i.e., he/she has gotten your goat or he/she is getting your attention in a really spectacular way. (2) Firmly grasp the arm of the child and, without comment, lead him/her to the time-out area. Your grasp on the child should be firm but should never cause pain. (3) The procedure should be explained to the child in advance. "Billy, from now on when you do _____, you will come with me to the time-out room." The target behavior should be very clearly explained to the child. (4) Accept no argument from the child. This is a case where you are always right. If he/she argues, ignore it. (5) Do not attempt this technique with children whom you are not physically capable of escorting to time-out. Trying to lead a hostile, six foot four inch, 240 pound male out of class when you are five foot two and 100 pounds may lead to a confrontation that will be highly counterproductive. (6) The time-out room must not be threatening, scary or aversive to the child. The room should be well lit and well ventilated. There should be a seat for the child and it should be at least large enough for an adult to walk in and feel reasonably comfortable. A six by eight room with a seven or eight foot ceiling is adequate. (7) The time-out room must not be a reinforcing place. That is, going to time-out should not be something that the student perceives as reinforcing. The room must be *dull*. There should be no toys or other possible playthings. (8) Unless there is some extenuating circumstance (e.g., an inhalation device for an asthmatic) the child should not be allowed to take anything with him/her to the time-out room. (9) A stay in time-out should not last longer than a few minutes. Once the target behavior stops occurring, the child should never be made to stay longer than another five minutes in time-out. You can tell whether or not the behavior has stopped by listening at the door or peeking in momentarily. (10) When the child is released from time-out he/she should be escorted back to his/her seat without any fuss or muss. Inappropriate behavior upon reentering the classroom should result in a return to time-out immediately without comment by you. (11) The entire procedure including how the child will leave and re-enter the room must be very clearly explained to the child. (12) Check in advance with the administration of your school and the child's parents before initiating such a procedure. Make sure that the parents understand what time-out is and that it is not some horrible punishment.

Well, time-out seems like a rather complicated process and it is, if done correctly. It is highly effective when it is used properly. We only recommend it for severe behavior problems that are not amenable to change through some of the other techniques we describe. There are some very real logistic problems we must address ourselves to in order for you to use this technique should the need arise.

(1) Not all classrooms will be built with an easily accessible room such as a large, well-lit closet or office area that you can use for time-out. If this is the case and you do want to use the technique, we suggest that you partition one of the corners of your classroom (6 ' × 8 ' or larger) for a time-out area. Such partitions have been built from old shipping cartons (the kind that washers and dryers come in) or from pieces of plywood, siding, etc., nailed to a frame. Such a corner partition should always be well lit and nonaversive. Children should never be frightened to be in such an area, nor should their parents feel that the place is aversive. However, the time-out area should screen off all vision of the classroom and of all other children. The entrance should be wide enough for you to enter but should be located where no window or door is visible. Soundproofing such an area is impossible but you can direct your other students not to attend to noises they hear from the student in this area or to talk about the child while he/she is in this area.

(2) You must be willing to keep track of children's behavior to determine whether or not time-out is effective. If it is not effective over a period of two weeks (ten class hours) you should consider other alternatives.

(3) Under no circumstances should you use any area for time-out that could be perceived by anyone as an area that is threatening to the child. Time-out has gotten a bad name because of the carelessness or callousness of some teachers who have shut children up in dark broom closets, locked them into storage trunks and generally scared the daylights out of small children with no thought given to why the technique is used. It is never used to punish. It is used to "cool off" a child and to remove him/her from an environment that has been reinforcing inappropriate behaviors.

(4) *You must seek (and have) parental and school administration approval to use this technique.* Show them the area you will use and give a demonstration. You are not out to "get" a child with such a technique; it is merely a way of reducing inappropriate behavior. If you find you cannot live up to the guidelines we have provided for the use of time-out, don't try it.

113

GROUP CONTINGENCIES

A second way to get at removing peer reinforcement for inappropriate behaviors is to institute group contingencies. Group contingencies commonly are a statement of what the consequence of a group's behaviors will be. We urge that only reinforcers be considered, as group contingent punishment can result in outcomes we don't want to have happen in our classrooms.

Group contingent punishment amounts to setting punishing consequences contingent for an entire group as the result of any one person's behavior. "If anyone talks during this period then everyone will be kept in from recess," is a common statement of group contingent punishment. Group contingent punishment is a highly punitive measure likely to evoke strong feelings among the group. Imagine, if you will, the impact of group contingent punishment on a class of students that has received punishment several days in a row for the behavior of one or two persons. Students are apt to be upset and dubious of the likelihood of their not being punished. They may begin to wonder that value there is in their being "good" because they are going to be punished anyway.

Group contingent reinforcement, on the other hand, is a statement of reinforcers the entire group can obtain if each member of the group will behave appropriately. No attempt to punish is made. Rather than saying "something bad will happen to everyone if even one person is bad," you are saying "everyone will be rewarded if everyone does good." If someone misbehaves, then, you are not punishing the entire group for one person's misbehavior, rather, you are withholding a reward, something they wouldn't have had anyway had you not implemented the group contingent reinforcement procedure.

For example, you may set up a reinforcer for the whole group (early recess, a free period, free time at the end of a period, etc.) contingent *on every member of the group* meeting a certain goal. This goal should be easily accessible by students and should be directed at the target behavior you are trying to extinguish. "If everyone will work without talking for the next ten minutes, we shall have an early recess," is one typical such statement of group contingencies. Group contingencies to get at an inappropriate behavior work best if they are administered on a daily basis. Doing it once in a while is not likely to have much effect. In other words, the students should expect that each day the target behavior will have a group contingency tied to it. And, when the group does not meet your goal, they do not obtain the reinforcer.

Some guidelines to follow in using group contingencies are: (1) Think small. Do not make it impossible for your students to reach the goal and to receive the reinforcement. Five or six days in a row of not being able to meet the goal will destroy the effectiveness of this procedure. (2) Think positive. Do not punish the group for the behavior of one person. What you want to do is to provide a reinforcer for the behavior of a group including the target person. If they do not obtain the reinforcer they will not be punished, they just won't attain a privilege. (3) Make sure you are consistent. Allowing privileges when the goals have not been met will not do anything to enhance this procedure. (4) If the target person takes delight in frustrating the entire group by his/her inappropriate behavior, deal with him/her individually, (5) Give the technique a chance. Let the students decide how to deal with the person keeping them from their goal on their own. Try it for a few days before you scrap it. (6) Don't let student reactions to the target student's behavior get out of hand. We were once involved in one group contingency concerning basketball practice for a group of nine boys. When they were thwarted three days in a row by the same person, he mysteriously showed up the next day with two black eyes. Although he did stop his "disruptive" behavior, such a reaction should never be allowed to happen. (7) Very slowly and gradually move your criteria up. For example, if you are working on talking behavior, you may start with ten minutes of nontalking and gradually, over several weeks, move to 30 minutes. Never put the goals out of reach of the children.

Group contingencies are an indirect way of lowering the levels of inappropriate behavior among some students in your classroom. Most of your kids will probably behave appropriately without the group contingencies. You are instituting peer pressure to modify the one or two or three target students who are performing the inappropriate behaviors. Don't worry that many of your students are "getting something for nothing." Over the long haul removing inappropriate behaviors will save you class time and improve the efficiency of classroom time usage by students even if you give up ten minutes now and then for free time or other reinforcers. Group contingencies are not bribes. Bribes are illegal or unethical payments for illegal behaviors. Bribes also come before a behavior, "I'll give you free time now if you promise not to talk during the principal's visit next period." Bribes do not work; contingencies do.

THE PREMACK PRINCIPLE

The Premack Principle was developed by Dave Premack and amounts to the notion that high frequency behaviors can be used as reinforcers for low frequency behaviors. That is to say that behaviors that children greatly enjoy can be held contingent on the performance of behaviors that children do not greatly enjoy.

So far we have allowed ourselves to spend most of our time talking about how we can extinguish inappropriate behaviors in students. While the

Premack Principle can be used to decrease some inappropriate behaviors, this decrease is a function of the increase of appropriate behaviors.

The procedure is really very simple. By observation you identify those high frequency behaviors children choose to engage in when given choices. These high frequency behaviors are then utilized as the contingent reinforcers for the performance of some low frequency behavior you intend to increase. When you were younger and were faced with "You can't go out and play until you make your bed," you were being given first-hand experience with the Premack Principle. Going out to play was a high frequency behavior held contingent upon your making the bed, a low frequency behavior.

For example, suppose you are having difficulty with some of your children not cleaning up after certain activities in class. These cleaning up behaviors are low frequency behaviors. One way to increase these low frequency behaviors is by setting high frequency behaviors contingent on the performance (to some criteria you and the students can agree on) of the low frequency behavior. The high frequency behavior may be playing a game, watching a film, doing art work, or whatever behaviors you have observed previously to be the kind of behaviors that your students enjoy.

The Premack Principle must be used consistently to have an appropriate effect. Sporadic use, once a week, twice a month, will have little or no value. You must implement the procedure and stay with it. You must be very careful to choose behaviors that are truly reinforcing to students as your contingent reinforcers. If you choose "studying quietly," you are likely not to have very much effect on behavior at all.

The Premack Principle can be implemented via individual or group contingencies. How you choose to use it is a function of the behavior you wish to change and the students you are working with. Regardless of which approach to the Premack Principle you choose, however, you must very clearly explain to your students how the high frequency behaviors will be administered and exactly the form in which the low frequency behaviors must appear. Ambiguity has no place in a behavior change process.

ASSIGNING RESPONSIBILITY

One of the most frequent complaints we hear from teachers is the fact that things happen in a classroom and that nobody will accept responsibility for what has happened. Desks are defaced, tables are written on, drains are stopped up, materials "disappear" from certain areas and so on. You probably clearly remember the cry of the outraged teacher, "Who did it?" (Our apologies to Mr. Roberts.) This "Who did it" behavior can and should be avoided. The best way to do it is to assign students responsibility for different materials in the room. If something happens to the materials they are responsible. This technique is not "fair" but then life in general isn't fair.

To even things up a bit you can rotate responsibilities on a weekly basis so that all the students have responsibilities at different times. If the laboratory table has been carved in, you know who is "responsible" whether or not the responsible person actually did the carving or not. This is a common occurrence in adult life. You will be responsible for what happens in your classroom even if someone else was the source of some problem.

Well, this assigning responsibility sounds really nice but how do we make it work? We make it work by instituting real and artificial contingencies. If your school has a policy of student payment for damages to school property, this becomes an aversive stimulus for students to avoid. Other, positive contingencies, points towards a grade, free-time privileges, etc., can be held contingent on the proper treatment of items in your room. You will, of course, have to very carefully define what is "proper treatment" in terms that allow for no ambiguity.

How do you get the other students who are not at the moment "responsible" to go along with the procedure? Well, their time to be responsible will come. This whole business is something that they must work out for themselves. The responsible person may just physically not allow the abuse of school property or he/she may inform the student who is defacing property that he/she will be reported to you so that you will know who to come to when you want the damages paid for. However your students work it out, it will remove the problem of "who is responsible."

There are a couple of tips about checking up on this defacement of property that you may find valuable. Where defacing school property (or making messes or leaving garbage, etc.,) is a problem, check the area before class starts. It only takes a minute to walk around the class and note (on a pad of paper) the condition of the different areas of the classroom. Then, a couple of minutes prior to the end of class, you may check the room again. Any changes for the worse are the responsibility of the student to whom responsibility has been assigned. Never accept any argument about "He did it," "She did it," "It was already there," and so on. You checked prior to class and you know that "it" wasn't there and you are not concerned about who did it, only who is responsible. This technique is particularly effective if you begin by assigning those students who you believe to have done most of the damage to responsibility. They will begin to learn some things about taking care of property.

CONTRACTS AND PROCLAMATIONS

Contracts and proclamations are more formal statements of "the way its going to be around here" than the techniques we have previously discussed. In this section we shall first describe behavioral contracts with an entire class. Secondly we shall briefly describe proclamations and lastly we

117

shall discuss individual contracts. You will find that the same operant principles we have adhered to throughout this chapter will continue to apply.

BEHAVIOR CONTRACTS FOR THE CLASSROOM

A behavior contract with a class of students is an agreement between you, the teacher, and the students of how a classroom is to be organized. Such a contract includes: (1) a list of behaviors that will result in reinforcement, (2) a list of behaviors that will result in punishment or a loss of reinforcement, (3) a thorough description of the consequences for appropriate and inappropriate behaviors, (4) how the consequences will be administered and (5) the signatures of both agreeing parties, the teacher and each student.

A behavior contract is an agreement entered into by both parties with full description and specification of the appropriate and inappropriate behaviors, how these behaviors will be reinforced or punished and the administration of the agreement. All contracts must be freely entered into by both parties. Students should have the right not to sign if they do not desire to do so. Contracts must also come up for renegotiation from time to time and it is a good idea to specify the date for renegotiations in the contract.

In essence, behavior contracts are formal agreements of what the consequences of behaviors are and how the consequences will be administered. The behaviors to be reinforced or punished are agreed upon in advance by you and the students and specified in a precise, unambiguous way. The reinforcers are negotiated between teacher and students and they are also clearly specified. The major differences between a contract and other techniques we have presented are: (1) a contract is mutually decided upon, (2) a contract generally includes many behaviors, (3) a contract is a formal statement, and (4) the students are aware of how the environment will be structured and have the right to opt not to participate.

The best way to get across the notion of a behavior contract is to present an example. Below you will see a sample contract for a Junior High School science class. In this case the immediate consequences for behaviors are the points that are gained or lost which serve as secondary reinforcers that can be traded in for other reinforcers.

A Sample Behavior Contract for Junior High

APPROPRIATE BEHAVIORS	CONSEQUENCES
1. Attending class (checked 15 minutes after the bell).	for attending—earn 1 point for not attending—0 points.

118

APPROPRIATE BEHAVIORS	CONSEQUENCES
2. Being on time (checked immediately after the bell).	on time—2 points late—lose 2 points
3. Bringing paper and pencil (paper clear, pencil with a point and eraser).	bringing materials—earn 2 points not bringing materials—lose 2 points
4. Bringing appropriate books (books announced previous day).	bringing books—earn 2 points. not bringing books—lose 2 points.
5. Taking the daily quiz (five minutes after the beginning of a class period). The quiz will be based on the previous day's lesson.	Each quiz will be graded for correctness by the instructor. Up to 10 points can be earned for correctness. Students will lose 2 points each time they are observed looking at another student's paper, their notes or their books.
6. Turning in homework. Homework will be taken up at the beginning of each class period.	When homework is taken it shall be scored for completeness only from 1 to 10 points. When homework is collected it will take the place of the daily quiz.
7. Finishing the daily classroom activity. This may be class discussion, a group activity, seeing a film, reading or written work.	Each classroom activity will be worth up to 10 points and will be scored by the instructor for completeness.
8. Weekly test (given each Friday made up of material from the daily quizzes and the classroom activities.	The weekly test will be worth up to 30 points. Students will lose 2 points each time they are observed looking on someone else's paper, their notes or a book.

INAPPROPRIATE BEHAVIORS	CONSEQUENCES
1. Hitting another student	lose 2 points
2. Throwing objects	lose 2 points
3. Loud talking or laughing	lose 2 points
4. Getting out of your seat without permission	lose 2 points
5. Chewing gum without permission	lose 2 points
6. Eating without permission	lose 2 points
7. Talking while the teacher is giving instructions	lose 2 points
8. Using dirty words or signs	lose 2 points

After a student has been penalized three times (losing 6 points) during a class period, he will be sent to the assistant principal for the rest of the period. If a student receives 10 penalties (losing 20 points) in class during a week, a letter will be sent to his/her parents (or guardians) describing the student's misbehavior.

Grades
Weekly grades will be determined on a point basis.
A = 145-130 points
B = 129-116 points
C = 115-101 points
D = 100-85 points
F = below 85 points
Daily grades may be determined on a point basis.
A = 24-27 points
B = 20-23 points
C = 16-19 points
D = 12-15 points
F = below 12 points
Privileges (reinforcing consequences to your readers)
In addition to grades, certain privileges will be based on the points you earn. If you finish the daily classroom activity and have earned at least 20 points on the previous class period, or at least 25 points on the Friday test, you may have the rest of the period as free time. During this free time you may do any one of the following things we agreed upon.

1. read comics
2. read magazines
3. read books
4. play games (those provided at the back of the room or those you have checked out with me)
5. draw
6. go to the gym
7. go to the library
8. talk quietly at the back of the room

Since some of the other members of the class will still be working on their assignments while you are enjoying free time, it is important that you be very quiet while you are engaging in free time. Any loud noise will warrant the loss of your privileges that day and the loss of 2 points for the next day.

Daily Procedure

If you are given written work for the daily learning activity and you feel you have completed it, you may turn it in to me and engage in your free-time activity, provided that you have enough overall points. If you like, the teacher will help you go over your things to see if your work is correct before turning it in.

If you are given group work or other kinds of activities, the teacher will let you know when you have finished. You will always have at least the last 10 minutes of the period free.

I, _____ (teacher), agree to abide by the conditions and consequences specified in this contract and agree to award grades and privileges according to the specification of this contract.

I, _____ (student), agree to abide by the conditions and consequences specified in this contract and agree to take the grade decided according to my own behavior and my performance on the quizzes and tests. The contract is to be renegotiated on _____ (date).

Signed _____ (teacher)

Signed _____ (student)

Such a contract always looks good on paper but is, in fact, hard to get working properly. To help you prepare a workable behavior contract, we offer some guidelines for you to follow.

(1) Always specify the behaviors that are included in the contract in a way that precludes any ambiguity. Behavioral specification here must be just as carefully attended to as in writing learning objectives or in defining behaviors for observation. One of the authors once included "bring a pencil to class" as part of a contract with an eleventh grade chemistry class. There wasn't any trouble with this until he started checking everybody's materials one morning and reached one young man who was feeling in each of his pockets for a pencil. Finally he whipped out a pencil stub, broken off at both ends. This stub could not be sharpened or used but it did have the term "number 2" visible on its side. He presented this as a pencil. This wasn't what the author had meant by pencil. He had visualized nice, long, sharpened pencils with erasers on them, but he was caught. The student clearly perceived the ambiguity of "bringing a pencil to class" and took advantage of it. At the next renegotiation period, that behavior was clearly specified, indeed!

(2) Student input must be obtained for a contract. A good way to do this is by providing the students with a sample contract to take home and look over the night before you negotiate your own. It is a good idea to have the behaviors in mind you want prior to your negotiations and to slip them in as you and the class talk over the contract. Be careful to rewrite the behaviors they suggest in behaviorally specified ways. Be careful to see that the various behaviors are weighted reasonably. Make sure that the reinforcers students suggest as consequences are reasonable. For example, if smoking is outlawed at your school, you cannot possibly let students out for a smoke break for doing good work. Don't feel uncomfortable about bringing up things on your own.

When you have a rough draft of behaviors, consequences and reinforcers, you can put your information into the form we presented above. (3) You must then provide one copy of the contract to each student. (4) You should sign each copy. (5) Students may sign or not sign but not signing merely means that they will go along without the reinforcing consequences of your new contract. They obtain none of the benefits of the contract and go along as they did prior to the contract.

(6) Reinforcers can take any form that is reasonable for your situation. Keep in mind that students frequently suggest things that they really won't want. Provide additional activities of your own devising to supplement the reinforcers they choose. Also remember that you must maintain the potency of the reinforcers. If reading magazines is one option you and the class have agreed upon, you must (or the students must) replenish the supply of magazines frequently. Once a student has read a magazine, it is not likely to be very reinforcing to read it a second time. All your reinforcers should be kept as novel as possible to avoid satiation. This is one of the biggest mistakes many teachers make.

(7) **Live up to your end of the bargain.** Nothing will ruin the effectiveness of a contract faster than your failure to hold up your end of the deal. How can you expect students to adhere to a contract that you will not adhere to?

(8) Be consistent. Check anything that must be brought to class at the beginning of the period at the same time every day. Have someone remind you if you tend to forget. Always give quizzes or take up homework at the same time each day. Always allow free time or other reinforcers at the same time each day.

(9) Weighing behaviors is difficult. You may feel that you need to revise your procedure after a while but worry not, it takes a few days to work the bugs out of any program. Weigh the most important behaviors the most heavily, the less important less heavily. It really doesn't matter whether you use points, chips, tokens or stars as secondary reinforcers, all are effective. Smaller children probably do better with stars or solid objects. Older children probably prefer points.

(10) As previously noted, if someone will not sign, he/she continues with the classroom organization prior to the contract and receives no benefit from it. He/she should be able to sign whenever he/she is ready.

(11) Somewhere you will have to keep track of all the points your students are earning. We suggest four methods that have worked well for other instructors:

(a)   List the children's names alphabetically on a portion of the blackboard for tallying daily and weekly points.

(b)   Tape an index card to the corner of each child's desk or work area and record the points here (or paste the stars down) as you pass by.

(c)   Have the students record their own points in either of the two methods suggested above. To insure accuracy, check some at random each day.

(d)   Use a combination of teacher/student tabulations. You may wish to tabulate quiz or test scores while the students keep track of other behaviors.

(12) Revisions of the contract or renegotiations of the terms in the contract should occur frequently enough so that all needed changes in a contract can be made. As some behaviors cease to occur and as others occur "automatically" you may wish to delete them from the contract and substitute other behaviors for them.

PROCLAMATIONS

Proclamations are identical to contracts except (1) only you have input; you make all the decisions, (2) no signatures are necessary and

(3) you are totally responsible for administering a proclamation. Other things should remain the same.

Which is superior? The evidence seems to indicate that both proclamations and contracts are highly effective ways of managing classroom behaviors. Most writers believe that students "feel better" about contracts than they do proclamations although the method you choose should be determined by the particular situation you are in. We have been acquainted with numerous teachers who started with a proclamation and after establishing its effectiveness moved to contracting.

INDIVIDUAL CONTRACTING

There will be many times during your teaching career when only one or two students will be an irritant to you. They may not do things you wish them to do, homework, reading assignments, etc., or they may be doing things you wish they would not do, the kinds of misbehavior we have discussed so frequently earlier in the chapter. You will, for various reasons, not want to engage the entire class in a contract or proclamation and the techniques we described for dealing with peer attention will not seem to fit either. In such cases we suggest that you consider individual contracts with these students.

An individual contract is an agreement between you and one student of how one or more (but preferably only one), behavior will be performed by him/her, how you will help the student perform such a behavior and what the consequences of the behavior will be. In the case of individual contracs we have found that the single most important component is the signature by you and the student. It is a method of obtaining a student's commitment in writing to perform a certain behavior or not to perform some behavior. Surprisingly, students who may balk at doing certain things in class or at home tend to take very seriously a formal agreement between themselves and the teacher. The contract should look like the contract we presented earlier for a class except for the fact that it will be much shorter and that it will include how you, the teacher, will help the student. Having the contract "look formal" is a great help to making the authenticity of the whole procedure more credible to the student. Type the contract from the rough draft (to be prepared as specified below) on bond paper and prepare a copy for you and the student. Throw in lots of "whereas's," "therefore's," "the party of the first part's," "the party of the second part's" and a few "henceforth's" to make the contract seem to be filled with legal jargon. Although the reinforcers are important, the impact of signing the document is the most important part of this technique.

An individual contract requires that you have a good rapport with the students. You should be able to sit down with the students and talk about what is being done or what isn't being done without the student balking.

You will have identified the behaviors you wish to change. You and the student should both recognize these behaviors from the way in which you have written them down. Again your writing must be absolutely clear.

When the behaviors have been agreed upon (at least when you and the student both can identify the behaviors) you should now try to identify possible reinforcing consequences for change. Have the student suggest some and you suggest some. Choose those reinforcers that the student desires but that are reasonable in your situation. Come to some agreement as to how the reinforcers will be administered. Put both the reinforcers and the method of administering them in writing.

Your next question should be, "How can I help you meet these goals?" Have the student suggest things you can do to help him/her meet the goals you have specified. Agree on reasonable behaviors that you can perform to help the student and put these in writing. Add a clause describing the fact that the student is not bound to the agreement unless you hold up your end of the bargain.

The next section of your contract should specify exactly what the student is to do, the consequences for his/her actions and your responsibilities. This is a restatement section that serves to clarify any questions from above. Take this rough draft and type it up as described previously. Then your signature as well as the student's should be affixed at the bottom of the document. Both of you should have one copy of the agreement. You should also specify when the contract will be renegotiated. If the student refuses to sign you should first try to have him/her sign a document testifying to the fact that he/she will not sign the contract and, if this doesn't work, you should return to the negotiations or to one of the other techniques.

Individual contracts are most effective if they are short-term (one week or less), if the reinforcers are readily attained and if only one behavior is described. Think small. Improving one behavior at a time is tedious but it is far more likely to be successful han if several behaviors are tried at once.

SUMMARY

In this chapter we discussed the influence of teacher behavior on student behavior and presented several ways in which you may gather data to perform such an analysis. Frequency counts, time interval and on-the-count assessments were described for gathering observational data. The gathering of teacher and student data for the behavioral analysis was described in three ways, simultaneous assessment, concomitant assessment and consecutive assessment.

You should be able to transfer tally sheet data into behavioral graphs and interpret behavioral graphs. The terms baseline, treatment condition and return to baseline were defined as was the use of an ABA design. Transcending all the observation and data gathering techniques was the notion of concretely specifying behaviors in unambiguous terms.

Several behavior change procedures were described along with guidelines for their use, time-out, group contingencies, assigning responsibility to class members for different areas of the classroom and the Premack Principle. Behavioral contracts for a class were described and proclamations were compared to them. Lastly, individual contracts were described.

Chapter 8
EVALUATION

The major emphasis of much of this book has been on those things we can do to help our students learn effectively and efficiently. One of our major concerns, repeated in each chapter, has been the evaluation of student learning. This chapter has been designed to provide you with additional information about evaluation in order to enhance your ability as an instructor even more. At the end of this chapter you should be able to:

1. Write brief statements defining process and product observation.
2. Write a statement defining reliability.
3. Write a statement defining interrater reliability and write the formula given for computing this reliability.
4. List and describe three ways of determining test reliability.
5. Write a statement defining validity.
6. Write a statement defining the term "norms."
7. List four characteristics of standardized tests.
8. List and describe three forms of intelligence tests.
9. Write statements defining intelligence and achievement tests.
10. List at least five advantages and disadvantages, five limitations and five points to consider for true-false tests.
11. List at least five advantages and disadvantages, three limitations and five points to consider for completion tests.
12. List at least three advantages and disadvantages, three limitations and five points to consider for multiple choice tests.
13. List at least five advantages and disadvantages, three limitations and five points to consider for matching tests.
14. List at least three advantages and disadvantages, five limitations and four points to consider for essay tests.
15. Write a statement describing how work samples are to be used for evaluation. Include three kinds of comparisons.
16. Write a statement describing how behavioral observations may be used for evaluations.
17. Write a statement defining norm-referenced and criterion-referenced testing.
18. Write a statement describing the purpose of grading and reporting results of school work.

127

OBSERVATION

One excellent method of assessment is the observation of student behavior. We discussed observation in great detail in our behavior analysis/classroom management chapter and also alluded to observation in each of the other chapters. To summarize, we can infer that learning has occurred by observing student behavior. If student behavior is different after a period of instruction, we can infer that learning has occurred. Observation of student behavior can take two forms, process observation and product observation.

Process observation amounts to the observation of a student during the process of completing some task. You may, for example, have your children take turns working math problems on the blackboard while you observe. This would, as you remember, be a type of formative assessment. As the children engage in the process of working a problem, you will be watching to see if they follow the steps in solving the problem which you have been teaching. You can readily watch the students perform each part of the overall process and determine which steps are completed appropriately and which ones are performed incorrectly or are left out. This kind of process observation allows you to provide additional instruction, prompts, hints and to generally make an assessment of how well the children are performing. This may give you valuable information about how meaningful the task is to the children. You could, if you so desired, rate the students you observe on each of the steps involved in the task and arrive at some percentage of overall task performance behavior.

Observation of products is an observation of the end result of behavior. This is commonly the kind of observation we make when we look at homework results, learning activity results or test results. All we see is the product and we get no sense of what behaviors the students performed in obtaining the product. We do, however, have the advantage of being able to spend all the time we wish in studying the product whereas process observation does not allow us time to study the process at our leisure.

Both process and product observation are valuable in evaluating students. Process observation, however, yields far more usable information than product observation. In process observation we see all the steps involved in arriving at the product while in the product observation we must somehow guess at the behaviors which resulted in the product we see.

You should keep in mind that our guidelines for developing operational definitions for behaviors we observe must be met in any observational setting we will be in. The quality of information we obtain through observation is a direct function of how well we have specified the behaviors we are observing. Any behaviors must be defined in concrete, unambiguous, observable and measurable terms.

RELIABILITY

The concept of reliability underlies all of the ways in which we gather data for the purpose of evaluation. An evaluation device (a test, an observation, whatever) is reliable if it measures whatever it does measure in a consistent way. Notice that accuracy or validity are not mentioned in the definition of reliability, only consistency.

An evaluation device you choose to use should yield about the same results any time it is used if that device is to be of value to you. For example, suppose you have devised a test to assess your student's ability to throw a baseball. That test should be reliable. That is, it should consistently measure the distance that a baseball is thrown. If student W takes the test on Monday and again on Tuesday, he should obtain about the same score both times.

The concept of reliability is fairly simple, a device measuring consistently whatever it does measure. However, the only way to determine if, in fact, a measuring device is reliable is by performing a statistical test. In this chapter we shall only describe one way of performing such a computation. Entire courses are devoted to measurement, evaluation and statistics.

INTERRATER RELIABILITY

It may be necessary, on occasion, for you to determine the reliability of your observations of student behavior. The question you are trying to answer is "Are my techniques of observation reliable; do I measure whatever I am measuring consistently?" The simplest way to calculate the reliability of observations is to use two observers and calculate the reliability of observations between the two observers. This is called interrater reliability. This calculation is based on the notion that if two observers observe just about the same things, the method of observation is reliable between observers and will also likely be reliable across time with one or more observers.

One way to calculate interrater reliability is to take the data from two observers in a consecutive or simultaneous observation setting and to divide the number of agreements they have on one behavior by the number of agreements plus the number of disagreements.

$$\frac{\text{number of agreements}}{\text{number of agreements} + \text{number of disagreements}}$$

For example, suppose observer A and observer B are tallying out-of-seat behavior for one student during an hour period. As you examine their tally sheets you see that they agree on 81 out of 100 observations. Plugging these numbers into our equation, we obtain:

$$\frac{81}{81 + 19} = .81.$$

In other words, our raters agreed 81 percent of the time in their observations. This technique will result in reliability scores of 0 to 1.00 or 0 percent to 100 percent agreement. Most psychologists agree that an 80 percent agreement or better is a good reliability, a 60 to 80 percent agreement is fair to poor and that agreements below 60 percent are unacceptable. (Please note that these values are peculiar to this technique and that there are no hard and fast rules for determining good or bad reliabilities.) If your reliability is below 60 percent, something must be done to increase the inter-rater reliability.

TEST RELIABILITY

You will use tests very frequently as means of assessing student learning. There are three ways in which such reliability comparisons can be made. In *test-retest* reliability we administer the same test twice to the same people. If the test is reliable, the results should be similar both times the test is given. Obviously, though, a test-retest procedure suffers from the fault that people change in between administrations of the test and that the results on the second administration of the test will be affected by the first administration. For example, if you are given a ten item, multiple choice test over a two thousand word essay on Monday and given the same essay and the same test Tuesday, you will likely not reread all that essay and are likely to remember the previous day's experience and answer in pretty much the same way that you did the day before. Hence, our computation of reliability is likely to be inaccurate because of such problems.

The best way to determine the reliability of a test is through the comparison of two *parallel forms* of the same test. That is, you construct two tests in the same way covering the same material and give one form one day and the other form on another day. If the tests are reliable the scores students obtain on the two administrations should be highly similar.

A third way to determine the reliabiltiy of a test is by the *split-half* method. In the split-half method you break up a test into two equal parts and compare the results on one-half of the test to the results on the other half of the test. The results of the two halves of the test should be highly similar if the test is reliable.

VALIDITY

Does a test measure what a test is supposed to measure? When we ask whether or not a test is valid we are asking whether or not that test measures what it purports to measure. A ruler can be said to validly measure length. That is, a ruler can be used to measure what it is that the ruler is said to measure, length. If we use a ruler to try to measure weight, however, we would conclude that the measure was invalid. No matter how well we measure the dimensions of some object with a ruler we cannot say that we have measured weight without some additional information, perhaps the density of the object. Even then our measure would be indirect.

All of us have taken examinations that we felt did not measure what they were supposed to measure. If we were asked to list, describe, compare and contrast some concepts and were then given a true and false test, we might very well argue that this test was not valid as it actually measured recognition and not listing, description, comparison and contrasting. Any assessment device that you develop, whether it is an observation form or a written examination should measure exactly what it is you say it should measure. A good assessment device is both reliable and valid but an assessment device may be reliable and invalid or valid and unreliable. We should strive to see that our assessment devices are both valid and reliable.

NORMS

As you enter the profession of teaching you will be confronted with the results of many kinds of standardized tests. Some of these will be intelligence tests, diagnostic tests, achievement tests, development tests, vocabulary tests, and so forth. You will need to be able to interpret the scores you see so that you may use them appropriately in any educational decisions you must make about students. One very important factor of such tests will be the norms on which the tests are based. Your ability to identify and describe norms from which test results are drawn will help you use the test results more efficiently.

A test is standardized (made standard) by giving it to large numbers of people for whom it is designed. For example, a mathematics achievement test designed for tenth graders is given primarily to tenth graders and probably also eighth, ninth, eleventh and twelfth graders. The results of these people's test taking are then used to make up "norms." A norm or normative score is that score on the test that an average or "normal" child of a particular age or grade level would be expected to make. On the mathematics achievement test above, a score of 90 may be the norm for tenth graders. In other words, an average tenth grader would make 90.

The same test may frequently be designed for use with children of different ages. If this is so, there will be a norm score for each age. Additionally, some tests have "college bound" and "noncollege bound" norms, boys' norms and girls' norms and so forth. It is especially helpful if a test provides you with a range of scores and the percentage of students in the norm group that made each score. If one of your tenth graders makes 120 on the mathematics achievement test, you may find that this score is made by only one percent of all tenth graders. Ninety-nine percent obtain scores below this level. Such normative information allows you some precision in the kinds of decisions you make about a child's educational programs. Generally, normative information is that information that represents how the norm group did on the test. You may then compare any student's score to the scores of the norm group and rate him/her with respect to that information.

We should point out that there has been a rather heated controversy in recent years about standardized tests and their utility with members of ethnic minorities. Many of the normative groups established for standardized tests in the 1940s and 1950s excluded members of ethnic minorities. Further, some critics of standardized tests point out that norms drawn from predominantly white, middle class children may not be useful in evaluating people from subcultures wherein social norms are different. We cannot possibly resolve this issue here nor can we even adequately set it out. You, however, should be careful to acquire the norms-technical manual of any standardized test so that you may keep in mind who the normative group was as you evaluate any one child's score.

STANDARDIZED TESTS

Any standardized test will have four characteristics that set it apart from nonstandardized tests. (1) Directions for administering the tests are uniform and do not vary. (2) The reliability and validity of the tests have been determined by trying the tests out on groups of persons for whom the tests are designed. (3) Directions for scoring the tests are uniform. Exactly the same scoring procedures are used each time the tests are scored. (4) The tests are based on standards of performance on the tests determined by the performance of the normative group. In other words, norms have been established for the tests and any one student's score can be compared to the norm group's results in order to evaluate his/her performance with respect to the group standards.

INTELLIGENCE TESTS

One commonly used form of standardized test is the intelligence test. According to Ronning (and other great psychologists), intelligence is the ability of a person to profit from experience. The greater the ability of a person to profit from experience, the greater the intelligence. Tests of intelligence are important to us for several reasons. (1) Intelligence tests are widely used throughout the American educational system. Whether we agree with their utility or not, they are used and we should have some knowledge of them. (2) A tremendous body of literature in educational psychology is based on the relationship of intelligence test scores to other factors such as achievement, personality type, special aptitudes and the like.

132

(3) Many important educational decisions such as tracking or grade placement, are based wholly or in part on intelligence test scores. (4) Intelligence tests are still one of the major diagnostic tools used to identify particularly bright and dull students. (5) Intelligence tests represent a very highly developed form of psychological and educational assessment that is frequently imitated by the developers of other forms of tests.

There has been a tremendous amount of heated debate among psychologists and educators over the usefulness of intelligence tests. Critics of the tests, with a great deal of support to back them up, charge that such tests are biased against ethnic subgroups, arguing that experience so greatly confounds test scores that the results are of extremely limited value. Supporters of the tests counter by arguing, again with highly impressive empirical evidence to support them, that the tests measure things that are not greatly affected by experience and do measure inherent mental ability. This "nature/nurture" controversy is not likely to be resolved in the foreseeable future and we must conclude that, at this point, intelligence tests provide only one rough indicator of intellectual ability.

Intelligence tests are designed to measure innate mental ability and not achievement. They are designed to measure the degree to which the test taker, in fact, can profit from his/her experiences. A good intelligence test should be able to identify a person with superior intelligence who has had no formal education just as well as a person with a college degree. That intelligence tests actually do this is debatable. Intelligence tests are not designed to measure what has been learned or what has been experienced but should measure a person's ability to learn.

There are basically three forms of intelligence tests: individual tests, group tests and multitest batteries. Individual tests include the Stanford-Binet and the Wechsler. Forms of these tests have been developed for use with people from preschool through adulthood. As the name indicates, individual tests are given by the administrator (usually a highly trained person, someone other than the classroom teacher) to one person at a time. Little writing is required and the answers are either given orally or through some task that can be observed by the administrator. In general, individual tests are preferable for young children (below the age of ten or so).

Group tests include the Lorge-Thorndike, the Henmon-Nelson, the Terman-McNemar and others. These are paper and pencil tests given to groups of people in one administration. These tests require that the examinees read the questions and write the answers. They are given to older children and may be followed up by individual tests.

Multitest batteries, exemplified by the Differential Aptitude Test (DAT), are really series of separate group tests that result in different scores for different abilities. They are highly similar to group tests except that they

133

yield several scores. The DAT, for example, yields eight different test scores: verbal reasoning, numerical reasoning, clerical speed and accuracy, spelling, language usage, space relations and mechanical reasoning. These are reported separately as though they were separate components of intellectual ability.

How do these tests relate to actual school achievement? The relationship varies from test to test and high intelligence as measured by a test is no guarantee of high achievement, but on the whole they relate fairly well to achievement. You must keep in mind the fact that intelligence test results should be used only as part of the assessment of any child's abilities. You should also keep in mind that each of the tests may define "intelligence" somewhat differently although most weigh numerical and verbal reasoning very heavily.

ACHIEVEMENT TESTS

Another commonly encountered type of standardized test is the achievement test. Achievement tests are tests of what children have learned in various subject areas. Achievement tests have been developed for almost every subject area we could imagine. Achievement tests (group tests, by and large) do not purpose to measure intelligence, rather they restrict themselves to measuring accomplishment in some area. The results you see will be based on norms and you should be able to interpret any one child's score by referring his/her score to the norms table.

TEACHER-CONSTRUCTED TESTS

The standardized tests described above are typically used by a school system on an annual or semi-annual basis. For the usual purposes of evaluating the day to day or week to week progress of students, the teacher is expected to construct tests and gather other information which will permit, finally, an evaluation of each student for the purpose of testing the child and (usually) letting his/her parents know how he/she is doing in school.

Several of the topics already discussed will be mentioned again. No matter what information a teacher uses to evaluate her/his students, the information must be valid for the purpose and must be obtained under conditions which insure its reliability. Thus, if you as a teacher wish to include "student attitude" as part of a grade in a course, you *must* be able to demonstrate first that attitude is important in judging the extent of meeting class objectives, and second, that your means of assessing "attitudes" is valid and reliable in at least one of the senses we have described earlier in this chapter. On the other hand, norms and a standardization population are not typically a part of the evaluation process we are concerned with in this section.

An important point to reemphasize is the relationship between the objectives given to students and the sort of evaluations (tests) used to assess the extent to which the objectives are reached. A seventh grade science teacher one of us knew told his class that his primary objective for the course was to "get students to use the scientific method in all aspects of their lives." Aside from some problems with this objective (see our chapter on behavioral objectives!), his examinations consisted solely of lists of terms for which he required definitions. In none of his examinations were students required to *use* the scientific method as a process. For his students, the objective of the course came to be "memorization of enough terms to pass the examination." Thus a course which ostensibly had a lofty objective became, in reality, one requiring laborious, rote memorization. If students are given objectives stating that they should list, define, describe, analyze or whatever, then the examinations should require that activity. If objectives and tests don't mesh (and all too often they do not) students rightly say that you have to "psych out" the instructor and try to guess what he *really* wants students to learn.

Given serious consideration of the points raised above, the methods teachers use to gather data for purposes of evaluating can be conveniently broken down into three classes: (1) "tests" of the types most frequently considered as either essay or objective; (2) work samples; and (3) behavioral observations. At the junior high and secondary school level, objective and essay tests are commonly used, while in the elementary grades (particularly grades K-3) work samples and behavioral observation are used. This division is unfortunate, because all three methods can be adapted and effectively used at all levels of instruction. Each of the three will be discussed in turn.

Objective and essay tests. Typically these tests are product observations which attempt to assess the outcome of a sequence or period of teaching. Each type of test has its advantages and disadvantages which will be specified below. In general, objective tests are particularly effective in obtaining evidence of student acquisition of factual material, including concepts and rules. It is more difficult, although not impossible, to construct objective tests which assess problem-solving skills. A chief advantage of the objective test format is the ease and reliability of scoring. If they are well constructed, a teacher must invest very substantial amounts of time in test item preparation. Essay examinations are particularly well suited to assessing organizational, analytical and problem-solving skills as well as "depth" of knowledge and understanding. Unfortunately, essay exams suffer from two serious defects: since they demand considerable time for response, only a few topics of a course can be sampled, and they are particularly difficult to score reliably. Depending upon the objectives given to a class, there may also be some question about their validity.

The following section represents a concise description of the various types of objective test formats, as well as the essay exam. It presents the advantages and disadvantages of each type of test item. If you use *any* of these test formats, this material should be carefully studied. Even if you do not intend to use them, you should be aware of the virtues and defects of the methods. As a final point, in the writers' judgment each major format (objective vs. essay) takes about the same amount of teacher time when the entire process of test construction, administration and scoring is considered. Time gained in scoring objective test items is gained at the expense of time required to construct good test items (it should be noted that the test item pools supplied by many textbook publishers are of dubious quality). At the same time, time gained in the preparation of two or three well-constructed essay questions (usually sufficient for 60 to 90 minutes of student response time) is, of course, lost in an extensive time required for grading.

COMMON TYPES OF TESTS—BY TEST ITEMS

The True-False Test
Uses and advantages:

1. The true-false item is widely used and is therefore well known to students. This is an advantage in that the students know how to answer the item concerned, but it also has a negative aspect. Students soon learn the inherent weakness of true-false items and are able to obtain high scores by noting the grammatical construction, the choice of words, the other clues.
2. Because it is easy to construct, the true-false test is used extensively. Because it is overused, the quality is often doubtful.
3. It can be used to sample a wide range of subject matter. A large number of test items can be answered in a short time—three to five per minute for average students.
4. It can be scored quickly and objectively.
5. It is a good instrument for promoting interest and introducing points for discussion.
6. It can be constructed as either a simple factual question or as a thought-provoking statement.
7. It is an effective substitute for a multiple-choice item when only two choices govern a point or a fact.

8. It can be used as a "cluster" to check several points concerning a particular concept, principle, or science unit. This type is effective in revealing the student's complete understanding.
9. Modified true-false items (requiring the student to tell why an item is false) require the student to exercise judgment and understanding instead of mere memorization.

Limitations:

1. A true-false item is of doubtful value for measuring achievement.
2. Guessing is encouraged even though correction formulas are employed. Many of the items can be answered correctly without any knowledge of the subject matter involved.
3. It is difficult to construct items that are completely true or completely false without making the response obvious.
4. Ambiguous statements, unimportant details and irrelevant clues are difficult to avoid.
5. Unless a large number of items is included in the true-false test, it is likely to be low in reliability.
6. Minor details tend to receive as much credit as significant points.
7. It is difficult to construct items when the subject matter is in any way controversial.

Points to consider in constructing true-false items:

1. Make approximately half of the items true and half false, and avoid following a pattern in arranging the items.
2. The method of indicating responses should be as simple as possible.
3. The "lifting" of statements directly from textbooks should be avoided.
4. Use direct statements—make the point of the item obvious.
5. Avoid catch questions and specific determiners.
6. True statements should not be longer than false statements.

Recall-Type Tests

Simple Recall—Who is the President of the United States? _____
Completion—_____ is the President of the United States.
Uses and advantages:

1. It is relatively easy to construct and is applicable to any field in which achievement is being measured.

137

2. It demands accurate information of the who, what, when, where type.
3. Recall items can be substituted for matching items.
4. When the variations are used, a wide range of subject matter can be sampled.
5. Well-prepared items minimize the guessing factor; hence, it has a high discriminating value.
6. It is particularly adapted to measuring the application of certain knowledge involving arithmetic computations, formulas, and measuring instruments.

Limitations:

1. Because it is relatively easy to construct, this type of item is used excessively.
2. Unless care is used in construction, an item may measure native intelligence rather than achievement in subject mastery.
3. Scoring may be quite subjective.
4. It may be time-consuming for the student who knows the material being tested but has difficulty recalling the exact word or words needed to fill in a specific blank.

Points to consider in constructing recall-type items:

1. Direct questions are preferable to statements, particularly with younger pupils.
2. Make questions or statements as specific as possible.
3. Place the response blanks at or near the end of the statement.
4. Be sure there is only one correct response for each blank.
5. Limit all enumeration type items to six or eight things to be listed. Give one point of credit for each blank to avoid partial or fractional scores.
6. Avoid using an enumeration-type item when the parts must be listed in order. Use the true-false or multiple-choice item instead.
7. Leave plenty of space for making responses, but do not give clues by using variable length lines.
8. Do not overmutilate statements—there must be sufficient key words in the statements to indicate the desired response.

Multiple-Choice Items
Uses and advantages:

1. Application of facts can be measured by well-constructed items.

138

2. It ranks high in discrimination, reliability, and validity.
3. It can be scored rapidly and objectively.

Limitations:

1. Unless well constructed, the item measures memorization only.
2. It is difficult to make the decoy choices plausible though incorrect.
3. It is difficult to construct a good item so that one and only one response is the correct one.
4. The multiple-choice test is space-consuming and time-consuming.

Points to consider in constructing multiple-choice items:

1. The stem of the item should contain a central problem and should be as specific, clear, and brief as possible.
2. All items should be practical and realistic.
3. Include no responses that are obviously wrong or that include clues.
4. Have the same number of optional choices in each item—three or four is the usual number for junior high school and senior high school.
5. Scatter the correct responses. Avoid developing a pattern of correct responses.
6. Place the choices at the end of the incomplete statement.
7. If the choices consist of a series of figures, put them in order.
8. Do not use a multiple-choice item when a simpler type will be equally as effective.

Matching Tests
Uses and advantages:

1. A large number of responses can be included in a small space and with one group of directions.
2. The matching item can be used for testing various outcomes. Some typical matching items are: terms with definitions, symbols with their proper names, causes with effects, principles with situations, and problems with their solutions.
3. It can be made totally objective and easily and quickly scored.
4. When properly constructed, the guessing factor is practically eliminated.
5. It is especially applicable for measuring the ability to recognize relationships and make associations.

Limitations:

1. Because the phrases must be short, the matching exercise is a poor measure of complete understanding and interpretation.
2. It encourages the memorization of facts.
3. Because it is easy to construct, it tends to be used when another type would provide a more valid and reliable measure.
4. It is susceptible to irrelevant clues which are subtle and difficult for the test maker to detect.

Points to consider in constructing matching items:

1. Responses should be limited to not less than five and not more than twelve in each matching exercise.
2. Place the column containing the shorter items on the answer side of the page. Include at least one extra choice.
3. Place the entire exercise on one page.
4. Identify the columns by appropriate headings, and use the column headings in the directions for clarification.
5. Use only homogeneous or related materials in any one exercise. Placing the answer responses in alphabetical order usually scatters the responses sufficiently to prevent a pattern of response. Number answer responses should be in order of size.
6. Use capital letters to label the parts in the answer column.
7. Check for determiners or clues. While making the scoring key, check each individual statement with all the answers to make sure that no answer could be used with the statement for which it is not intended.
8. Provide a line or parentheses beside each problem statement for the student to indicate his response. Arrange these answer spaces in a column for ease of scoring. Insist the student use capital letters to indicate his response choice, since they are easier to distinguish from each other than lower case letters.

Essay Examinations

Uses and advantages:

1. The essay examination measures best in these areas: (1) interpretation of functional information; (2) ability to think and reason; (3) aspects of work habits, and (4) philosophy.
2. Knowing that an essay test is to be used causes pupils to employ desirable study habits such as making outlines, taking extensive notes, and making summaries.

3. Essay tests have a secondary value in measuring the ability of the student to organize and discriminate.

Limitations:

1. Limited sampling of subject material causes low validity.
2. Objectivity is reduced because of the emphasis put on the irrelevant factors of spelling, quality of hand-writing, and English usage.
3. It overrates the importance of knowing how to say a thing and underrates the importance of having something to say.
4. Reliability is low because of the shortness of the test and the subjectivity of the scoring.
5. It is time-consuming for both pupil and teacher.

Points to consider in preparing:

1. The age of the student should be borne in mind—younger students should not be expected to write at great length.
2. As nearly as possible, the questions or problems should be of equal length and difficulty.
3. Avoid weighing questions or problems by assigning a definite number of points, but if it is necessary, arrive at the number of points by establishing the number of facts called for in the item.
4. In scoring, prepare a key showing the points of information expected in each question or problem. Grade all papers for a class in one sitting and without interruption. Grade all number 1 items, then proceed to grade all item 2 questions and problems.

Work samples. Work samples include exactly what the name implies: Actual examples of work done by a student. These are collected systematically and filed (usually chronologically) in a folder for each student. At the end of some specified period (usually a six, nine or eighteen week marking period) the work specimens are examined. Several sorts of comparisons are possible: (1) the student's work in arithmetic, as one example, may be examined over time to answer the question "how much progress has the student made in six weeks (or whatever the time period) in achieving certain objectives"; (2) the work of the *same* student in several areas (arithmetic, spelling, art, etc.) may be examined to look for patterns of strengths and weakness, and possibly to guide the teacher in deciding in what areas the student needs more help or to devote additional time; (3) the teachers may compare students with each other in a "normative" manner for purposes of assigning differential grades. The first two suggestions above are crude attempts to "freeze" process observations and record them. For example, quality of homework in arithmetic (with whatever formative information present on the work sheet) handed in to you in September can be compared with the quality of the work handed to you in October. If you collect and file enough of these bits of data, you can begin to find patterns of recurring errors, which can lead you to diagnose particular instructional treatments for each child in a class.

Work sample procedures are appropriate at almost all grade levels. In the secondary school English program, for instance, a teacher may wish to collect writing samples from students. Each student might be required to write, say, a descriptive paragraph each Friday for twelve successive weeks. This sort of sample might provide *both* student and teacher with clear evidence of progress (or its lack) in more effective writing skill. Similar projects could be developed in social studies by asking students periodically to analyze important "social" problems and after a period of time examine them for greater "depth," or sophistication, of analysis. We urge you to note the need to specify to students the objective of the task if, indeed, the work samples are to be evaluated over time for "more sophisticated levels of analysis." Courses of study at the junior or senior high school which are "product-" oriented afford particularly easy and appropriate work sample opportunities. Thus industrial education activities such as woods or small engine repair; home economics activities such as sewing; business activities such as typing and shorthand all naturally produce materials which can be cataloged chronologically and examined at specific points. These sorts of evidence are particularly impressive to both student and teacher in answering questions such as "What am I learning in this course?"

The third use of work sample materials, that is, the comparison of one student to another, poses certain problems. In many instances the work samples saved may differ from child to child. As we have already noted, some students enter a class performing at levels far above (or below) other children in the class. Is it fair to compare these children? This difficult question will be addressed (although not fully answered) in the section of this chapter on norm-referenced vs. criterion-referenced testing.

To summarize, then, the work sample process is simple, perhaps deceptively so. For each student the teacher systematically gathers products which are dated and filed or stored for later examination. At the elementary level this may require several folders (for each of the major activities of the self-contained classroom) for each student. These products must be gathered systematically for all children. Methods must be found to insure that you have enough samples to reliably estimate any change in student performance over a 6-12 week period. At a minimum, in the writers' judgment, this would require one product for each week for each subject matter. While this may sound like a formidable task, we should point out that the student may provide help by maintaining his/her own folder—a process not without some dangers, though!

Finally, the information (products) collected must be related to the sorts of judgments the teacher wishes to make at the end of the grading period. Hence judgments about improvement in handwriting skill should (obviously) be based upon (a) samples of student handwriting and (b) a set of criteria which validly assess handwriting skill. The same requirement holds if you are judging "creativity" in story writing, spelling improvement, laboratory skills, or whatever.

Behavioral observations. This last form of data for evaluation is closely related to the work sample process, but attempts in many cases to get at slightly different objectives. For many teachers student "attitude" toward learning is an important variable. Frequently, however, teachers have no systematic way of assessing this variable. As a consequence, the teacher "intuitively" assesses each student. An alternative to this is to keep consistent records (behavior samples) of observations made in the course of daily instruction. Such observations could take the form of very brief notes about each of five or six different children for each day of the week. Thus observations written on each of six different children for a school week would insure some behavioral record for each student in a class of thirty. The content of the notes would vary with the objective of the teacher. If work habits are of concern then notes indicating the extent to which a particular student "got down to work on an assignment" or instances of disturbing or disruptive behavior, etc., might be appropriate. Such record keeping might identify recurring patterns of student behavior which might necessitate changes in the ways in which a class is managed. For example, if a particular student exhibits disruptive behavior each time he is required to read aloud in class, and if your records provide reliable evidence for this recurring behavior, you may wish to initiate a set of teaching procedures which will alleviate the incidence of disruptive behavior. Initially this could consist of not asking the student to read aloud until you have had opportunity to work with her/him individually to find out if fear of humiliation, shyness, a speech defect, or whatever, is evoking the undesirable behavior. As chapter seven on behavior management indicates, record keeping and systematic intervention are very solid tools for teacher use.

It must be emphasized that problems of reliability and validity are potentially severe with this technique. The individual differences in student behavior may result in some very fat folders of behavioral descriptions for a few "active"(!) students, and practically no information for other students. Furthermore, the teacher's own reaction to students may affect the manner in which behavioral observations are recorded and interpreted. Nonetheless, the technique is a valuable one in providing evidence for evaluations which are frequently made on very scanty, subjective grounds.

NORM- VS. CRITERION-REFERENCED TESTING

In evaluating student performance every teacher has two basic choices. The first, and until recently the most common, choice is to judge the performance of a student against either other students in a class (as in the case where a set of test grades are "put on a curve"), or where a standardized test provides information (norms) against which each student may be judged. This approach, called the norm-referenced approach, has the advantage of telling each student how he compares to other students in his class or of his age or grade level. It is basically, then, a process of comparing students to each other and evaluating them accordingly. The second choice, less frequently used in the past, requires the development of an age or grade appropriate set of behavioral objectives for which a teacher can establish reasonable, nonarbitrary and predetermined cutoff scores. Each student is then evaluated against the cutoff criterion score and thus either meets the criterion or fails to meet it.

Norm-referenced testing. A chief advantage of this method of testing is its familiarity to students, parents, and the public generally. When a student receives a grade of 70 on an examination where the average is 80 and the highest score 95, he/she can make very direct comparisons of his/her performance to that of other students. Parents understand the test result because for most of them it is a system with which they are familiar through experience. A further advantage of the system in a competitive society such as ours is that the system gives very clear evidence of how one stands in the competition for "good" grades. Whether this is educationally desirable remains to be proved! At the same time, teachers may become dissatisfied with the norm-referenced system when class performance on a 100 item test averages only 40 points, with a range of scores from 20 to 50. Clearly one can compare students, but many teachers become uneasy about assigning a high grade (an A perhaps) to a score of 45 or 50 on a 100 point exam. To what extent has the whole class failed to meet desired objectives?

Criterion-referenced testing. Where it is possible to set clear, unambiguous objectives, such as in a typing class where a teacher sets the criterion for performance at 50 words per minute with not more than five errors on a three minute speed test, this form of testing has a very useful role. Here the emphasis is on meeting the objective, not on competing for an A. To a large extent the criterion-referenced system tends to maintain focus on accomplishment of objectives rather than on competition for grades. At the same time, it should be said that many students are uncomfortable with this system. Even using a Pass-Fail system (a crude criterion-referenced system potentially), the writers find that many secondary and college students ask "What do I have to do to get a high pass" (or an A). Most clearly, criterion-referenced tests permit a teacher to define for her/himself and for a group of students precisely what they are to learn and the criterion against which they will be classed as successful. Some students respond to this very effectively, others less so. As hinted at above, parents and others outside the school system are unfamiliar with the system with the result that report cards carrying criterion-referenced performance data may not be understood.

Criterion-referenced testing procedures have been criticized because of their seemingly limited applicability. Critics assert that it is very difficult to specify the criterion performance for complex learning tasks such as problem solving, creative productions and the like. It should be pointed out that norm-referenced examination systems are no more successful in measuring these sorts of outcomes. Complex human performance will remain a difficult area for assessment and one with which every teacher will, sooner or later, have to wrestle.

MARKING AND EVALUATING

One of the most difficult of all teacher tasks is that of equitably evaluating the performance of each student and conveying that information in an understandable form to students and parents. The most common form of marking (grading) is some variant of the standard A, B, C, D, F scale where the work of some fixed grading period is summarized into a letter scale system in which the middle category is seen as "average," while letters above or below represent varying degrees of success or failure. Substituting words such as "Superior, Excellent, Satisfactory, Fair, Needs to Improve" fails to change the system, although this is a common device in the elementary school. The chief problem of this system is the lack of definition, or the arbitrariness, of the criterion of "average" or "satisfactory." How much, for example, is "average" a function of the general achievement level of a group? Isn't it quite possible that average in one class might be excellent in another?

Teachers have attempted to deal with this problem in a number of ways. In the elementary schools, a common practice is to substitute a parent conference for the report card, at least for some of the reporting periods. This has the double advantage of giving the teacher opportunity to talk with parents and also to show the parents samples of their student's work. These samples, when compared with work completed earlier by the child give a parent a sense of how their child is performing and improving. In other schools the child is evaluated descriptively in two or three brief paragraphs. This report permits the teacher to briefly describe both strengths and weaknesses of the child without necessarily formulating these into "letter" grades. For a busy teacher this is a substantial writing task.

The writers have no easy solution to the problems of evaluating students and reporting the results. As might be expected, we lean toward the criterion-referenced testing method. When using that scheme, time, rather than student ability or prior knowledge becomes important. Thus, an objective may be completed satisfactorily by some students in 30 minutes, but by others in as long as two or three days. Properly established, every student should be able to reach criterion, although it may be in vastly different amounts of time. These time differences become a real challenge to the organizational skills of a teacher. In spite of our preference, we also recognize the difficulty of establishing clear performance criteria in some aspects of school performance, and also recognize the resistance of parents and the public at large to changes from the conventional, widely-accepted, norm-referenced system.

SUMMARY

The purpose of this chapter is to bring to your attention the issues and problems related to the substantial task of evaluating and reporting student performance. We have outlined and briefly discussed the major issues and presented you with a number of techniques and alternative methods. For further, more complete information we urge you to consider taking a course such as tests and measurements, measurement and evaluation, etc. The tasks presented in this chapter are too important to be left to teacher whim or personal preference.

Chapter 9

AN INTRODUCTION TO MAINSTREAMING

The topic of mainstreaming is not an afterthought attached to this book in an arbitrary way. Mainstreaming, the process and the law, is a fact of life in the United States and its impact on instruction, class composition and teacher duties is truly important. After completing this chapter you will be able to:

1. Write a brief statement describing the basic requirements of the mainstreaming laws.
2. Write a brief paragraph defining the process of mainstreaming.
3. Write a brief statement summarizing why mainstreaming is being implemented in the schools.
4. Write a brief paragraph describing primary prevention.
5. Write a brief statement describing multidisciplinary assessment.
6. Write a brief statement describing multifaceted assessment.
7. Write a brief statement describing behaviorally-oriented assessment.
8. Write a brief statement describing naturalistic assessment.
9. Write a brief statement describing assessment in contrived settings.
10. Write a statement defining continuous assessment.
11. List the members of the multidisciplinary team and very briefly describe each member's duties.
12. Write a statement summarizing placement. List at least three placement options.

MAINSTREAMING: THE LAW AND THE PROCESS

The mainstreaming laws are currently "on the books" in 48 out of 50 states. They are rooted in the 14th Amendment to the Constitution and have resulted directly from Supreme Court decisions in the late 1960s and the early 1970s. Mainstreaming laws are state laws as opposed to federal laws and, as a result, there are some variations from state to state. However, the intent of mainstreaming laws is the same in all states. The intent is that every child who is a resident of the state be afforded a public education within regular classrooms or at least within the regular school complex regardless of whether the child has any sort of emotional, social, physical, intellectual or environmental handicap. In other words, regardless of whether or not a child has a handicap, that child shall receive a public education in public schools and in the "normal" classroom where at all possible.

The reason for such laws is simple. Some children were being denied their rights to a public education in the United States and others, although educated in a public system, had their civil rights violated by being separated from their peers without just cause. The mainstreaming laws exist to insure equal educational opportunities for all children. The laws presume that the inherent worth of all children is the same and that a handicap, regardless of its nature, is not reason to restrict any child's rights to a public education and to *equal* public education.

The laws say that each child shall receive a public education, regardless of any handicap, and further state that where possible, each child shall be a part of the regular classroom setting with his/her peers. What does this mean in terms of the requirements or the law? (1) Each child, to the extent possible, shall be enrolled in a regular school program. (2) Each child between the ages of three and six must be screened for any possible hearing, visual, medical, physical, psychological, educational or environmental handicaps. (3) Those children identified as having a handicap must begin receiving services (hearing aids, glasses, therapy of various sorts) designed to correct or reduce the handicap. In most states the eligible ages for such treatment are three to twenty-one. (4) Some criteria must be established by the local educational agencies for singling out those children who will need a more thorough evaluation than those suggested in requirement three above. (5) Labelling is forbidden other than as a basis for developing educational programs for children who have been identified as having handicaps. (6) An *individual* educational program must be devised and implemented for each child identified as having a learning handicap. (7) The child must be placed in his/her educational program. (8) All educational placements must be considered temporary and each child's program must be reviewed at least three times a year with the possibility of changing the educational program under consideration. (9) The "fault" is not within the child. "Fault" is an irrelevant consideration. (10) Teacher education must be changed to meet the needs of handicapped children. In some cases additional personnel must be hired by school systems, in others currently employed personnel must upgrade their education. (11) Where necessary, the actual physical construction of school buildings must be changed to accommodate children with physical handicaps. (12) New materials and educational equipment may need to be purchased to accommodate the needs of children. (13) The parents of the handicapped children must be informed of all school actions with respect to their children and further, must be involved in any and all decisions. They have the right to question, challenge or refuse any school decisions. (14) Each local school system must develop and submit its plan for implementing the mainstreaming program for approval by statewide educational agencies. Compliance with all thirteen of the requirements listed above must be documented.

THE PROCESS: SCREENING, REFERRAL, PLACEMENT

The process of mainstreaming can be summed up with the following list of components of the overall procedure: (1) screening and primary prevention, (2) multidisciplinary assessment, (3) multifaceted assessment, (4) behaviorally-oriented assessment, (5) naturalistic assessment, (6) continuous assessment. These six components, which we will expand on below are present in one form or another in each state's laws. They summarize how each child is to be evaluated in terms of the kind of educational program he/she will receive.

SCREENING AND PRIMARY PREVENTION

In mainstreaming, screening means what the term implies. It is the process of identifying children in need of special help prior to the beginning of an education. Many school systems have traditionally screened children for auditory and visual problems prior to entering school and have then reported to the parents what the parents must do to correct the problem. In mainstreaming, screening is more accurately a part of preventitive actions taken by the school rather than the parents.

Primary prevention includes screening but goes somewhat further. The mainstreaming laws are written with the knowledge that the sooner problems are identified, the more effective and less costly will be programs designed to help children overcome these problems. The major emphasis here is on identification of problems during preschool and kindergarten that may cause problems in later educational experiences. Children who are so identified (or where no formal identification process exists, all children) should be screened medically (e.g., brain damage, physiological disorders, vision problems, auditory problems, motor control and other possible forms of structural damage) and psychometrically (e.g., emotional stability, family relationships, social behavior problems, evidence of any pathology, intelligence and so forth).

The earlier such identification can be made, the greater the likelihood that programs designed to help children overcome these problems will be successful. *Such programs will also be less expensive than if identification occurs later in a child's program.* Additionally, primary prevention reduces the possibility of children having unfortunate or damaging experiences in school as a result of their problems. Feelings of self-failure, self-doubt, shame, anger, guilt, embarrassment and the like that can easily result from not performing well in school as a result of some problem should be greatly reduced. No matter how else we look at it, school should never be a source of noxious experiences for children that result in reduced learning capabilities among students.

MULTIDISCIPLINARY ASSESSMENT

The inclusion of multidisciplinary assessment reflects the powerful feeling among educators that one person alone does not have the right to restrict assessment to himself/herself. Behavior can easily be demonstrated to be situation specific. The kinds of behaviors seen in a classroom, for example, are specific to classrooms and may not be seen in a psychologist's office, at home or at work. Multidisciplinary assessment must include separate assessments made by special education specialists (such as a school psychologist, a guidance counselor, a special education teacher or a social worker), the child's classroom teachers (all of them if there is more than one), someone from the school administration, any other adults that come in contact with the child on a regular basis and the parents.

This multidisciplinary assessment process does not guarantee that a correct decision will be made about children but it greatly increases the likelihood of decisions being based on all the pertinent data about any given child. The variety of observations on any child is increased by such a process and the possibility of making an accurate appraisal is greatly enhanced.

MULTIFACETED ASSESSMENT

The multifaceted assessment portion of the mainstreaming procedure merely means that assessment of a child must take many forms including but not limited to (1) standardized tests, (2) naturalistic observation, (3) samples of the child's work, (4) interviews with adults that come in contact with the child, and (5) direct observation in as many settings as possible. This multifaceted assessment is included because accurate assessments cannot be made on the basis of only one set of data. IQ tests, for example, may be used, but only as one component of the overall assessment. An IQ test by itself does not provide enough information to allow intelligent decisions. A number such as 95 written on a piece of paper says something with respect to the test it was drawn from but it says nothing about how a child actually functions in a classroom setting.

BEHAVIORALLY-ORIENTED ASSESSMENT

Behaviorally-oriented assessment is an assessment of behaviors that are defined in clear, concrete and unambiguous ways. Basically, the procedures we described for defining behaviors to be observed are the procedures that must be used for mainstreaming assessments. Terms such as "disruptive," "hyperactive," "hostile," "retarded" and the like are not appropriate. Clearly defined behaviors of the sort we described in chapter six must take their place.

NATURALISTIC ASSESSMENT

The component of naturalistic assessment is quite straightforward. It is the requirement that children be observed in "natural" settings such as the home, the neighborhood, the playground and, of course, the classroom. Naturalistic assessment is required because children behave differently in artificially contrived environments such as counselors' offices, formal meetings and the like.

ASSESSMENT IN CONTRIVED SETTINGS

Assessment in contrived settings such as a principal's office is commonly of little value because of the situation specificity of behaviors. We are all aware of children who behave like perfect angels in the principal's office while driving us up the wall in our classrooms. Contrived settings may be necessary for interviews, meetings or the administration of various kinds of standardized tests but they must be augmented by naturalistic assessment.

CONTINUOUS ASSESSMENT

Assessment must be a continuous process, following each child throughout his/her educational career. Assessment cannot stop just because a child has been referred and placed. Children change. Disabilities are overcome. Disabilities develop later in some children than in others. Some programs are not exactly what children need. The only way to ensure that every child has obtained the best possible education is to continue to evaluate children throughout their educational careers.

THE TEACHER'S ROLE

We have briefly outlined the mainstreaming law and given a description of what this law requires. How do these things affect the role you play as a teacher? (1) If the mainstreaming program is initiated in your school, you will become (at times) a referring teacher and thereby part of the multidisciplinary team that makes referral and placement decisions about the child you have referred. Participation in such a team approach alone changes your role. (2) You must be proficient at gathering and interpreting behavioral data. That is, you must be capable of gathering student behavior data in the ways described in our behavior analysis and classroom management chapter. (3) You must be capable of implementing, to some degree, the decisions made by the multidisciplinary team. (4) You must be capable of working with the consulting teacher who has the responsibility for your students who need special services. (5) You must have the kind of behavior management skills to allow "mainstreamed" children to enter your "normal" classroom for varying amounts of time each day without being

151

ostracized by their classmates. (6) You must have skills in individualizing instruction as per our discussion in chapter five. Let us examine in greater detail how your role will be changed from the traditional and thereby continue to describe the mainstreaming process.

THE TEACHER AS A TEAM MEMBER

If a mainstreaming program exists at the school you teach in, you will become part of the primary prevention program. Your observations of student behavior (behaviorally specified, of course) will often be the first step in identifying those children in need of special help. Over the course of a few years, you will identify children with hearing, speech, vision and behavior problems. Upon identifying these children, you must put the referral and assessment process in gear. (Note: This text is not designed to give you skills in identifying children in need of special help. Identifying children with disabilities is a difficult task, one that takes considerably more preparation than this brief introduction to mainstreaming allows. Our apologies, but one book or one course cannot possibly do everything.)

Typically, you would start the referral process by first gathering behavioral data taken from the student you have identified. When you have gathered sufficient data to "make a case" (enough data to allow outside parties to see the need for referral that you see) you will approach the member of your staff charged with organizing the multidisciplinary team. This person will commonly be a member of the school administration, a school psychologist or a guidance counselor. If you and this person agree that a consideration of referral is an appropriate step, the multidisciplinary team should then be formed.

The multidisciplinary team, that group of persons charged with the responsibility of making an assessment of the child and placing the child in an educational program appropriate to his/her needs, is commonly composed of the referring teacher (you), a school psychologist, the principal or his/her designate, a guidance counselor, a school social worker, the consulting teacher, any other interested adults and the parents. This team must first decide whether or not to refer a child; if the decision is affirmative, an assessment of the child must be carried out leading directly to a placement of the child in an educational program designed to meet the child's specific needs. Describing the responsibilities of each person on the team should help clarify how the team works and what your relationship to such a team will be.

The principal or a person representing the principal is the person commonly responsible for notifying all the personnel involved of their duties. This person may serve as the chairperson for the committee and must see that the parents are informed of what is going on, must secure parental permission and must act to safeguard the rights of the child. This person is the administrator of the committee.

The guidance counselor represents the counselling and guidance program of the school. This person may be involved in personal counselling, with the student or in a guidance-oriented function. Additionally this person or his/her designate may be involved in gathering some naturalistic observation data from the student. The guidance counselor may also gather some data via the administration of standardized tests of various sorts. Typically the guidance counselor functions in ways to help the student adjust to his/her placement via counselling but the referral could be for counselling as a placement in conjunction with "normal" classroom activities or special classroom activities.

The school psychologist is that person most frequently charged with performing psychometric evaluations of students ranging from intelligence and achievement tests to some of the personality assessment devices. This person is frequently the psychological diagnostician but can also be extremely helpful in actually helping to write educational programs for the student. Many school psychologists will also be involved in gathering naturalistic behavioral data about the students they are working with.

The school social worker, in those systems where one is available, is the person charged with school-home liaison duties. This person can gather observational data in the home or in the neighborhood and may be involved in the placement decision when the person must see that the parents implement certain changes. There are some student learning disabilities which are a function of parental behavior. This person can report on conditions in the home and neighborhood and may be involved in changing these conditions.

The consulting teacher (sometimes called special teacher or resource teacher) is that person who will likely be visiting and implementing the educational program for a child. This person should have special training in the teaching of disabled or exceptional children and must have the skills necessary to develop instructional programs. This person will also be coordinating the classroom teacher's efforts and his/her own in working with the child once a placement is made. In short, this person is an instructional specialist for the teaching of disabled students and is the consultant for teachers without such special training.

The referring teacher (you) is responsible for demonstrating that a referral is necessary. You must have gathered behavioral data to support your ideas about the necessity for such a referral. During the assessment phase, you must either gather the classroom data (behavioral data, work samples and so on) or supervise a person that will do this for you. During the placement phase you are responsible for meeting with the consulting teacher and coordinating your work with the student and the work of the

153

consulting teacher. You must implement the student's educational program in your classroom (for the times when the student is present) and arrange for a social and psychological climate which the "special" student can benefit from. You remain on the team throughout the time you work with the student or until he/she passes to the responsibility of another classroom teacher.

The parents must be fully informed of a pending assessment for referral and have the right to serve on the multidisciplinary team as equal members. They may give whatever input they see fit and can obtain additional, out-of-school, assessments of the child to be used by the team. They may legally refuse assessment, referral and placement. No action can be taken without their consent.

Other members of the team may be suggested by any member of the team or the child himself/herself. Persons that come in contact with the child in various settings may be asked to come in and provide information about their observations of or interactions with the child. Such team members may include the family minister, a school cafeteria worker, a coach at the YMCA or the bus driver. These people commonly are only present during the assessment stage of the meetings either before placement or when the placement is being evaluated.

THE TEACHER AS A GATHERER OF BEHAVIORAL DATA

In addition to being involved in the mustidisciplinary team, you will be called upon to gather behavioral data any time you wish to initiate a referral or when a referral has been initiated and you are a part of the data-gathering team. The means by which you can gather behavioral data have been set forth in a previous chapter.

THE TEACHER AS AN IMPLEMENTER OF
EDUCATIONAL PROGRAMS

Each child who is referred, assessed and placed in an educational program will receive an individual placement. That is, his or her program is likely to be unique and will certainly be somewhat different from those things other children are doing. Whatever kind of program is likely to be unique and will certainly be somewhat different from those things other children are doing. Whatever kind of program is decided upon, you are responsible for administering it in your classroom. This may mean participation with the larger group at times and at other times it may mean that this child will need individual instruction. You must have the teaching and management skills to let this happen.

WORKING WITH A CONSULTANT

Once an educational placement is decided upon it can take two forms, an educational intervention or a noneducational intervention. You will likely not have any change in your teaching role if a noneducational placement (personal counselling, medical treatment, etc.) is involved. However, for an educational intervention, you will have to change how you teach to the extent that the "mainstreamed" child can benefit from your instruction. It is recognized that you as a classroom teacher may not have the kinds of skills to write or devise special instruction for students requiring special help. This is where the consulting teacher comes in. He/she commonly devises such instruction in conference with you and gives you detailed guidelines for implementing the instruction. To receive maximum benefit from such a consultant you must be able to work to another person's specification and to implement things another person has developed.

Your relationship with this person is all important. You will not have the time, resources or practice in developing instructional approaches for "mainstreamed" children. This is the domain of the consulting teacher. She/he will devise the instruction in consultation with you and you will implement it. Your job and the student's educational experience will both be enhanced if you can maintain a good working relationship with this person.

THE TEACHER AS A BEHAVIOR MANAGER

As we shall see when we outline the "levels of intervention," a student may be placed in an educational program which requires that part of her/his day be spent outside the "normal" classroom and the rest be spent in your classroom. There is no question but that other children will be aware of any student's differentness. When a child is gone part of the day for some "special" program, all the other children will be aware of this fact. You must have the kind of behavior management skills to allow any students receiving "special" educational assistance to be accepted by the other members of your class. Such children cannot be alienated by other members of the class or much, if not all, of the value of the special educational programs will be lost. Overriding all your skills in the area of behavior management is your personal commitment to the worth and inherent value of each child. Your attitude will determine to a large extent the ease or difficulty "mainstreamed" children have in entering your classroom on a part-time basis.

THE TEACHER WITH INDIVIDUAL INSTRUCTION SKILLS

As mainstreaming is implemented to a greater and greater degree, the need for teachers to be skilled in individual instruction will increase. Mainstreaming gets at the fact that different children have different educational needs. The most effective way to meet this problem of teaching children who have different needs is through individualized instruction. You will be in the position of having to individualize instruction for "mainstreamed" students and as a result of this demand will probably want to individualize the instruction your other students receive. Your role will be somewhat different than the "traditional" teacher's role because you will need to be able to perform the skills we summarized in chapter four at a high level of proficiency.

PLACEMENT

After the referral and assessment process has been completed for a child, the next step is placement in an educational program designed to meet that child's specific needs. Such placements may vary from remaining in the "normal" classroom full time with some special help (counselling, medical therapy, individualized learning activities in the classroom) to total removal from the "normal" classroom which is commonly reserved only for those children who are so severely handicapped that they cannot benefit from instruction in "normal" classrooms.

Briefly, the options are (1) program enhancement in the normal classroom, (2) augumentation of "normal" classroom activities with visits from specialized teachers who provide extra instruction in some areas (e.g., reading, speach pathology, etc.), (3) special instruction outside of the classroom with a "special education" teacher for less than one-half of the school day, (4) augumenting the "special" classroom with "normal" classroom less than half a day for those activities from which the student can benefit), (5) augumenting the "normal" classroom with other professional agencies' services outside the school (e.g., psychiatric services, physical therapy, etc.), (6) a full-time placement in "special" education classes, (7) special day schools for severely handicapped student, and (8) a visiting teacher who provides the child with instruction at home. Regardless of the level of intervention chosen by the multidisciplinary team, assessment must remain constant and the child's progress in the program must be frequently evaluated to determine if changes in placement are warranted.

SUMMARY

In this chapter we very briefly outlined the law and the procedure of mainstreaming with respect to the impact it will have on your role as a teacher. We have barely skimmed the topic of mainstreaming and did not attempt to deal with such crucial topics as diagnosis, support services or kinds of instructional programs for children. Our intent was merely to introduce you to the concept of mainstreaming.

Chapter 10
EDUCATIONAL PSYCHOLOGY AND EFFECTIVE TEACHING
or "What the Hell Difference Does All This Make?"

That question with the dubious grammar is not raised in jest. You have at this point just about completed one or more courses in educational psychology, so it's time to take stock.

"Taking stock" means at least four separate acts or steps:

1. Identifying what has been mastered thus far.
2. Estimating the worth or value of that which has been learned by comparing with a criteria.
3. Looking ahead to see what additional understanding and skills are needed to become an effective teacher.
4. Making a plan for use of remaining time in teacher education to achieve the objectives of becoming an effective teacher.

In other words, it is time to evaluate past learning experiences and to look ahead to the next experiences. This chapter will provide readers with a number of exercises for doing just that. As the reading and the worksheet exercises at the close of the chapter are completed, much more will be learned about the process of *effective* teaching as revealed by several research projects and ways can be visualized in which the learnings from educational psychology can be used further to help one develop into an *effective* teacher, which is assumed to be the goal of students in teacher education. That is, it is assumed that all students in teacher education *intend* to teach in ways which lead to learning and development of their students.

Some Preliminary Questions to Be Answered

Before going through the four steps described above, it is necessary to consider some prior questions. For instance, before going to all the trouble of making a self-improvement plan, should one not first ascertain whether or not schools and formal education themselves have an affect on the development of children and adolescents? After all, if schools and formal education have no effects, there is no point in looking for teacher caused effects. In a similar vein, if schools and formal education *do* have effects, one needs to determine if the effects are due to teachers or to the influence of

157

peers, of home background, or if they are just a matter of innate capabilities of children and youth. Assuming for the moment that teachers do make a difference, is it their "personality," their "natural bent," their "IQ," the specific methods they employ, or their skills that "cause" some teachers to be effective and a lack of skills that "causes" other teachers to be ineffective?

This last question is the one you will want to ponder. A corollary question is: "Can one *learn* to be an effective teacher as a college student or, is effective teaching an *instinctive* matter, or an *artistic* skill (such that it can only be developed through trial and error), or possibly, is effective teaching a set of skills and habits that are derived only from inborn abilities and talents, and is not really *learned* or *developed* at all?

If effective teaching skills cannot be developed through formal education, then some very profound thinking must take place in teacher training institutions, both by faculty and by students. Teacher preparation programs will need to become much better at identifying college freshmen who have a high probability of becoming effective teachers and rejecting of those with low potentials for becoming effective teachers, rather than continuing in *training and educating* teachers.

Are schools and formal education effective in influencing student development? To be completely logical, one should complete the question by stating "compared to—" with an alternative to schooling being posed. For example, "Are schools and formal education effective in influencing student development when school graduates are compared to children and youth educated at home, or around the village fountain by the tribal elders? The quality of the evidence is not good; certainly it is not conclusive, but such as it is, it indicates that school and/or formal education do make a difference.

Green et al. (1966), for example, studied the children of Prince Edward County, Virginia, which closed all public schools from 1959-1964 to avoid racial integration. When the development of children who stayed in the county but who did not attend school was compared with that of children who either attended private schools or moved to other counties, a clear difference emerged. The children who did not go to school were, in many instances, severely regressed in their intellectual development and required much remediation to "catch up" with their peers. A second study conducted by Schmidt (1966) in a South African community found essentially the same results as did a study by Vernon (1969) in Nigeria and Senegal, South Africa. Differences in intellectual development as measured by IQ tests and tests over school subject achievement consistently favored those who attended school. Some of the nonattenders actually decreased in IQ as they grew older.

These studies may, as mentioned previously, be methodologically poor and the results biased. The studies did not control for differences in family behaviors and quite possibly the apparent resulting differences in development might have very little to do with formal education or its lack. It may be that the *families* are differentially reinforcing certain behaviors in the children and this differential reinforcement is the crucial factor in development rather than formal education.

These studies are also not to be taken as indicating that sound intellectual development *cannot* occur elsewhere than in the schools. It can and does. In the Australian "outback". for example, where children live on ranches or "stations," hundreds of miles from each other and from schools, intellectual development apparently proceeds apace with that in more urban settings, despite the fact that the outback children never see the inside of a school. They receive some instruction by radio and the state provides materials which are used in a self-instructional way but the learning is homecentered rather than school centered.

The studies above simply indicate that intellectual development is not as *likely* to occur outside the formal education process. A careful look at the Australian outback homes probably would reveal many facets of what we would regard as formal education including parents who serve as teacher surrogates. They set schedules, obtain needed supplies, discuss lessons, coach their children, reinforce them with praise, correct their mistakes, etc. In fact, it is very likely true that it is this structure and personal guidance that are the essential "influence factors" in any formal educational program. And they do not "just happen." At least, the Prince Edward County and South African studies suggest they do not occur spontaneously with any frequency in homes and communities. It is very likely that the majority of parents in the United States would not expend the necessary time and energy over a long enough period of time to insure their childrens' intellectual development.

This failure could be a critical matter, especially if there is any validity to the idea that some learnings need to occur during rather restricted periods of life. Children dependent on preoccupied, unmotivated or unskilled parents might well miss crucial learning periods and never catch up. In conclusion (for which the evidence is not too strong), there are indications that severe risks will be run by any group of parents who elect to use homebased and nonformal education for their children. The probabilities are substantial that many children will suffer losses of intellectual development that will not be completely "repaired" by later learning experiences.

Do teachers make a difference, or are seeming effects of education due to home environment, the influence of peers or to innate capabilities of children? The safe answer here is: "They all make a difference." In other words, development of children and youth *is* influenced by the quality of teaching they receive, and the stimulus-modeling effects of peers, and the rewards and punishments, and the examples they receive in the home, and by their innate ability and individual motivations (interest, attitudes, fears, etc.). It is a *safe* answer because it is easy to imagine a particular instance where any one or several of the factors were so out-of-phase that learning obviously could not take place. It is not a *good* answer, though, because it does not help determine what portion of the variations in student development are associated with variations in quality of teaching.

There have been some studies which seem to indicate that variations in achievement grow principally out of differences between schools, characteristically located so that they served students of a narrow band of socioeconomic levels, parental educational levels and cultural value patterns. The chief research of this type is the now famous *Equality of Educational Opportunity,* the so-called "Coleman Report" prepared by a research group under the direction of James Coleman, a Harvard sociologist (Coleman et al. 1966). Similar analyses of related data by Mosteller and Moynigan (1972) and Jencks et al. (1972), tend to lead to conclusions that schools and teaching as such accomplish very little other than to provide a baby-sitting service while keeping the young from competing in an already tight labor market.

The Coleman report was a very large scale inquiry involving 4,000 schools with all the teachers and administrators, and over 645,000 pupils at all grade levels. The principal data were students' scores on standardized achievement tests on successive years. Secondary data consisted of information on the schools, the neighborhoods, parental characteristics, aspirations and attitudes of pupils. These data were subjected to a variety of sophisticated analyses to determine if schools were or were not providing pupils with equal educational opportunities.

The findings can be summarized in seven main points:

1. Minority students consistently performed less well than did majority students.
2. The quality of educational service varied markedly between schools across the entire country.
3. The differences between schools seemed to make little difference in how much children learned.
4. The significant differences in learning were related to student background factors—home, parents, neighborhood, etc.
5. School quality, while not as significant across the board, *did* make a difference in the accomplishment of minority students. In other words, students from the majority culture tend to be largely unaf-

160

fected by attending low quality schools, but children from minority and disadvantaged homes can be *positively* influenced by attending higher quality schools which expend more money on special services.

6. Achievement of students within schools was positively related to backgrounds and motivations of *other* students in the schools. Thus, students from disadvantaged homes placed in a school populated by students who are high achievers, will tend to do better.

7. Where there was found to be higher average quality of teachers in a school, achievement of students tended to be higher. Here again, the relationship was more marked for disadvantaged, minority students than for white, majority students. This was interpreted by the Coleman group as "a cumulative impact of the qualities of teachers in a school on the pupils' achievements" (Coleman et al. 1966, p. 22).

Thus the Coleman report gives only token support to the notion that differences in teaching make a difference in student intellectual development. The research design, unfortunately, lumped all teachers in each school into an anonymous "average" and thereby considerably reduced variations or even cancelled out differences in teacher quality. This possibly weakened what could have been the strongest finding of the entire study. That is, had they compared the achievements of students taught by the teachers identified as "highly qualified" with the accomplishments of the students of less well qualified teachers, then it is possible that that difference would have exceeded all other differences found in the study.

As it is, the recommendations growing out of the study have dealt with busing students, not with improvement of teaching, thereby attempting to equalize educational opportunities by obtaining a more heterogeneous mix of peers and not by improving teaching as such. There have been many criticisms of the Coleman report, although the major findings have withstood the attacks. In the present writers' view, it is simply a *partial* study—it did not carefully search for all the factors which could significantly affect and eventually equalize student achievement. The conclusions and recommendations from the study can, therefore, be only partial solutions to the problem of improving education generally.

Christopher Jencks and his associates took another tack in assessing the effectiveness of education and instruction. Rather than achievement test scores, they used criterion measures that related to "success" in American life, i.e., cognitive skill, educational level attained, occupation and income. They asked the overall question: "Are variations in individual success related more to pupil intelligence, pupil social background, school quality, racial segregation patterns, or to the use of ability tracks as a plan for curriculum?''

Their first finding was not unexpected—there are shocking differences in status, income, and opportunities in America. The differences are interlocked to the extent that if an individual has an excess of one, the chances are he will have excesses in all others.

Secondly, they determined that life success is largely an outgrowth of native ability (IQ) and social background. However, there was a substantial amount of success that could not be attributed to these factors. Good, Biddle, and Brophy (1975) point out that Jenck's use of the term *luck* to "explain" the variations due to unknown factors is unfortunate, to say the least. It is quite possible, they point out, that variation in a pupil characteristic of *persistence* could have accounted for as much of the variance in success as ability or social background; so, in the present writers' view, the Jencks report, too, is only a partial study with limited recommendations.

Thirdly, Jencks and his cohorts found that factors of school quality (curriculum, special services, etc.) have little to do with pupils' life success. Rather, they argue that schooling differences only *reinforce inequalities in American life, and do nothing to equalize opportunities.*

Fourthly, the Jencks group found nothing to suggest we should stop trying to improve schools and education. They argue that we should continue to try to improve, and especially to integrate, the schools. This could serve to reduce racial prejudices in future generations.

Fifthly, they believe it is futile to depend on schools to achieve equality in the society. The only way Jencks and his group can see for that to occur is to redistribute wealth. The Jencks report, then, becomes a blueprint for society as a whole and for social reform, not a plan for improving schools.

The two studies discussed here illustrate a central fact about all research findings (and therefore about conclusions and recommendations). They are limited by what researchers elect to measure when they plan their research. To some degree, what one elects to measure as an investigation depends on personal values, perhaps on personal dislikes or preferences, and one's personal goals. Neither Coleman nor Jencks were, or are, involved with public school *teaching.* They, therefore, were not interested in laying a research basis for improving instruction and they did not pose research questions or use measures that led to recommendations for *improving instruction.*

There are researchers with interests in improving schools by improving instruction, however, and they have found that teachers *do* make a difference. That is, they have found that in schools there are typically some teachers who, with some regularity, prepare students to do better on measures of achievement than do other teachers. The differences are large enough to be significant in several ways. The best way to dramatize the difference is to project an instance whereby a student is fortunate enough to be enrolled only in classes taught by effective teachers for his entire school career. He would probably excel over students enrolled in a succession of classes under less effective teachers by a matter of "achievement-years." This difference would be enough to significantly reduce any restrictions on learning associated with socioeconomic distinctions, IQ differences, special services in schools, etc. Fortunately, these investigators have not only shown that teaching quality is a prime factor in the accomplishments of students, they have used measures which permitted them to analyze teaching styles so as to provide a rather detailed picture of the instructional activities that add up to *effective teaching.*

What is it about teachers and teaching that makes instruction effective? This question (or its numerous variations) has intrigued educational researchers for decades. Literally thousands of studies have been carried out to find the answers. To many early researchers it seemed obvious that teacher personality, or intelligence, or attitudes, or education, or personal background would be key factors that influence how well children develop.

Research conducted by these investigators tended, therefore, to be concerned with *teachers* not *teaching.* The research was based on an assumption that teaching behavior was highly correlated with or "caused by" teachers' personal characteristics, and that effective teaching behavior is a product of such intrapsychic characteristics as "democratic personality," warm and loving temperament, "positive attitudes," or "good self-concept." Or, poor teaching is assumed to be an outgrowth of "authoritarian personality," "needs to dominate," "negative attitudes," etc. Teachers' academic preparations were also supposed, by early researchers, to affect how well their students learned (teachers having *high* grades or a liberal arts degree would likely prove more effective than those with average grades or B.S. Ed. degrees. (Or perhaps it was the other way around. It is possible to be too bright and too sophisticated to relate to public school students according to some theorists.)

In the main, research on teacher characteristics has yielded no useful findings. As long ago as 1953, the *Committee on Criteria of Teacher Effectiveness* of the American Educational Research Association noted that the combined effect of forty years of such research was not enough to help school administrators select teachers or in granting them tenure, nor were state agencies better able to certify teachers as being competent, moral, or otherwise suitable for teaching nor are colleges aided in designing teacher-preparation programs. It would be difficult to find forty years of more futile research, it seems to the present writers.

Later research, though in many ways equally futile, did shift to factors

163

other than the teacher. These were the early "process" studies which tested new curricular innovations and new "methods." The "new math" and P.S.S.C. Physics curricula are examples of the former and "discovery" and "discussion methods" are examples of the latter. Class size, various scheduling schemes, and other, more or less random factors were investigated to ascertain what, if any, relationship they had to student learning.

By and large, these studies yielded a mixed bag. Some factors had an effect on student learning some of the time, but not at other times. Some had an effect with certain learners, but not with others. Perhaps more significantly, some studies indicated that methods, class size, etc., were effective only in interaction with certain other conditions. In fact, it became widely accepted that teaching method was a matter for personal choice by teachers; each teacher had his or her own "best" method.

In the main, this research has been much more heat generating than enlightening. Teachers and theorists have tended to become zealots: espousers of this or that method or classroom arrangement. Arguments abound on whether or not two or more teachers should "team" a course or if one teacher should continue to hold sway but make extensive use of special resource materials to "mediate" learning. The zealots, as is true of "true believers" everywhere, ignored research findings that indicated special methods, special classroom arrangements, special approaches and techniques were not particularly different in their effects. Children learned in the less directive, more open, situations, but so did they in the more direct or closed classrooms. No special method or arrangement or scheduling procedure has made consistent improvements in instructional effectiveness (Gage 1963).

The failure of the teacher characteristics and early teaching process studies to yield useful information is probably a function of four defects in the research: (abstracted from Dunkin and Biddle 1974):

1. The research ignores the actual activities that occur during instruction and learning. None of the studies looked at what actually was going on when the teacher, the students, and the material came together in the classroom. These are the events that count. These are the events that determine how student time is used, what occupies his attention and what consequences are experienced for correct and incorrect, thoughtful or impulsive responding. In short, this is where teaching and learning occur and these early studies ignored these events.

2. These early researchers tended to use a "shotgun" approach to research, largely unguided by theory. Consequently, they correlated whatever measures they had (personality tests, IQ tests,

164

college grades, etc.) with whatever measures they could devise of teaching effectiveness (principal's ratings, students' evaluations, peer ratings, etc.) with little or no rationale. Consequently the relationships have been just about at chance level and the studies never resulted in measures that would *predict* teacher performance.

3. Many of the studies used unreliable means of assessing teaching effectiveness as rated by principals in one school's system but not as effectiveness was rated in another school system.

4. Many researchers apparently considered the factors that constitute good effective teaching to be universal. That is, they operate predictably in all places at all times and under all conditions. The assumption of universality overlooks the obvious fact that what works in elementary school will not likely work in high school, and ignores the patent evidence that students of differing backgrounds have learned to respond differently to different stimuli. In other words, effective teaching is related to the *context* in which it occurs.

Fortunately, over the past ten to fifteen years, the substantial number of studies on teaching (alluded to previously) have concentrated on identifying salient features of effective teaching—where effective teaching is rather reliably estimated by measures of student response or development. So prevalent have these studies become, that entire reviews are devoted to them (see Medley and Mitzel 1963; Biddle 1967; Nuthall 1968; Rosenshine 1971). One review publication (Simon and Boyer 1970) describes over 70 different systems for observing and measuring events within the classroom. With such "microscopes" the instructional process can remain a completely artistic mystery no longer.

The observational scheme and predictor variables in this more recent research are not selected randomly, or through a "shotgun approach," rather, researchers are using basic and applied theory to direct their attention and observations to relevant events. Operant theory, for example, directs attention to the antecedent, cuing, acts and consequating, reinforcing and punishing, acts of teachers. Cognitive theory directs attention to the activities of the teacher that provide organization and structure or "meaningfulness" to learning experiences. In short, the attention is on teaching behaviors and their relationship to learning products or outcomes.

The knowledge produced by research involving direct observation of teaching behavior and noting correlated differences in student development, is not yet sufficient in scope or of adequate reliability to answer *all* or even *most* questions about teaching. Nor is it a basis for making recommendations to school administrators as to what individuals are best to hire, retain or promote. Neither is it possible to develop a teacher preparation program using research findings to establish behavioral goals and objectives. These must await a larger and firmer data base.

At this point, the findings are only intriguing and suggestive to people who make decisions about teachers and teacher preparation. They can, however, be used by individual teachers in evaluating the use or potential applications of their formal, professional learnings and skills as procedures for aiding children and youth in mastering learnings. The research also can aid teachers in defining what further skills and understanding they might reasonably expect to pursue in their remaining courses and preparatory experiences.

One series of studies, for example, by Kounin and a group of colleagues (1970) attempted to locate the differences between effective and ineffective teachers in terms of their dealing with classroom behavior problems. They found, to their supprise, that there were no discernible differences! What was noted, however, was that effective teachers were much more successful in preventing behavior problems in the first place! Once misbehavior started, though, they were no better at dealing with it than their less effective colleagues.

Much of the preventative success seemed to stem from effectiveness in keeping children actively engaged in lessons and seatwork and thereby reducing boredom and restlessness. They did this by: (1) organizing and planning so that transitions between activities were smooth and well explained, (2) pacing work well, keeping something going even for the most rapid learner, (3) using combinations of activities to maintain involvement. In other words they planned assignments for differing levels of ability.

A more general set of teacher behaviors were classed by Kounin as "withitness." This refers to a category of behaviors that kept the teacher in close touch with how *each* student was progressing and that led to an anticipation or very early detection of trouble spots. Add to this an ability or a willingness to respond *immediately* and the affective teachers nipped developing problems in the bud.

Kounin's findings should be no surprise to anyone familiar with research in behavior modification techniques. It appears that the effective teachers were successful in presenting *cues and prompts* for appropriate responding and were *differentially reinforcing behavior other than* time wasting and disruptiveness. "Withitness" suggests that effective teachers had a variety of discriminated responses developed into a wide spectrum repertory. That is, a number of pupil behaviors served as clear signals to the effective teachers that they should *act quickly,* as opposed to the less effective teachers who were not responding discriminatingly to the cues for *im-*

mediate response and disruptive behavior continued to accelerate and expand in their classes at a higher frequency.

While Kounin's findings appear to be clear and straight-forword (even simplistic and commonsensical), when one moves into the cognitive area, the picture becomes very much more complex. There are few one-to-one relationships between teacher behavior and pupils' cognitive development. Most relationships interact with other factors. A particular behavioral-style of teaching that is most effective for lower S.E.S. (Socioeconomic status) students but will be less effective for middle and upper S.E.S. students, is an example of such an interaction. Other research indicates that a particular style tends to be more effective for secondary students but not for elementary students, while some patterns of teacher behavior are more effective for helping students learn mathematics while others appear more effective in English or reading class.

The result of this complexity is: effective teaching for cognitive development requires teachers to hit upon "mixes" or "combinations" of styles which are then integrated or "orchestrated" to fit a particular learning context. The analogy of teachers managing cognitive learning experiences, to that of symphony conductors composing and conducting a symphony is rather apt and is widely used (c.f. Dunkin and Biddle 1974; Brophy and Everston 1976; and Good and Brophy 1977). Both the conductor/composer and the teacher are taking separate entities of known effect and combining them into shifting, fluid patterns to achieve an overall effect on learners and listeners.

This shifting and combining is not, or at least *should* not be, a random, purely extemporaneous process. If there is one aspect of effective teaching that stands out, it is that such teaching is highly *intentional* on the part of the teacher. The teacher *plans* for things to happen, usually with considerable attention to detail. Extemporaneous behavior, while it may "feel good" and is assumed to be a mark of a "natural teaching talent," is not especially consistent with effective instruction. Effective planning is a process whereby teachers orchestrate their knowledge about students, the nature of their subject matter, and availability of special resources, etc., into a symphony of activities for their students.

Planning which is rational—that is, which is aimed at achieving defined and prescribed outcomes, is a process of making decisions among alternatives. Every instructional plan can be expressed in dozens of ways so that a final plan always represents a choice (in reality, a whole series of choices). In a very true sense, any act of a teacher can be performed in a different way, or a substitution could be made. For example, a math teacher hears a student insist to a classmate that an incorrect solution to a problem was correct. The teacher may decide to do nothing or he may decide to correct the student. He/she may correct him now, at the end of the period or tomorrow. The teacher may smile as he/she corrects the student or he/she may frown or even express no feeling. He/she may actually compliment the student for recalling the incorrect procedure, while still pointing out that the solution is incorrect. There are many alternatives from which the teacher may select at each decision point. Some may be helpful to the student, that is, help him to master mathematics objectives, others may be deleterious, that is, making mastery more difficult and making retention of new learnings less certain.

What is not apparent, perhaps, is that the teacher may make the choice on any one of several reasons or bases:

1. The teacher may be feeling sad and moody or bright and cheerful, but, whatever, the choice is based on teacher mood.
2. The teacher may not expect a particular student to learn anyhow since he has a low IQ.
3. The teacher may have read a report of a well-designed research which indicated that ease of learning and retention for students like those in his class tended to be greater if the teacher responded to errors in a particular way, so he/she elects to apply the research proved procedures.
4. The teacher may recall that a favorite teacher of his/hers "always" said certain things when students made errors in discussion so he/she attempts to do things just like his/her old mentor.

Obviously, one would hope that the teacher would not be so unprofessional as to simply act as he/she felt, and one would question the competence of a teacher who responded to set expectations for students who have relatively low measured IQs. One would hope that teachers would decide on the basis of research, research that indicated students similar to the one in question generally learned and retained better when teachers responded in certain ways.

The matter of teacher decision-making is the subject of an exercise entitled "Worksheet on Teacher Decision Making." It has been designed to broaden your grasp of the centrality of decision and choice making. If your instructor is assigning the exercise, turn to it at this point.

The decision-making exercise should have illustrated several points about teacher decision making as the class discussed their responses to the problem situations.

1. That there are a diversity of choice points in teaching.
2. That different alternatives have different consequences of effects on student learning.

3. That, in some cases at least, research or extrapolations from research can be helpful in selecting appropriate responses.
4. That, lacking research or experience, people tend to make choices among alternatives in somewhat random ways.
5. That there is a need for teachers to know what research findings say about teacher decisions in order to make sound decisions.

The next few pages will introduce you to a series of studies that suggest a research basis for making a wide variety of decisions about what acts or behavioral styles you may use as a teacher. The list of stylistic behaviors is certainly not complete: not nearly enough research has been done to answer all the questions. Also, space limitations require the authors to be selective so not even all those teaching stylistics that have been researched are incorporated here.

We shall begin by looking at a stylistic that may be labelled "relating to children." Traditional wisdom suggests that the teaching-learning relationship is a loving, affectional relationship. Is that true? Research says only in a limited sense. If we compare the relationship established by teachers whose students seem consistently to learn more than average with teachers of students who consistently learn less, the findings are that effective teachers:

1. Are matter-of-fact about their students, showing no tendencies to sentimentalize about them. They do not excuse or defend students for inappropriate or less-than-wise decisions. They recognize erroneous student responses for what they are—a signal that learning has been incomplete and needs strengthening. They do not especially try to read "meaning" into or to interpret student errors.
2. Despite the matter-of-fact approach, effective teachers tend to be classed as warm and tolerant. Apparently they do not take students or themselves too seriously. They can laugh and enjoy students. Most of all, the notion of "warmth" indicates friendly interest—a fair amount of time listening to students and to exulting over student success but not necessarily pity over student losses or failures.

These descriptions of effective teachers should not surprise students of educational psychology. The matter-of-fact teacher is cued to respond more by student achievement or achievement-related problems so, attends more to and differentially to student *achievement*-related behavior. In attending differentially, the teacher is more likely to describe and specify clearly just what is expected of students (an example of cuing and prompting by use of

169

objectives). The somewhat relaxed, amused, tolerant response to student behavior probably means that the teacher is not getting angry, exasperated or defeated, and then communicating these feelings to students (which may be the case with many ineffective teachers). The teacher who is communicating such feelings to students will tend to make students act in avoidant ways. They may be nervous and "fidgety" (anxious—from the viewpoint of other theories). They may "daydream" or "not concentrate." (They may have "unsatisfied needs" according to some psychologists.) The upshot being, the more emotionally reactive teacher, by setting up an avoidant situation reduces students' "time on and attention to learning tasks." It is no wonder the nonsentimental, matter-of-fact, tolerant, achievement-interested teacher is more effective.

The matter of teacher attending-to-achievement requires further consideration. Most teachers think, from their study of reinforcement theory, that positive teacher response to pupil achievement will tend to somehow "fixate" achievement so they "praise" or give other approval signals to students who evidence learning or effort. Does research confirm this practice?

Not entirely. Some studies show that effective teachers may use praise less fullsomely than the ineffective teachers, so learning is not especially increased by increased *amounts* of praise.

Significantly perhaps, it has been noted by some researchers that teacher praise is more effective in reinforcing performance of slow learners and lower socioeconomic status students. Middle and upper S.E.S. and faster learning students' performance is increased by feedback that errors have been made.

The matter of teacher praise is perhaps clarified by findings that teacher praise, to be effective, must be used *contingently* and with *pupils who have teacher praise and approval as learned or secondary reinforcers*. Teacher feedback of error performance, on the other hand, is used by effective teachers for pupils who have apparently learned previously to achieve as a means of avoiding the failure that is implicit within negative feedback.

As might be expected, many of the slower learning and lower S.E.S. students do not perform better following negative feedback. They possibly (probably?) have learned to avoid failure by avoiding the entire school situation or by "giving up," rather than by correcting their performance.

As a tentative conclusion, we may hypothesize that you as a teacher may become more effective, that is, increase student learning by:

1. Learning to identify students who respond to teacher praise/approval and those who respond positively to negative feedback.

170

2. Learning to apply praise and to give negative feedback contingently to achievement or its lack.

There seems to be no question that teachers are very much in control in the classroom. Even in the most "child-centered" classroom, children and adolescents spend a majority of their time looking at, listening to and responding to, teachers. Teachers initiate most learning activities and preselect most materials. Teachers determine when to move to other subjects or topics and when a pupil or class has achieved objectives. Are there differing styles or decisions here and do the differences make a difference in how well pupils learn? In other words, are effective teachers characterized by one pattern and less effective teachers by another pattern?

As a general rule, research supports the idea that teachers should manage classrooms in ways which lead students to be more active and involved, rather than just passive recipients of information. That is, teachers who: (1) use small groups to encourage more student participation and who (2) ask open questions which require students to give their own example of concepts, apply principles to specific problems or to evaluate and formulate their own positions tend to have pupils who learn more.

This is not a universal rule though. Some pupils have not developed basic "expressive skills," even by high school age. These pupils are still at a "receptive verbal learning" level. They can probably learn from *hearing about, reading about, seeing demonstrations of,* but they will need considerable skill development before they can learn from exercises which require them to generate verbal analyses, describe applications or use criteria to evaluate and synthesize. The effective teacher probably requires these students to repeat learnings rather than analyze, synthesize, apply or evaluate. These pupils, especially, are not asked to *initiate* learning activities such as field trips, lists of examples to define concepts or to describe unique applications of principles until they have developed greater verbal skills.

The varying of a basic instructional procedure to accommodate to the capabilities of students, as described in the preceding two paragraphs, is one instance of teachers acting to individualize instruction: tailoring of procedures to enable all students to learn and develop.

The general importance of individualization has been dramatically illustrated by a number of studies. Keele (1973) for example, found, with a group of twenty-eight elementary school children who were individually tutored (even by paraprofessionals of minimum training), that achievement in reading was markedly accelerated over that of twenty matched children who were taught by regular class methods. The improved reading achievement was found on all five of the separate measures of reading level and comprehension!

171

More evidence as to the importance of individualizing of instruction by teachers is provided by Sears et al. (1972) After the first year of a five year study they concluded that:

1. School achievement is improved when teachers direct more time and attention to individual learners than to groups or to the class as a whole.
2. School achievement is improved by relating such attentions to students' performance and work rather than to their overall behavior.
3. The achievement is improved by making arrangements for providing periods of *undivided* attention to individuals' work and progress.
4. However, teacher attention, especially information-giving, is most effective for increasing achievement when given in a public way. Apparently, students learn better when the teacher directs information to the solving of an individual's problem than they do when information is "broadcast" to a group to be simply "remembered."

Individualization through a contingency contracting procedure, as advocated by Homme (1970), has been investigated for its effects on learning. Despite some indications that the use of material rewards tends to reduce the influence of something called "intrinsic" reinforcement, research tends to support use of classroom contracting as an effective means of increasing achievement.

Thompson et al. (1974) for example, showed that teachers can master the contracting procedures. Their classes demonstrated afterwards that students spent more time on tasks and there were fewer class behavior problems than before contracting was introduced.

Note that the contracting procedure (and most behavior modification procedures such as "token economies") leave the teacher free to make very separate decisions about learning experiences for individual students. In fact these procedures require the teacher to make such decisions.

This is in contrast with some of the so-called "package" curricula available to schools such as IGE (Individually Guided Education) and IPI (Individually Prescribed Instruction).

Good et al. (1975) interpret the results of a series of studies with the IGE system as indicating the individualization appears to be effective in most but not all schools and they wonder if students of various response patterns differ in their response to the structure and materials of the planned program. It is possible, of course, that the program structure prevents teachers from making needed adjustments for many individual students and for entire groups of students of certain backgrounds.

Shimron (1973) conducted evaluation studies of the IPI program which requires students to follow a set pattern of experiences but allows them to vary their pace. They can ask for special help from teachers, who are then able to make some adjustments in the program.

Shimron found, however, that fast learning students typically spent *twice* the amount of time as did slower learning students suggesting a great difference in the interest value of the program materials. He also found that the faster students asked for and received more teacher attention, so that teacher time was under the control of students rather than teacher analysis of pupil need.

Clearly, the individualized curricula packages do not reduce requirements for spontaneous teacher response to individual student needs. The programs, in the hands of responsive teachers, may prove to be more effective than other kinds of traditional programs in the hands of the same teachers, but such has yet to be demonstrated.

Just what is involved in the process of individualization either in a traditional classroom or in a package curricula classroom? The following list of teacher procedures and behaviors is a description of a minimum (but necessary) set of activities and behaviors:

1. Teacher effectively communicates (explains, describes or demonstrates) what is expected of each student on each assignment or activity and reduces or increases expectations according to pupil progress.
2. Each student knows that he can receive help from the teacher or other persons *when he needs it.*
3. Student progress is checked and students are held accountable for their performance.
4. Classroom rules and regulations set up a procedure for students to follow in receiving help but also protect the teacher as he or she acts to assess performance of groups of students.
5. Classroom procedures establish optional activities for students who complete assignments early.
6. Teachers provide rapid feedback to students using some paper, pencil (formal) assessment procedures, but also many observational measures to give students information on achievement-related behavior such as "I see you're now using an outline to organize your thoughts. That should be a help."
7. The teacher has more advanced materials and assignments available for faster learning students and a procedure for students to follow to initiate the advanced assignments.

The demands of individualization on teachers to "diagnose and evaluate" individual progress raises a number of significant questions. Should, for example, such diagnoses and evaluations be based on standardized or teacher-made tests or should informal measures be used rather than formal? Should IQ tests be used to predict pupils' potentials? Should measures be norm-referenced or criterion-referenced? Should tests be given frequently or very seldom?

When effective teachers are queried on these matters, they tend to deemphasize standardized achievement testing and other means of taking formal measures of student progress. They considered these measures to simply confirm what they had already assessed through close, but informal, *observations* of students. Brophy and Everston (1976) note, however, that when formal achievement measures are used, the students of these teachers uniformly score higher than do students of other teachers.

The effective teachers of lower S.E.S. students were especially critical of standardized and teacher-made tests. They considered them useless for purposes of making instructional decisions, because the tests assumed that the students had basic abilities that just were not there.

Notice that in emphasizing informal observation methods, these effective teachers were almost forced into use of criterion-referenced measurement. That is, there is no precise, easy way to "norm reference" a set of observations about a student completing an assignment. Note too, that the more observational process encourages teachers to attend more to actual progress and permits attending on a very frequent basis so that feedback can be given students at times when it is most effective, that is, when feedback functions as a reinforcer or to correct error-behavior before it becomes firmly established as a "habitual" response of the student. Traditional testing practices (weekly, quarterly, and semester exams, for example) on the other hand, do not actually function as, or provide reinforcing or corrective feedback for pupils. They simply do not occur close enough in time to actual student effort to master objectives.

The requirement to individualize according to student characteristics has generally been interpreted to mean that instruction should be altered to a mode or form that permits students to use whatever abilities they might have to achieve the most that they can. In other words, if a student has difficulties in learning from reading, instruction for him should make maximum use of visual and/or oral modes and rely on printed modes only at some minimum level.

The notion of learning style has been extended beyond the matter of learning *competency,* to include personal *preferences* as well. At the present time, many instructional theorists are postulating that there are several individual learning "styles" which should be determined by teachers as a basis for planning instruction.

174

At the present time, there appears to be no indication that "effective" teachers are those who have mastered a formal system for classifying students by their learning "style." This is not to disparage the notion of learning style, nor to discourage continued research on the relationship of these learner variables to mastery of objectives.

There is one concern of the present authors, however, about the "learner style" concept itself. There is somewhat of a tendency to consider the responses which comprise a style to be immutable. In other words, once an individual develops an ability to learn best through a particular mode, he or she is forever at that mode.

This is unfortunate. It seems more likely to the present writers that learning style responses are themselves learned behaviors and also that different styles are more appropriate in some situations and other styles are more appropriate in others. This opens the intriguing possibility that effective teachers will prove eventually to be those who help students learn a variety of styles or abilities-to-learn through various modes. A student who has learned diverse styles could, then, learn from lectures or from demonstrations or from correspondence courses or from experimenting and trying out: whatever mode happened to be available. In many respects, it seems that ethical and moral considerations rule out simplistic catering to restricted student learning styles that are a function of impoverished learning opportunities.

The same ethical and moral considerations require teachers to systematically design learning experiences for increasing the diverse response capabilities of students presently limited by their backgrounds, in addition to increasing their cognitive skill base.

It should be apparent at this point that effective teaching involves work, effort and close attention. Indeed, one group of investigators concluded that effective teachers always *referred* to teaching as work, they organized their time to make work efficient, they were active much of the day getting ready for upcoming classes, they maintained schedules, etc. Less effective teachers, on the other hand, saw teaching as a chore perhaps, but perceived it more simplistically as a baby-sitting or child-tending chore, as not having many work-type requirements. The less effective teachers tend to devote more time and energy to entertaining children, maintaining order, or even time-killing. Most noticeable of all, they do not tend to give time and energy to *individualization* of instruction but (apparently) minimize such effort by keeping entire classes functioning pretty much as a unit or whole.

For students in teacher education it is difficult to realize the work, effort, time and energy involved in being an effective teacher. It can be visualized (vaguely perhaps) by thinking for a moment about how much effort there is in making individual diagnoses of children's achievement levels and learning problems, in obtaining or preparing individual instruction

175

materials, in giving individual assignments and correcting individual errors. Then compare this with the amount of effort expended by the teacher who teaches classes as groups. The amount of effort to individualize should become immediately apparent. Most of the energy outlay, of course, is expended in just staying alert, attending to children's responses, particularly to "error" or "inappropriate" responses and quickly devising corrective measures. It is the unremitting demands for close attention to individuals that make general alertness and high energy level at prerequisite for effective teaching.

CONCLUSION

One way to achieve closure for the preceding discussion is to point out some conclusions the research does *not* support and then examine what seem to be implications for students in teacher education from remaining conclusions.

First of all, there is nothing in the research to suggest that effective teachers and less effective teachers are diametrically opposed on any behavioral dimension. In truth, the difference is probably one of one group employing a particular approach or strategy in a certain way a greater percent of the time or with a greater frequency than do the others. In other words, effective teachers behave in effective ways more often than do ineffective teachers and, perhaps, with better timing. The chances are, the less effective teachers have some skill in and do actually use most of the same teaching behaviors as do effective teachers. The effective teacher *too*, from time to time, uses some of the practices that characterize less effective teachers.

In other words, the difference is a matter of frequency and timing. To change less effective teaching into more effective instruction, it is only necessary to alter the frequency of certain behaviors and learn the discriminations necessary to combine the behaviors into a "package" that is a best mix for a particular group of students studying a particular subject under particular circumstances.

There is nothing in the cited research that suggests that increased frequencies and timing skills are dependent on "personality," "IQ," special "sensitivity," or any other innate characteristic and, therefore, are not learnable. The teacher responses all appear to be modifiable.

The same general conclusions apply to students in teacher education. There is a reasonably good chance that many of the effective teaching behaviors are already established to some degree as a part of every student's repertory when they start their formal education. There are probably many of the less effective responses established also. The problem for teacher education, then, is to alter frequencies and to establish cues for timing of responses.

Of course, there are some specific task skills which will not be present at any level. Such skills as record keeping, preparing audiovisual materials, conferring with parents, directing a play, demonstrating a laboratory procedure, using the Dewey Decimal system, etc., must be learned, partially from models. In case of less complex task skills, verbal descriptions of models from texts and lectures will provide all the cuing that is needed. For the more complex task skills, it will probably be necessary to observe "real live teachers" as they go through the various acts, then practice the task skills in an actual task setting.

The question for each student at this point is, how do I make the best use of my time in the future to alter frequencies of critical behaviors that are related to effective teaching and also gain the task skills needed to go along with the more general approaches and strategies? Obviously, methods courses and student teaching will provide many opportunities. There are, however, some steps that each student in teacher education can and should take on their own to increase the likelihood that they will achieve the goal of being an effective teacher.

That is the thrust of the next section—so read on.

PLANNING FOR BECOMING AN EFFECTIVE TEACHER

It is now time to return to the four steps set forth at the first of this chapter:

1. Identifying what has been learned thus far.
2. Estimating its worth—comparing with a criterion.
3. Looking ahead to see what additional learnings and skills are needed to become an effective teacher.
4. Making a plan to follow in becoming an effective teacher.

The research findings given in the first part of the chapter provide a basis for carrying out the four steps.

A series of worksheets or exercises have been prepared to lead readers through the steps. These are found at the end of the book. They should be examined carefully at this point. Note that the series of worksheets asks you to:

1. Decide from the research on teaching patterns which ten are most important. You will, of course, want to keep in mind that the idea of *importance* means "instrumental in increasing pupil achievement."

2. Analyze each of the ten patterns to identify critical specific skills that make up the overall pattern.
3. Estimate how much of the skill required for effective teaching has already been accomplished.
4. Decide roughly how much or what level of skills is needed to be a fully effective teacher: the "ideal" level.
5. Note the difference between present skill level and the ideal level.
6. State the differences as personal objectives.
7. Develop a plan to achieve the objectives.

Setting Personal Objectives

Obviously, at this point, readers are in a position to plan critical aspects of their own curriculum for the next year or so and perhaps even for longer than that, if it is assumed thay will continue learning, developing higher level skills during their first few years of actual teaching.

The first step will be recognized as a process for setting some personal development goals and objectives. It is analogous to the social studies teacher who sets goals for her/his pupils by asking the question, "What skills and understandings do these young people need in order to understand the political system of the country and how to make it serve them?"

Step two is a type of "task analysis," a procedure whereby complex behaviors are broken down into simpler, more readily learned behaviors.

Steps three, four and five can be referred to as a "needs assessment" procedure. It functions to identify specific deficiencies in skills and knowledge. That is, when one's skills and abilities are compared to a standard, it is possible to determine in what areas one "needs" to develop more skills and abilities and how much skill and ability are "needed" to achieve goal levels.

The alert reader recognizes this as a means to set specific objectives for oneself and to thereby plan a course of experiences for learning the skills and developing the abilities.

It is suggested that readers work through the process of deriving or establishing personal development objectives in small groups and with considerable guidance from instruction. This should be completed before planning is attempted.

Making a Personal Plan

Achieving the developmental objectives set through the preceding steps will require considerable time, although there is some likelihood that the act of setting a particular objective will be all that is necessary for achieving the objective in some instances. The author has noticed that when most beginning counselors, for example, state that they are going to "increase the

178

amount of time they *listen* to clients," they usually become much better listeners at once. Presumably, stated objectives will function to cue behavior changes in teachers just as they do for counselors.

However, stated objectives do not function equally well for all people for all behaviors. For example, some counselors stated the objective of "increased listening to clients" but "forgot" or impulsively dominated the discussion and did more talking than their clients. Hellervik (1968) reports on a process by which he "reinforced" counselors in training by flashing a light for the counselors to see (but the client could not) when they had been actively listening for increased periods of time. Other studies have reported on bug-in-the-ear (a small radio receiver with an earphone) procedures for cuing and reinforcing student teachers who are mastering a new technique. The supervising teacher views the student teacher through a one-way-vision screen then makes suggestions via radio to the student teacher and offers praise or constructive criticism while class is in progress.

Generally speaking, the counselor and teacher behaviors set as objectives in these studies have increased in frequency in exactly the same fashion as does the behavior of children reinforced in behavior modification studies.

Probably of more interest and of considerably greater importance to readers of this chapter is the *fact that teachers can use reinforcement principles on themselves to increase desired behaviors or to decrease unwanted responses*. This procedure, which has become quite well accepted by behavior modifiers in the past five years has been termed *self-management*.[1]

In self-management, an individual who can analyze his or her own behavior to identify the controlling cues and consequences, alters the cues and consequences to change the behaviors. Thus Hector (1976) trained a number of neophyte counseling psychologists to record the frequencies with which they made certain kinds of responses to their student clients. The results clearly indicated that the self-recording led to an increase in the frequencies.

Graduate students of the present authors have set up successful self-modification programs for:

1. Asking more open-ended, discussion type questions rather than yes-no type answers.
2. Stopping more frequently to ask students for their questions.
3. Improving a number of study behaviors, note-taking, following a schedule, etc.

---

1. The basic procedures and supporting research for self-management has been described by Mahoney and J. Cousin in *Self-Control: Power to the Person.*

4. Providing students with verbal praise or approval.
5. Getting papers graded in a more timely fashion.
6. Reducing "gushiness" and seeming "insincerity" after a student complained about her habit.
7. Several behaviors related to marriage and family living.
8. Some students have successfully used self-reinforcement procedures to reduce timidity, stage-fright, and test "panic."

There are some applications of self-management procedures that are quite complex. However, the majority are relatively simple as in the following case report of a college-level study-skill client.

The student, a sophomore, was not a strong student in any sense of the word. In a preliminary "needs" assessment it appeared that he had practically none of the behaviors that characterized effective students. One marked deficit was his ability to "concentrate" on reading assignments. He reported that he often read and reread a single page (up to four repeats) because his "mind would wander" and he would reach the bottom of the page with no recall of what he had just read.

It was estimated from an observation of his reading that the student probably could attend to most reading materials for about seven to eight lines then he began thinking about something else. The overall goal was set for him to read an entire chapter with no day-dreaming and specific objectives were set to increase concentration to cover five-ten lines more at a time until an entire page was read; then he was to increase the number of pages gradually until he could concentrate for an entire chapter.

He maintained a chart of his successes. The line on the chart kept going up day after day until at the end of three weeks the overall goal was reached! Needless to say, he was trained in other study-skills at the same time. For each skill objective, the client was given a self-monitoring procedure. He even began treating the self-maintained charts as a "token" system. He would permit himself to smoke a cigarette, for example, only after completing so many pages of reading without day-dreaming!

As a result of the cuing from the behavioral descriptions of effective study (through study-skill objectives) and the reinforcement records and charts, there was a remarkable change in his study behavior. His grades reflected the more systematic efforts and, surprisingly, the amount of time he spent on studies actually decreased!

The above example of self-management can be followed rather exactly by readers in planning their own future development into effective teachers. Note that the student set his goals by referring to research findings of what effective students do, just as is suggested here that prospective teachers set their goals based upon research into what effective teachers do. Note that analyses are performed to identify study-skill needs or deficits and that the specific behavioral objectives were set through a process analogous to that susggested for teachers. Next note that the process of developing each study-skill was planned for as a separate procedure involving separate cues and reinforcers.

To assist readers in setting up a similar procedure for themselves, two sets of worksheets have been included in the set at the end of the book.

The first is a worksheet for planning a "practice" or "pilot" self-management project. To complete this worksheet, plan (with assistance from your instructor) a one or two week "experiment" in modifying your own behavior.

The second worksheet leads you to develop a more general plan for yourself—one that can be implemented as you continue your program in teacher education. It (the plan) is a procedure to be followed in the increasing effective teaching behaviors and decreasing ineffective behaviors.

We now return to the ungrammatical question which formed the subtitle to this chapter—just what the hell difference does educational psychology make?

Perhaps as you go through the process of planning your own learning and then implementing the plan, the answer will become clear.

SUMMATIVE EVALUATION

You should now be able to respond to the following items at a 100 percent accuracy rate. In each instance, be careful to read the directions and respond in exactly the way called for by the instructions. You may set your own conditions for the task. Your responses should be written directly on the book. That's right, write in the book. After you have checked your work and find it to be successful, take a break and reward yourself with a pat on the back, a cold beer or a nap. If you make some errors, reread the chapter and try again. It may help for you to write comments in the margins of the text as you go back through it.

Set One: On the following questions, restatements of the objectives set out at the beginning of the chapter, write your responses immediately below the question.

1. Write a sentence telling what instructional objectives are.

2. Give five possible differences between long-term and short-term (behavioral) objectives.

3. List the three components of a behavioral objective.

4. Write a sentence telling what learning is.

5. Write a sentence describing the accessibility of learning to an observer.

6. List three uses of behavioral objectives.

7. Write one behavioral objective, containing the three necessary components of behavioral objectives for: (a) concept learning, (b) skill learning, and (c) value learning.

8. List the five guidelines for learning activities.

9. Describe the learning activities you would use (including the five guidelines for learning activities) for the three objectives you listed for question seven above.

10. List the three forms of evaluation of learning.

11. Describe the three forms of evaluation you would use for each of the three behavioral objectives-learning activities you have developed for questions seven and nine above.

Set Two: You will see ten short-term objectives listed below. In the space provided under each one indicate whether or not the objective is appropriately written and list, if necessary, those incorrect or missing components of the objectives.

1. The students will thoroughly know the concept of photosynthesis. They will demonstrate their knowledge on a written examination in class.

2. The students will identify the seven factors imperative in the downfall of the Persian empire on a multiple-choice test in class.

3. The students will perform three of five jumping jacks correctly in physical education class.

185

4. The students will understand the number 7.

5. The students will become less prejudiced.

6. The students will list and describe the seven Cardinal sins. They must list at least six without misspelling any words.

7. The students will be aware of the constitutional duties of the Vice President of the United States.

8. The students will properly construct a distillation apparatus at a 100 percent accuracy rate in the laboratory prior to a lab quiz.

9. The students will state the need for wearing goggles as a safety precaution. They will do so on a written quiz in the lab period and must list at least three reasons for wearing goggles to have their responses be accepted.

10. The students must demonstrate a thorough conceptualization of the properties of irridium. A formalized recitation period shall be the location for the assessment of their relative levels of cogency in this knowledge area.

SUMMATIVE EVALUATION

Chapter 3

1. Write a statement defining entering behavior.

2. List at least six factors to be considered in entering behavior.

3. Write a statement defining task analysis.

4. Write a statement describing the relationship between task analysis and entering behavior.

5. Write a statement describing the relationship between entering behavior, task analysis and behavioral objectives.

6. Write a statement describing how task analysis proceeds from behavioral objectives.

7. Perform a task analysis for the following behavioral objective: Students will define the concept of "over" verbally and identify when one object is "over" another. The criteria for acceptance shall be the correct identification of twenty examples of "over" and "not over" out of a possible twenty-five. They must delineate between "above," "on," "below," and "over" in their definition. The assessment will take place in a class meeting with each child responding orally.

8. Perform a task analysis for the following behavioral objective: The students will correctly tie their shoelaces in class, at least three of four times.

9. Perform a task analysis for the following behavioral objective: The students will learn to like the Strauss waltzes. This will be determined by having them choose, freely, in music class to listen to whatever they want and if they choose a Strauss waltz, the objective has been met.

10. Rewrite a behavioral objective for hypothetical students based on their entering behavior and the task analysis you have performed for questions number seven, eight and nine above, assuming any missing prerequisite behavioral component of the overall task.

11. Write a statement outlining the steps you will follow in bringing students from their entry level to the place at which your original behavioral objective was written.

When you have finished, refer to the text of the chapter to check your work. If you estimate that you have attained 90 percent agreement or more, take a break and reinforce yourself by smiling at yourself.

SUMMATIVE EVALUATION

Complete the following questions and then check your answers by referring to the chapter. If you achieve a 90 percent agreement with our statements under whatever conditions you have set for yourself, reinforce yourself with a pat on the back.

1. Write a statement defining thinking.

2. Write a statement defining memory and forgetting.

3. Write a statement defining a concept.

4. Write a statement defining a rule.

5. Write a statement defining a problem.

6. List at least two ways in which concepts may be taught.

7. Task analyze a concept learning task appropriately, establish a behavioral objective for teaching the concept and present a teaching strategy for meeting the objective.

8. Identify a problem, task analyze it into the appropriate rules and concepts, prepare behavioral objectives and a teaching strategy which will teach students to deal effectively with, or to solve, the problem.

9. List at least four ways for improving the efficiency of reading.

Suggested Readings:

Bourne, L. E., Ekstrand, B. R. and Dominowski, R. C. *The Psychology of Thinking.* Englewood Cliffs, New Jersey: Prentice-Hall, 1971.

Gagne, R. *Conditions of Learning,* third edition. New York: Holt, Rinehart and Winston, 1977.

SUMMATIVE EVALUATION

Below you will see eleven questions. Answer each in the space provided and then refer to the text material to check your answers. If you determine that you are 90 percent accurate or better, under the conditions you have set for yourself, become self-actualized and reinforce yourself. If you have any trouble, review the chapter or refer to the following readings.

1. Write a statement describing the Diagnostic-Prescriptive Teaching method.

2. Outline the four steps in the Diagnostic-Prescriptive Teaching method (DPT).

3. Outline your role in the DPT process.

4. Outline the role your students must play in DPT.

5. Describe the process of "making prescriptions."

6. Describe the way in which a classroom should be physically arranged to allow the best use of DPT.

7. Describe the logistic problems involved in the exchange and storage of DPT materials.

8. Describe your role as a tutor.

9. Describe the process of peer tutoring.

10. Describe the importance of observation, providing hints, prompts and help in general and keeping track of what all students are doing.

11. Describe two forms of keeping track of student progress.

Suggested Readings:

Charles, C. M. *Individualizing Instruction.* St. Louis: Mosby, 1976.

Glover, J. A. and Gary, A. L. *Mainstreaming Exceptional Children: How to Make It Work.* Pacific Grove, California: Boxwood, 1976.

Howes, V. M. *Individualization of Instruction.* New York: MacMillan, 1970.

SUMMATIVE EVALUATION

Below you will see a series of questions, restatements of the objectives at the beginning of the chapter. Answer each one in the space provided and then refer to the readings in the chapter to check yourself. If you answer 90 percent of them correctly or see that your agreement with our responses is 90 percent or better, take a break and reinforce yourself. If you have difficulty, refer back to the chapter or the books on the recommended reading list at the end of the questions.

1. Write a statement defining operant theory.

2. Write a statement defining the term "stimulus" and give an example of a stimulus.

3. Write a statement defining the term "neutral stimulus" and give an example of a neutral stimulus.

4. Write a statement defining the following terms and give an example of each:
   (a) reinforcing stimulus

(b)   positive reinforcer

(c)   negative reinforcer

(d)   primary reinforcer

(e)   secondary reinforcer

5. Write a statement that delineates between the terms reward and reinforcer. Provide an example of each term.

6. Write a statement defining the following terms and provide an example of each.
   (a)   escape behavior

   (b)   avoidance behavior

7. Write a statement defining the term "punishing stimulus" and give an example of a punishing stimulus.

8. Write a statement that delineates between how the term punishment is defined by operant psychologists and by lay persons. Give an example of each use of the term.

9. Write a statement defining the term "eliciting stimulus" and provide an example of this term.

10. Write a statement defining the term "discriminative stimulus" and provide an example of it.

11. Write a statement defining the term "shaping" and provide an example of shaping.

12. Write a statement defining the term "stimulus generalization" and provide an example of this term.

13. Write a statement defining the term "response generalization" and provide an example of it.

14. Write a statement defining the term "stimulus discrimination" and provide an example of stimulus discrimination.

15. Write a statement defining the term "schedule of reinforcement" and provide an example of a schedule of reinforcement.

16. Write a statement defining the term "extinction" and provide an example of extinction.

17. Write a statement defining the term "spontaneous recovery" and provide an example of spontaneous recovery.

18. Write a statement defining the term "internalized reinforcement" and provide an example of internalized reinforcement.

Recommended Readings:

Ackerman, M. J. *Operant conditioning techniques for the classroom teacher.* Glenview, Illinois: Scott, Foresman, 1972.

Glover, J. A. and Gary, A. L. *Behavior modification: enhancing creativity and other good behaviors.* Pacific Grove: California: Boxwood, 1975.

Madsen, C. H. and Madsen, C. K. *Teaching/discipline.* Boston: Allyn and Bacon, 1970.

Reynolds, G. S. *A primer of operant contitioning.* Glenview, Illinois: Scott Foresman, 1975.

EXERCISES ACCOMPANYING
CHAPTER 7

The numbers listed below represent the total number of behaviors observed each day. Construct a behavioral graph including both axes, a plotting of the data points and a connecting line drawn between the data points. The solution appears on the next page.

Days	Behaviors
1	14
2	16
3	12
4	19
5	21
6	12
7	10
8	6
9	5
10	3
11	12
12	10
13	14
14	15
15	16

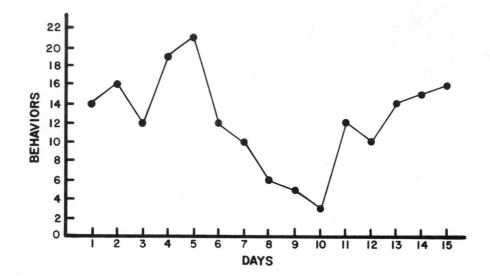

Interpret the following behavioral graph.

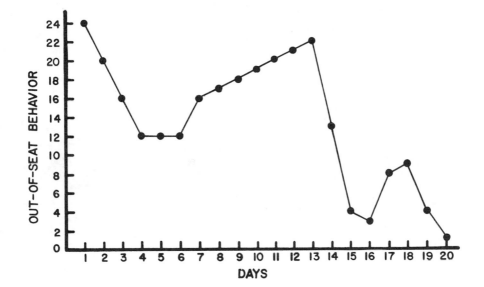

Plot the following data points on a graph of your own construction. Refer to the solution on the next page to check your work.

Teacher Attending Behavior		Student Noisemaking Behavior	
Day	Behaviors	Day	Behaviors
1	10	1	14
2	12	2	15
3	14	3	16
4	8	4	10
5	0	5	14
6	0	6	8
7	0	7	6
8	0	8	5
9	5	9	5
10	7	10	9
11	12	11	14
12	15	12	16

Exercise 7.4

Interpret the graph you have constructed for exercise 7.3.

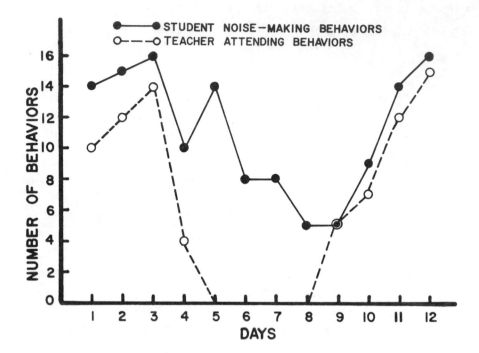

SUMMATIVE EVALUATION

Below you will see a series of questions and exercises based directly on the objectives from chapter seven. Please respond to them in the space provided and then refer to the chapter to check your work. If you determine a 90 percent mastery based on your comparison of your responses to ours, take a break and obtain some positive reinforcement. If you do not attain 90 percent mastery, review the chapter carefully and try again.

Some readings that may help you attain 90 percent mastery are listed at the end of the questions.

1. Write a statement describing what impact teacher behavior has on student behavior.

2. Write a statement describing how you may change a student's behavior by changing your own.

3. Upon reading about a "problem behavior," you will be able to define that behavior or a portion of it in observable terms.

   Sam has been a "problem student for Mr. Di Dactic this semester. He is rebellious and disruptive. Mr. Dactic also reports that Sam hits other students, scoots his chair around, makes noise and is out of his chair a lot. Define this rebellious and disruptive behavior by specifying four behaviors you could assess.

211

4. Write a statement describing a frequency count and list its disadvantages.

5. Write a statement describing time interval assessment and list its advantages and disadvantages.

6. Write a statement describing "on-the-count" assessment and list its advantages and disadvantages.

7. Write a statement describing (a) concomitant assessment, (b) simultaneous assessment, and (c) consecutive assessment.

8. Upon being given data, you will be able to reduce it to a graph format.

Construct a graph and plot the following data:

Days	Behaviors
1	15
2	17
3	12
4	10
5	9
6	10
7	11
8	13
9	17
10	21
11	19
12	14
13	8
14	6
15	5
16	1
17	2
18	5
19	9
20	11

The solution appears on the next page.

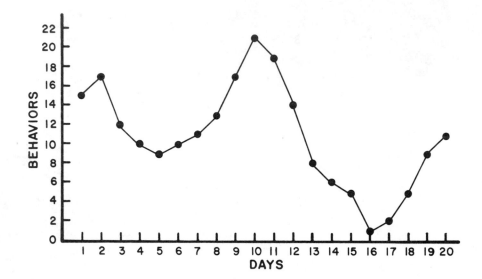

Interpret (describe in writing) the graph you constructed for question eight.

Analyze the graph labeled question eight.

Analyze this graph.

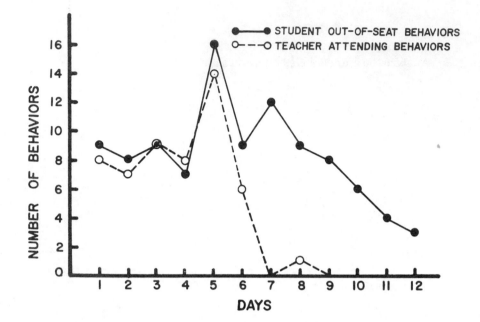

9. Upon seeing a graph of behavior you will interpret it correctly.

10. Upon being given a graph of teacher and student behaviors, you will analyze the effects of teacher behavior on student behavior.

11. Say what a "baseline," "treatment condition" and "return to baseline" are. Provide an example of such a triad.

12. Say why an ABA design is commonly used in behavior change procedures.

13. Write a statement describing the usefulness of a "return to baseline condition" for teachers not conducting an experiment.

14. Write a statement describing "time-out" and describe an appropriate time-out room and the procedures to be used in placing a person in time-out.

15. Write a statement defining group contingencies. Provide an example of group contingent reinforcement.

16. Write a statement describing the Premack Principle and describe an example of the Premack Principle in use.

17. Write a statement describing what "assigning responsibility" is and why it is used. Provide a hypothetical example of this technique.

18. Write a statement describing what a behavior contract is. List three differences between a behavior contract and the other techniques described in this chapter.

19. List all necessary components of a behavior contract.

20. Describe the procedure for initiating and implementing a behavior contract with a class of students.

21. Write a statement describing the relationship of reinforcement potency to behavior contracts.

22. Say what a proclamation is and compare and contrast it to a contract.

23. Write a statement telling what individual contracting is and what the necessary components of an individual contract are.

24. Describe how you might devise an individual contract with a hypothetical student.

Suggested Readings:

Glover, J. A. and Gary, A. L. *Behavior modification: Enhancing creativity and other good behaviors.* Pacific Grove, California: Boxwood, 1975.

Herman, T. M. *Creating learning environments.* Boston: Allyn and Bacon, Inc., 1977.

Kolesnik, W. B. *Learning: Educational applications.* Boston: Allyn and Bacon, Inc., 1976.

Williams, R. L. and Anadam, K. *Cooperative classroom management.* Columbus, Ohio: Charles E. Merrill, 1973.

SUMMATIVE EVALUATION

Chapter 8

Respond to the following questions in the space provided and then check your answers against our statements in the chapter. If you achieve a 90 percent agreement under whatever conditions you have set for yourself, choose a reliable and valid way to reinforce yourself.

1. Write brief statements defining process and product observation.

2. Write a statement defining reliability.

3. Write a statement defining interrater reliability and write the formula given for computing this reliability.

4. List and describe three ways of determining test reliability.

5. Write a statement defining validity.

6. Write a statement defining the term "norms."

7. List four characteristics of standardized tests.

8. List and describe three forms of intelligence tests.

9. Write statements defining intelligence and achievement tests.

10. List at least five advantages and disadvantages, five limitations and five points to consider for true-false tests.

11. List at least five advantages and disadvantages, three limitations and five points to consider for completion tests.

12. List at least three advantages and disadvantages, three limitations and five points to consider for multiple choice tests.

13. List at least five advantages and disadvantages, three limitations and five points to consider for matching tests.

14. List at least three advantages and disadvantages, five limitations and four points to consider for essay tests.

15. Write a statement describing how work samples are to be used for evaluation. Include three kinds of comparisons.

16. Write a statement describing how behavioral observations may be used for evaluations.

17. Write a statement defining norm-referenced and criteria-referenced testing.

18. Write a statement describing the purpose of grading and reporting results of school work.

Suggested Readings:

Kolstoe, R. H. *Introduction to statistics for the behavioral sciences.* Homewood, Illinois: Dorsey, 1973.

Thorndike, R. L. and Hagen, E. *Measurement and evaluation in psychology and education.* New York: Wiley, 1969.

Tuckman, B. W. *Measuring educational objectives.* New York: Harcourt, Brace and Jovanovich, 1975.

SUMMATIVE EVALUATION

Below you will see a list of twelve questions. Answer them in the space provided under the conditions you have set for yourself. Check your answers against the text and reinforce yourself by playing some canasta or ping pong if you determine that you meet a 90 percent correctness level. If not, review the chapter or read the suggested reading listed below.

1. Write a brief statement describing the basic requirements of the mainstreaming laws.

2. Write a brief paragraph defining the process of mainstreaming.

3. Write a brief statement summarizing why mainstreaming is being implemented in the schools.

4. Write a brief paragraph describing primary prevention.

5. Write a brief statement describing multidisciplinary assessment.

6. Write a brief statement describing multifaceted assessment.

7. Write a brief statement describing behaviorally-oriented assessment.

8. Write a brief statement describing naturalistic assessment.

9. Write a brief statement describing assessment in contrived settings.

10. Write a statement defining continuous assessment.

11. List the members of the multidisciplinary team and very briefly describe each member's duties.

12. Write a statement summarizing placement. List at least three placement options.

Suggested Reading:

Glover, J. A. and Gary, A. L. *Mainstreaming exceptional children: How to make it work*. Pacific Grove, California: Boxwood, 1976.

SUMMATIVE EVALUATION

Chapter 10

The following materials accompany chapter ten and should be completed as you finish the chapter. As there is no formal summative evaluation, you should ask yourself the questions set forth at the beginning of the chapter. Your answers will be your response for you to evaluate.

WORKSHEET
TEACHER DECISION MAKING

Teaching is decision making—decision making means making choices from among alternatives. This is an exercise in making choices. The choice-making is to select one teacher behavior from three alternatives on the basis that the selected behavior will have an effect on pupil behavior.

In the spaces below and on the following page are brief descriptions of a classroom situation with a description of a teacher response to that situation. In line with the above thinking, the teacher response was a choice and it had an effect on pupils' behavior.

You are asked to write in the space after each situation:

1. Your estimate of the effect of the teacher response on student behavior.
2. Two alternative responses the teacher might have made.
3. A rating for each alternative—estimating whether or not the effect on pupils' behavior would tend to be for: increased achievement, decreased achievement, no difference.

Work in groups of two or three and bring your worksheets to class prepared to defend your judgment!

Situation 1:

Classes are changing and students are arriving in their next hour classes. Mr. Smith, 8th grade social studies, stands looking out window ignoring noise and confusion for several minutes before attempting to get pupils' attention.

Probable effect _____

_____

Alternative teacher behavior #1 _____

_____

    estimated effect _____

_____

Alternative teacher behavior #2 _____

_____

    estimated effect _____

_____

Situation 2:

    Seven of ten students missed three quiz items having to do with concept of *analysis*. Teacher changes class plans and discusses errors, further defining terms and getting students to give examples. Continues for five minutes then resumes original plan.

Probable effect _____

_____

Alternative teacher behavior #1 _____

_____

    estimated effect _____

_____

Alternative teacher behavior #2 _____

_____

    estimated effect _____

_____

Situation 3:

    Paul, a ninth grader, tries to answer a teacher's question even though it is obvious he does not know the correct answer. It is his first attempt in two months to enter the class discussion. The teacher smiles at him and then changes the wording of his obviously wrong answer so that it is correct, then goes on to another discussion question.

Probable effect _____

_____

Alternative teacher behavior #1 _____

_____

    estimated effect _____

_____

Alternative teacher behavior #2 _____

_____

    estimated effect _____

_____

Situation 4:

    Teacher finishes presentation twenty minutes early. Tells class of 35 ninth graders from lower S.E.S. families that they can "use remaining time anyway they wish—just keep the noise level down."

Probable effect _____

_____

Alternative teacher behavior #1 _____

_____

estimated effect _____

_____

Alternative teacher behavior #2 _____

_____

estimated effect _____

_____

WORKSHEET

Assessment of Present Level of Personal Development of Effective Teaching Skills—Stylisitcs

On the following pages are a number of blank rating scales which appear as follows:

Def. & Examples	0	1	2	3	4	5

The blank space to the left of the rating scale is for you to enter the categorical name of a set or style of teacher behaviors. On the first page, write ten behavioral categories that, from your reading, appear to be most significant teacher behaviors. Then under each scale define the category by noting specific examples of the behavior. On the next page note ten behaviors that should be conspicuous by their *absence* from teaching style—then define by examples as you did on the positive behavioral categories.

Next, rate your development in two ways. Make an x over the position that reflects your *present* level of understanding and skill. Then mark an ! over the position that you think should be your level before you start to teach.

Use the following ratings to indicate levels of development.

Mark "0" if the behavioral category is largely just a term to you—you can't even recognize the behavior when you see it.

Mark "1" if the behavior is reliably *observed*. Level 1 development is the ability to observe the behavior and discriminate it from other behaviors and to agree with other observers also to "talk about" the behavior.

Mark "2" if the behavior can be observed and discussed with a knowledge of what effects it should have on pupils' learning or classroom behavior.

Mark "3" if the behavior represents a series of acts that can be demonstrated on demand. That is, if someone asks for you to "show" the behaviors, you can do so and they will be obviously a part of the set or category.

Mark "4" if the behaviors are "automatic" and "smooth." They are elicited by the cuing acts of students and by teacher's own plan—they are not performed just on demand.

Mark "5" if the behaviors are automatic and smooth *and* slightly changed from time to time to both provide variety and to make them fit either special groups of students or better serve differing types of learning.

Rating of Personal Development

(Definitions and examples)

1. _____

| 0 | 1 | 2 | 3 | 4 | 5 |

2. _____

| 0 | 1 | 2 | 3 | 4 | 5 |

3. _____

| 0 | 1 | 2 | 3 | 4 | 5 |

4. _____

| 0 | 1 | 2 | 3 | 4 | 5 |

5. _____

| 0 | 1 | 2 | 3 | 4 | 5 |

6. _____

| 0 | 1 | 2 | 3 | 4 | 5 |

7. _____

| 0 | 1 | 2 | 3 | 4 | 5 |

8. _____

| 0 | 1 | 2 | 3 | 4 | 5 |

9. _____

| 0 | 1 | 2 | 3 | 4 | 5 |

10. _____

| 0 | 1 | 2 | 3 | 4 | 5 |

WORKSHEET

Self-Analysis Description of Behavioral Style and Skills I Need to Develop to Be an Effective Teacher

From the self-assessment worksheet, prepare a brief description of the kinds of behavior you hope an impartial observer would note as being characteristic of you during your first year of teaching. Indicate in a general way which four or five you will need to work on *most* during the next two years in order to achieve.

WORKSHEET

Plan for Practice or Pilot Experience Self-Management

Fill out in duplicate—submit one to instructor, retain the other.

I. *Problem behavior*—describe behavior and situations where it occurs.

II. *Baseline*

III. Is behavior change a matter of reducing a behavior, increasing a substitute behavior (PRD) or simply strengthening a weak behavior?

IV. Procedure for bringing about a change.

V. How is behavior change to be evaluated?

Signature _____

Instructor _____

Date _____

FINAL WORKSHEET

Plan for Self-Managing Development of Selecting Skills
of Effective Teaching

I. What skill developments do I probably need to emphasize in order to be classed as an effective teacher?

1.

2.

3.

4.

5.

II. What present stylistic behaviors do I need to reduce in order to be an effective teacher?

1.

2.

3.

4.

5.

III. What is my general plan for increasing the "effective-teacher" stylistics?

1. Baselining

2. Defining the specific examples to be baselined.

3. Noting occurrences of the exemplary behaviors.

4. Reinforcing the exemplary behaviors.

5. Evaluating the effects of the increased stylistics.

   (a) for pupils of differing ability levels.

   (b) for pupils of differing backgrounds.

(c)   for differing types of learning.

6.   When and under what conditions will practice, monitoring and self-reinforcement be attempted?

IV. What is your general plan for reducing ineffective behaviors by self-management procedures?

1.   Baselining procedures

2.   Define specific examples of stylistics to be baselined.

3.   Will differential reinforcement procedures of response suppressing procedures be used?

4. General procedures for suppressing responses

5. General procedures for *Reinforcing Other Responses*.

6. Evaluating effects of reducing the specific exemplary behavior.

   (a) on pupils of differing ability levels.

   (b) on pupils of differing backgrounds.

   (c) for differing types of learning.

REFERENCES

Anderson, R. "Learning in discussions: A resume of the authoritarian-democratic studies." *Harvard Educational Review.* 29, 1959. 201-15.

Biddles, B. J. "Methods and concepts in classroom research" *Review of Educ. Res.* 37, 1967. 337-57.

Brophy, J. Colosimo, J., and Carter T. "Applying a contingency management system to all students in each classroom in an elementary school." *Research Report, The Research and Development Center for Teacher Education.* University of Texas at Austin, 1974.

———and Evertson, C. M. *Learning from Teaching.* Boston: Allyn and Bacon, Inc., 1976.

Coleman, J. et al. *The Equality of Educational Opportunity.* Washington, D.C.: Supt. of Documents, U.S. Gov't. Printing Office, 1966.

Dunkin, M. J. and Biddle, B. J. *The Study of Teaching.* New York: Holt, Rinehart & Winston, 1974.

Gage, N. "Paradigms of Research in Teaching." *Handbook of Research on Teaching.* Chicago: Rand, McNally, 1963.

Good, T. L., Biddle, B. J. and Brophy, J. E. *Teachers Make a Difference,* New York: Holt, Rinehart & Winston, 1975.

Good, T. L. and Brophy, J. E. *Educational Psychology: A Realistic Approach.* New York: Holt, Rinehart & Winston, 1977.

Green, R. et al. "The educational status of children during the first year of school following four years of little or no schooling." E. Lansing, Mich.: Michigan St. Univ., 1966.

Hector, M. A. Counselor Training: *Changing Counselor Behaviors Through Self-Management.* Paper presented at AERA Nat'l. Conv. San Francisco, California, 1976.

Hellervic, L. "An Operant Conditioning Approach to Changing Counselor Interview Behavior." Unpub. Ph. D. diss., Univ. of Minn., 1968.

Homme, L. et al. *How to Use Contingency Contracting in the Classroom.* Champaign, Ill.: Research Press, 1970.

Jencks, C. et al. *Inequality: A Reassessment of the Effect of Family and Schooling in America.* New York: Basic Books, 1972.

Keele, R. A. "A Comparison of the Effectiveness of Remediation of Non-Readers by Trained Mexican-American Aides and Certified Teachers." Paper presented at the annual conv. of AERA, New Orleans, La., 1973.

Kounin, J. *Discipline and Group Management in Classrooms.* New York: Holt, Rinehart & Winston, 1970.

Medley, D. M. and Mitzel, H. D. "The scientific study of teacher behavior." in A. A. Bellack (ed) *Theory and Research in Teaching.* New York: Teachers Col., Bureau of Publications, 1963.

Mostetter, F. and Moynihan, D. *On Equality of Educational Opportunity.* New York: Random House, 1972.

243

Nuthall, G. A. "Studies of Teaching: Types of Research on Teaching." *New Zealand J. of Ed. Studies,* 1968.

Rosenshine, B. *Teaching Behaviors and Student Achievement.* London: Nat'l. Foundation for Ed. Res., 1971

Schmidt, W. "Socieoconomic status, schooling, intelligence and scholastic progress in a community in which education is not compulsory." *Pardogogica Europa.* 1966.

Sears, P. et al. "Effective Reinforcement for achievement behavior in disadvantaged children. The first year." *Tech. Report No. 30.* Stanford Center for Research and Development in Teaching. Stanford University, 1972.

Shimron, J. *Learning Activities in Individually Prescribed Instruction.* Paper presented annual conv. of AERA, New Orleans, 1973.

Thompson, M. et al. "Contingency management in the schools: How often and how well does it work?" *J. Amer. Ed. Research Assoc.* Vol. 11, 1974.

Vernon, P. *Intelligence and Cultural Environment.* London: Methuen, 1969.